Bridges

Readings for Writers

Bridges
Readings for Writers

DONNA GORRELL
University of Wisconsin, Milwaukee

Little, Brown and Company
Boston   Toronto

Library of Congress Cataloging in Publication Data
Main entry under title:

Bridges: readings for writers.

　　Includes index.
　　1. College readers.　　2. English language—Rhetoric.
I. Gorrell, Donna.
PE1417.B712　　1984　　　808'.0427　　　84-19458
ISBN 0-316-32136-2

Copyright © 1985 by Donna Gorrell

All rights reserved. No part of this book may be reproduced in any form or by any electronic or mechanical means including information storage and retrieval systems without permission in writing from the publisher, except by a reviewer who may quote brief passages in a review.

Library of Congress Catalog Card Number 84-19458

ISBN 0-316-32136-2

9　8　7　6　5　4　3　2　1

MV

Published simultaneously in Canada
by Little, Brown & Company (Canada) Limited

Printed in the United States of America

Acknowledgments begin on page 282.

*In memory of my dad, Ray Ketelboeter,
for encouraging me from the very beginning.*

Preface

Most good writers have this in common: they pay attention to what they read—how the writer puts words and sentences and paragraphs together, how a word looks on paper, what a paragraph looks like. And they emulate the work of other writers—perhaps not altogether consciously, yet still patterning their writing after other writing. Good writers usually observe writing conventions without thinking about rules. Inexperienced writers, on the other hand, all too often do not have "models" in their heads of what good writing looks like, not because they don't read but because they may not pay attention to writers' ways of achieving effects.

Bridges is designed to span this gap by enabling inexperienced writers first to read like writers and then to write like writers. For, as they learn to see what they read with the perception of writers, they also see their own writing more clearly. They move from inexperience as writers to a new confidence that comes from knowing how to communicate ideas in a publicly effective form.

My aim in this book, then, is to get less experienced writers to notice conventions of writing, to become aware of the options available to them, and then to transfer their consciousness of these conventions into original writing. To achieve this aim, twenty-five essays have been selected for their interest, ease of reading, and serviceability as models. Most have not been anthologized before. Each is complete, and each is the basis for a writing assignment.

Writing teachers will find the chapters rather tightly structured as they progress from reading assignment to writing assignment, yet each chapter has a flexibility that allows experienced teachers to employ their individual teaching styles. The preliminary apparatus is based on the assumption that active involvement in reading leads to better comprehension; as a writing teacher I am convinced that this "better comprehension" means better understanding not only of what writers say but of how they say it as well. Each chapter, therefore, is focused on both form and substance; in each I give a biographical-rhetorical background, suggest content by means of the vocabulary list, and send the reader into the passage searching for answers to the preview questions. Because this active involvement in reading is practiced regularly, it usually transfers to other reading. The questions for discussion following each essay function as a bridge between the reading and the writing. These bring up both what the writers say and the means they use for saying it. Frequently the discussion following a question actually answers that question in order to lead to further discussion.

The next two sections might be used in the order given or reversed. First is the sentence-patterning exercise, which lifts a sentence from the reading for use in imitation. These exercises teach various ways in which to phrase sentences as well as how to punctuate them. We ask for strict imitation but open the way as well for freer patterns. Some teachers may prefer to put off the sentence patterning in order to go directly from the questions to the writing assignment, thus taking full advantage of their interrelatedness. Actually, the writing assignment is the heart of each chapter. Utilizing the reading as a model, it provides topics for writing, ways of exploring ideas, and guides for revision. The assignment may also address organization, coherence, audience, and other rhetorical considerations.

The theoretical underpinnings of this book are eclectic, drawing from one or another rhetorical theory according to its appropriateness for the specific writing assigned. Invention, for example, may be tagmemic when the subject's relation to change and other subjects is fitting, but at other times it might use free writing, journalistic questions, or other techniques. The revision questions are likewise assignment-specific. Students thus learn about the many ways of exploring ideas and revising writing, yet repeating key concepts emphasizes the continuing need for exploration of ideas and revision of writing, as well as showing how the various ways of doing them are connected. Teachers will also find that the revision questions lend themselves well to writing workshops, providing students with ways of looking at writing done by others as well as their own.

The essays in this book are arranged according to difficulty of the reading and writing assignment together with consideration for a logical order in the sentence-patterning exercises. Other arrangements are effective too, and some assignments can be skipped without loss of continuity. At the back of the book are several reading assignments discussing aspects of writing. These essays are accompanied by neither writing assignments nor the apparatus of the main part of the book; they can be used at any time and in almost any order. Other practical features are an index and a glossary defining some of the terms used in this book.

The modeling approach employed in *Bridges* has advantages for teaching basic writing. It not only provides students with examples of how an assignment can be done but also assists them in learning how to read the models—in recognizing which features of other people's writing can serve them in their own writing. They actually do come to think of themselves as writers—in association with other committed writers like Bertrand Russell or Loren Eiseley or George Gaylord Simpson. My colleagues and I have seen this contagion happen with students who used a rough-draft version of this book in their basic writing classes. In their next writing class they had confidence in their ability to write (knowing full well the imperfections in their written products), and they actively led class discussions about writing. Moreover, they no longer needed models. Using models did this for them: it eliminated some of the hit-or-miss in their writing efforts and convinced them that they could be effective in expressing their ideas on paper.

I am indebted to a number of people for their assistance in the production of this book: to my daughters Lynn, Louisa, and Michele for performing the tedious task of proofreading; to my husband, Ken, for being always ready to listen; to several colleagues at the University of Wisconsin-Milwaukee for offering comments to help me through revisions—Margaret Mika, Marilyn Gius, and David Martin; and to the students at UWM who learned to write better and read better as they used a rough-draft version of this book. I am also grateful to those who reviewed an early draft and provided me with helpful suggestions: Elizabeth Balser of Fairmont State College, Susan Helgeson of Ohio State University, Cecilia Macheski of La Guardia Community College, William R. Siebenschuh of Case Western Reserve University, and Judith Stanford of Merrimack College. Finally, I want to thank those at Little, Brown and Company who carried the book through production: Joseph Opiela, Molly Faulkner, Julie Winston, and Allison Hoover.

Contents

Introduction   1

1. **What I Have Lived For**
   BERTRAND RUSSELL   5

   The essay is a three-point, five-paragraph exposition. The discussion explores coherence. Sentence patterning: coordinated independent clauses.

2. **Shearing Sheep in Patagonia**
   GEORGE GAYLORD SIMPSON   14

   The essay narrates a story. Sentence patterning: quoted dialogue, stressing tense; coordinated independent clauses.

3. **The Beginning of a Word**
   J. WALLACE HAMILTON   22

   The essay defines a word through examples. Sentence patterning: the semicolon between independent clauses; comma-spliced and run-on sentences.

4. **Spelling Is Nonsense**   DONALD E. P. SMITH, EDITOR   30

   The essay describes a process for improving spelling. The assignment calls for a how-to essay with numbered steps. Sentence patterning: the semicolon between independent clauses.

5. **The Great Process**   TOM SCHWABE   39

   The student essay describes the student's writing process. The assignment discusses the process and assigns a similar essay. Sentence patterning: transitional adverbs.

xii Contents

6. **Good and Bad** PAUL ROBERTS 48

    The essay attempts to persuade readers that correctness in language depends on a given speech community. Sentence patterning: the colon followed by a series.

7. **Mr. McElroy** MAYA ANGELOU 57

    The essay describes a person remembered from childhood. Fragments are discussed. Sentence patterning: nonrestrictive relative clauses.

8. **Summary of "Take This Fish"**
    L. DANIEL ROSIN 64

    The student essay summarizes Samuel H. Scudder's "Take This Fish and Look at It." Summary is discussed and assigned. Sentence patterning: coordinated verbs.

9. **Echoes of Grief** DORIS LESSING 75

    The essay narrates an incident from childhood. The discussion stresses the need for clearly establishing a setting. Sentence patterning: coordination in a series, prepositions.

10. **Blubber on Ice** ROBERT CUSHMAN MURPHY 83

    The essay uses present-tense verbs to describe a habitual process. Sentence patterning: nonrestrictive participial phrases.

11. **Why the Sky Looks Blue** SIR JAMES JEANS 90

    The essay explains through analogy. Sentence patterning: restrictive relative clauses.

12. **Lift Your Feet** ANDREW WARD 99

    The essay shows the effects of a single cause. Sentence patterning: the introductory participle as the modifier of the subject of the sentence.

Contents   xiii

13. **Letter of Complaint**   106

    The letter registers a consumer complaint. The assignment stresses accuracy and attention to details. Sentence patterning: this *with a clear reference.*

14. **The Arctic Storm**   FRANKLIN RUSSELL   113

    The essay narrates the progress of a storm. The discussion stresses objectivity. Sentence patterning: nominative absolutes.

15. **What Color Is an Orange?**   JOHN McPHEE   121

    The essay explains its subject by means of contrast. The discussion treats paragraph development. Sentence patterning: subordinate clauses at the end of sentences.

16. **Three Disciplines for Children**   JOHN HOLT   129

    The essay develops its subject through classification and division. The discussion treats paragraph development. Sentence patterning: introductory subordinate clauses.

17. **Preface to *Reversals***   EILEEN SIMPSON   139

    This essay on dyslexia presents three causes—or reasons—for a single effect. Sentence patterning: introductory what *clauses.*

18. **The New Ambidexters**   ELLEN GOODMAN   147

    The essay defines a word by contrasting the political Right and Left. The assignment suggests a newspaper article. Sentence patterning: writing and avoiding fragments.

19. **Ticaspleeze and Trees**
    MICHAEL D. McCARTHY   158

    The student essay shows how figures of speech can enhance descriptive writing. Sentence patterning: introductory participial phrases.

20. Ticaspleeze and Trees (Revision)
MICHAEL D. McCARTHY   168

Three drafts of the student essay show progressive movement to finished essay. Sentence patterning: appositive and alliterative repetition.

21. The Bounty of the Sea   JACQUES COUSTEAU   188

The essay employs a cause-and-effect chain of development and is highly persuasive in intent. Sentence patterning: introductory if *clauses, inset* by which *relative clauses, and* not only . . . but *structures.*

22. Reading by Leaps and Bounds
FRANK SMITH   197

The essay relates some facts about reading by defining a word; in development it uses process, contrast, and effects. Sentence patterning: restrictive relative clauses, two of them coordinated.

23. The Hidden Teacher   LOREN EISELEY   207

The essay is the narration of a dream. Sentence patterning: emphasis through repetition.

24. Beginning   ISAAC ASIMOV   215

The essay contrasts the Biblical and scientific views on the beginning of all things. Sentence patterning: parallel structure.

25. Play in Ancient Greece   EDITH HAMILTON   225

The essay is a combination of causes, classification, examples, comparison, and effects. Sentence patterning: subordination and coordination.

ESSAYS FOR FURTHER READING

26. **Theme Writing**   DOROTHY CANFIELD FISHER   235

    The essay encourages student writers to overcome inertia by plodding ahead with the writing task and to revise thoroughly.

27. **Probing for Ideas**   FRANK J. D'ANGELO   239

    The essay states that topics *are ways of thinking, of exploring ideas, and of organizing essays.*

28. **Developing a Paragraph from a Topic Sentence**   JIM W. CORDER   244

    The essay illustrates paragraph writing with several examples.

29. **Specific Details**   DAVID SKWIRE AND FRANCES CHITWOOD   252

    The essay discusses specific details and how to use them.

30. **The Maker's Eye: Revising Your Own Manuscripts**   DONALD M. MURRAY   257

    The essay stresses that revision is essential to writing, but that the writer must learn what to look for.

Appendix A. Connectors and Their Uses	267
Appendix B. Glossary of Key Terms	270
Index	277

Contents
Arranged by Rhetorical Strategy

CAUSE AND EFFECT

12. Lift Your Feet   ANDREW WARD   99
    Shows the effects of a single cause.
17. Preface to *Reversals*   EILEEN SIMPSON   139
    Gives three causes or reasons for a single effect.
21. The Bounty of the Sea   JACQUES COUSTEAU   188
    Employs a cause-and-effect chain of development.

CLASSIFICATION

16. Three Disciplines for Children   JOHN HOLT   129
    Discusses classification and division.

COMPARISON

11. Why the Sky Looks Blue   SIR JAMES JEANS   90
    Explains the difference between analogy and comparison.
15. What Color Is an Orange?   JOHN McPHEE   121
    Uses contrast to develop the subject.
18. The New Ambidexters   ELLEN GOODMAN   147
    Defines by contrast.
24. Beginning   ISAAC ASIMOV   215
    Contrasts two views of the same subject.

DEFINITION

3. The Beginning of a Word   J. WALLACE HAMILTON   22
    Defines through examples.

Contents Arranged by Rhetorical Strategy

18.	The New Ambidexters ELLEN GOODMAN *Defines through contrast.*	147
22.	Reading by Leaps and Bounds FRANK SMITH *Defines by process, contrast, and effects.*	197

DESCRIPTION

7.	Mr. McElroy MAYA ANGELOU *Describes a person remembered from childhood.*	57
9.	Echoes of Grief DORIS LESSING *Narrates a story rich in description.*	75
19.	Ticaspleeze and Trees MICHAEL D. McCARTHY *Student essay shows how figures of speech can enhance descriptive writing.*	158

EXPOSITION

1.	What I Have Lived For BERTRAND RUSSELL *Uses three-point, five-paragraph exposition.*	5
22.	Reading by Leaps and Bounds FRANK SMITH *Uses process, contrast, and effects to define a word.*	197
25.	Play in Ancient Greece EDITH HAMILTON *Uses causes, classification, examples, comparison, and effects to explain the point.*	225

LETTER

13.	Letter of Complaint *Registers a consumer complaint in business letter form.*	106

NARRATION

2.	Shearing Sheep in Patagonia GEORGE GAYLORD SIMPSON *Narrates a story in the third person.*	14
9.	Echoes of Grief DORIS LESSING *Narrates an incident from childhood.*	75
14.	The Arctic Storm FRANKLIN RUSSELL *An objective observer narrates the progress of a storm.*	113

Contents Arranged by Rhetorical Strategy　　xix

23. The Hidden Teacher　LOREN EISELEY　　207
    Narrates a dream.

    PERSUASION
6. Good and Bad　PAUL ROBERTS　　48
    Attempts to persuade that a speech community determines correctness in language.
21. The Bounty of the Sea　JACQUES COUSTEAU　　188
    Uses vivid cause-and-effect development for purpose of persuasion.

    PROCESS
4. Spelling Is Nonsense　DONALD E. P. SMITH, EDITOR　　30
    Describes a how-to process with numbered steps.
5. The Great Process　TOM SCHWABE　　39
    Student describes his writing process.
10. Blubber on Ice　ROBERT CUSHMAN MURPHY　　83
    Uses present-tense verbs to describe a habitual process.

    SUMMARY
8. Summary of "Take This Fish"　L. DANIEL ROSIN　　64
    Student summarizes an essay.

Bridges

Readings for Writers

Introduction

People learn to write by writing and by observing the writing of others—in other words, by writing and by reading purposefully. Ordinarily when we read we look for meaning: we want to know what the writer has to say on a given subject, whether it's why nuclear arms should be limited, or how we might repair a garbage disposal, or why one nation is declaring its independence from another. But we don't *always* read for meaning. Sometimes, for example, we read for *errors,* as when we're proofreading. And at still other times we read for style—to observe how others put their words and sentences and paragraphs together to make up a coherent, whole piece of writing. This kind of reading leads to better writing.

Most people can improve their writing just by noticing what other writers do and practicing those things: how they use clauses or phrases, how they begin their sentences, what words they choose, how they connect their paragraphs, and so on. This book is designed to build writing skills through attention to the writing of others. The first twenty-five essays have two purposes: first, to be read—both for content and for writing style—and second, to serve as models for writing assignments.

Imitation of models is an effective way of improving writing. Just as you may try to improve your batting stance by paying attention to how George Brett stands at the plate and then trying to do as he does, you may also attempt to improve your writing stance by imitating how Bertrand Russell, as an example, positions himself in relation to his subject and audience, This book, in part, is meant to heighten your powers of observation while you read, so that you see not only what a writer says but how he or she goes about saying it. Then the book directs you to transfer your observations into a piece of writing modeled on the original.

Each chapter, therefore, has as its basis an essay to read and one to write. Other parts are designed to aid either the reading or the writing. You'll find that each of the first twenty-five chapters is made up of several parts.

1. *Biographical Sketch.* Each chapter begins with a biographical/rhetorical sketch about the author and the writing situation. This will assist you in relating the author to his or her work.

2. *Vocabulary Preview.* A number of words from each essay are defined according to meaning(s) that correspond to the context of the essay. You'll find that some of the words included in these lists, such as those in "Blubber on Ice" or in "Reading by Leaps and Bounds," are specialized terms for a given field. Others are words that you seldom encounter and consequently may not know. Still others are words that are probably already part of your active vocabulary. By reading these lists of words and their meanings *before* reading the essays, you accomplish two things:
    a. When you encounter an unfamiliar word while reading, you'll recall that you just saw it, even if you don't remember what it means. A quick glance back will give you the meaning.
    b. Also, the list of words serves as a sort of preview of the essay, giving you some idea of what to expect.

3. *Essay Preview.* These questions are meant to direct your thinking about the essay, to send you looking for answers as you read. Reading specialists tell us that we read with more comprehension when we preview the piece and seek answers for questions. So, as you read, actively look for answers to the preview questions.

4. *The Essay.* The essays come next, with lines and paragraphs marked for reference. You'll notice that the essays are short; that's so they can serve as realistic mod-

els for your writing. They're written on a variety of subjects, by a variety of authors, with a variety of patterns of development. Most of the writers are professionals but some are students.

5. *Questions for Discussion.* The questions for discussion that follow each essay deal with many aspects of the reading: its meaning, the way it is structured, its coherence, its word choice, its selection of details, and so forth. In addition, they lay the groundwork for the writing assignment that follows. These questions are not meant to be a quiz. Actually this section is a combination of questions and discussions that together encourage exploration of the essay and preparation for writing your own essay. As you read the questions you should remember to pause and think about the answers before reading on into the discussions. After you discuss the questions (in class) or think them through (at home, for class preparation), read on into the discussions, which will often stimulate further discussion or thought. The eventual purpose of both the questions and the discussions is for you to understand how one writer performed in a given writing situation and then be able to write in a similar way yourself.

6. *Sentence Patterning.* From each essay in Chapters 1 through 25 a sentence is taken to illustrate a pattern worth practicing. Some sentences use subordinate clauses and some participles, some are fragments, some take semicolons, and so on. Each sentence pattern is illustrated by a line diagram, and then a new sentence written on the pattern serves as an example of another way the same pattern might be used. You are asked first to *copy* the sentence exactly, in order to impress the pattern on your mind through the coordinated action of the hand and the eye. Then you are to write a sentence in imitation of the pattern, using your own ideas. For example, if the pattern sentence has a *who* clause, you write a sentence that has a *who* clause in the same position. Finally, you may take the imitation one step further. After the close imitation just described,

you may try writing sentences that more loosely imitate the original, using only some part of the pattern.
7. *Writing Assignment.* Each chapter concludes with a writing assignment that develops from the reading. It uses the reading assignment as a model, points out some central aspects of the model, and gives you some instruction on how to begin writing, what to consider as you're writing, and what to look for when you revise. The principle of imitation is applied again. Now you use the essay as a *model,* a guide. The result is that you should end up with an essay organized like the original, with your ideas supported as adequately as those of the original, with transitions linking your ideas, with a carefully phrased thesis statement, and with an adequate introduction and conclusion. Is all this too much to ask? Well, perhaps, but not necessarily when you have a model before you. Remember again the batter whose stance you imitate. You may not hit a home run the first time you imitate him, and maybe you never will, but if you keep working at it, you'll get a lot better. And unless you want to be a professional you don't have to hit like George Brett.

At the end of the book are five essays, Chapters 26 through 30, that give additional instruction in writing well, from how to explore a new idea to how to revise a rough draft. They supplement the instructions you'll find throughout the main part of the book.

So, as you see, this book is a *writing* textbook. It's a reader, yes, but each reading has as its ultimate goal a piece of writing. Each assignment will take hard work. If it's going well it can be fun; if it's not going well, think of it as a challenge to be met with ingenuity and persistence.

1

What I Have Lived For

BERTRAND RUSSELL

Bertrand Russell, an English mathematician and philosopher, lived from 1872 to 1970. He wrote numerous books in both mathematics and philosophy, taught at universities in England and the United States, and won the Nobel Prize in Literature in 1950. Russell is known also for his controversial beliefs on pacifism, communism, religion, marriage, and education—all subjects on which he has written. His autobiography, completed when he was ninety years old, is a three-volume compilation of letters he wrote and received throughout his lifetime. The essay below is his Prologue to the first volume. Writing in his old age, Russell summarized the meaning of his remarkable life.

Vocabulary Preview

line		
5	anguish	suffering, from physical or mental pain
6	verge	edge; brink
12	abyss	bottomless pit; hell
13	mystic	mysterious; filling one with awe or wonder
14	prefiguring	suggesting beforehand; imagining in advance
21	Pythagorean	concerning the philosophy of the ancient Greek philosopher Pythagoras, who described reality in terms of numbers
21	holds sway	controls; has power over

6 What I Have Lived For

22	flux	a continual change; a flow of energy
25	reverberate	to re-echo; to resound
29	alleviate	to reduce; to make more bearable

Essay Preview: Questions to Answer as You Read

1. What three things does Bertrand Russell say he has lived for?
2. For what three reasons did he seek love?
3. What three things did he wish to understand?

What I Have Lived For

1   Three passions, simple but overwhelmingly strong, have governed my life: the longing for love, the search for knowledge, and unbearable pity for the suffering of mankind. These passions, like great winds, have blown me hither and thither, in a wayward course, over a deep ocean of anguish, reaching to the very verge of despair.

2   I have sought love, first, because it brings ecstasy—ecstasy so great that I would often have sacrificed all the rest of life for a few hours of this joy. I have sought it, next, because it relieves loneliness—that terrible loneliness in which one shivering consciousness looks over the rim of the world into the cold unfathomable lifeless abyss. I have sought it, finally, because in the union of love I have seen, in a mystic miniature, the prefiguring vision of the heaven that saints and poets have imagined. This is what I sought, and though it might seem too good for human life, this is what—at last—I have found.

3   With equal passion I have sought knowledge. I have wished to understand the hearts of men. I have wished to know why the stars shine. And I have tried to apprehend the Pythagorean power by which number holds sway above the flux. A little of this, but not much, I have achieved.

4   Love and knowledge, so far as they were possible, led upward toward the heavens. But always pity brought me back to earth. Echoes of cries of pain reverberate in my heart.

Children in famine, victims tortured by oppressors, helpless old people a hated burden to their sons, and the whole world of loneliness, poverty, and pain make a mockery of what human life should be. I long to alleviate the evil, but I cannot, and I too suffer.

This has been my life. I have found it worth living, and would gladly live it again if the chance were offered me.

Questions for Discussion

1. Bertrand Russell's "What I have Lived For" is a near-perfect example of the five-paragraph essay. It begins with a precise, direct statement of thesis followed by three clear-cut paragraphs of discussion and is fitly ended with a forthright conclusion. Its simple outline follows:

   I. Introduction
      A. Thesis statement
      B. Writer's position on subject
   II. Love
      A. Ecstasy
      B. Relief from loneliness
      C. Vision of heaven
   III. Knowledge
      A. Hearts of men
      B. Stars
      C. Number
   IV. Pity
      A. Cries of pain
      B. Longing to alleviate evil
   V. Conclusion

   The number *three* seems to give the essay balance and order. The essay begins by indicating three points for discussion, and the paragraphs on love and knowledge are divided into three parts too. While the paragraph on pity is not divided into three, the final sentence in the paragraph has three coordinated statements. *Do you think the balance was a help to you as a reader, or was it too obvious as a structural pattern? Support your answer with your responses to specific parts of the essay.*

2. Not only does Russell carefully balance his points, he also carefully arranges them for maximum effect. He begins with the two passions he sought—love and knowledge—then contrasts the unsought passion, pity. The effect is another kind of balance, this time underscoring the concept that life consists of what seeks us out as well as what we go searching for. *Discuss what the effect might have been if Russell had started with pity and left the paragraph on love, his largest, till last. One reasonable way to organize an essay is to save the strongest point for last.*

3. Russell uses no specific examples in developing his paragraphs. *Do you think he should have? Does he make statements that demand illustrations?*

   For the most part, Russell explains his statements with specific language. He amplifies, for example, his references to ecstasy, loneliness, and the vision of heaven. Loneliness is "one shivering consciousness" looking over "the rim of the world into the cold unfathomable lifeless abyss." The vision of heaven is seen in "mystic miniature" and imagined by "saints and poets." *Find other instances of specific words that clarify Russell's statements.*

4. The thesis statement of "What I Have Lived For" (Russell's opening sentence) follows a common pattern: an assertion about the subject followed by the points to be discussed. A colon separates the two. It is also a well-phrased thesis statement because it does two things: (a) it presents the subject, and (b) it gives a point, or meaning, to the subject. In this essay the subject is "three passions in my life." The point is that these passions have governed Russell's life. So a statement like "There are three passions in my life" presents only the subject and, because it has no point, is not a thesis statement.

   Here's a thesis statement from another essay in this book. *What is its subject, and what is its point?*

   > There is an enormous difference between the Biblical statement of beginning and the scientific statement of beginning.

The subject of the essay that follows this thesis ("Beginning," p. 215) is the beginning of all things. The point is that the two statements about the beginning are different; as author Isaac Asimov explains, this difference accounts for all disagreements between Biblical and scientific scholarship.

Here's another. *What's the point?*

> I don't think we are turning to the right, or to the left. . . . I think most of us are turning ambidextrous.

In this statement of thesis (from "The New Ambidexters," p. 147), the subject is political inclinations, and the point is that most of us are turning to both the right and the left, thus being politically ambidextrous (able to use both the right and the left equally well).

The *point* is what gives us a reason for writing—and the reader a reason for reading. Essays with a point don't leave the reader asking, "So what?" A reader doesn't care how you define racism, for example, unless you provide some significance for your definition. This is what the point is—the significance of what you have to say.

5. Bertrand Russell, as an accomplished writer, effectively uses the devices of coherence to create an essay that "hangs together," in which all parts are clearly related to one another. The most fundamental device for achieving wholeness in an essay is a well-stated thesis. All parts of the essay then can be related to it by means of a repetition of its key words. Look again at Russell's thesis—the first sentence of the essay. Several of its words can be termed "key words" because the content of the essay depends on them. They are *passions, my life, love, knowledge,* and *pity. To see how Russell uses the repetition of these words to connect parts of his essay, glance through the essay again and underline each occurrence of these words or related words* (know/knowledge), *synonyms* (understand/know), *or pronouns* (this/love). You see that each paragraph picks up the key word of the thesis and repeats it in nearly every sentence. *Study the essay on page 10.*

What I Have Lived For

1   Three passions, simple but overwhelmingly strong, have governed my life: the longing for love, the search for knowledge, and unbearable pity for the suffering of mankind. These passions, like great winds, have blown me hither and thither, in a wayward course, over a deep ocean of anguish, reaching to the very verge of despair.

2   I have sought love, first, because it brings ecstasy—ecstasy so great that I would often have sacrificed all the rest of life for a few hours of this joy. I have sought it, next, because it relieves loneliness—that terrible loneliness in which one shivering consciousness looks over the rim of the world into the cold unfathomable lifeless abyss. I have sought it, finally, because in the union of love I have seen, in a mystic miniature, the prefiguring vision of the heaven that saints and poets have imagined. This is what I sought, and though it might seem too good for human life, this is what—at last—I have found.

3   With equal passion I have sought knowledge. I have wished to understand the hearts of men. I have wished to know why the stars shine. And I have tried to apprehend the Pythagorean power by which number holds sway above the flux. A little of this, but not much, I have achieved.

4   Love and knowledge, so far as they were possible, led upward toward the heavens. But always pity brought me back to earth. Echoes of cries of pain reverberate in my heart. Children in famine, victims tortured by oppressors, helpless old people a hated burden to their sons, and the whole world of loneliness, poverty, and pain make a mockery of what human life should be. I long to alleviate the evil, but I cannot, and I too suffer.

5   This has been my life. I have found it worth living, and would gladly live it again if the chance were offered me.

Sentence Patterning

Bertrand Russell's sentences have infinite variety. He uses short sentences effectively, but he has many long ones too, varying the patterns or, if he chooses, repeating them. The following sentence pattern is one that you are probably familiar with. It's a series of three independent clauses, joined with the coordinating conjunctions *but* and *and*.

Let's briefly discuss the punctuation. Usually when independent clauses are joined by coordinating conjunctions (*and, but, or, for, nor, so, yet*), the conjunction is preceded by a comma—as in Russell's sentence. However, when the clauses are quite short (as Russell's are), the commas are sometimes omitted. But Russell includes the commas. Now, this is his stylistic choice, and the fact that he uses them indicates his intent. They have the effect of slowing down the reading of the sentence and gaining emphasis for what it says. As an accomplished writer, Russell knew what effect the commas would have.

Read the sentence below and copy it exactly on a sheet of paper, observing the pattern. Compare the example sentence below with the pattern, and then write a sentence of your own.

SENTENCE

I long to alleviate the evil, but I cannot, and I too suffer.

PATTERN

I _____, but I _____, and I _____.

EXAMPLE

I tried to catch the bus, but I missed it, and I had to walk to school.

12   What I Have Lived For

Underline the words and punctuation marks that follow the pattern, as in the example sentence. After imitating the pattern closely, write one or two more sentences that are not so closely patterned but have two statements joined by a coordinating conjunction and a comma.

WRITING ASSIGNMENT

Russell states that his life was governed by "the longing for love, the search for knowledge, and unbearable pity for the suffering of mankind," and he claims further that his life was worth living. Remember that when he was writing he was an old man, a philosopher looking back nearly a century on a life that began in 1872. He had much in his life to remember. Your life is somewhat shorter than Russell's at the time of writing, but for the purposes of this assignment try to decide on three passions that govern your life. Rather than looking at the past, as Russell did, you may want to look at the present, or even project into the future. What is important to you? What are your goals in life? What do you "live for"?

Use Russell's essay as a model for your own. Write a thesis sentence that follows this pattern:

Three passions, ____[modifier]____, govern my life: _____, _____, and _____.

As Russell did, make your thesis the first sentence of your essay and follow it with a position statement (Russell's second sentence) that summarizes the effects these passions have on your life. As your passions will no doubt be different from Russell's, so will the effects.

Write an outline that follows the pattern of the one in Question 1, filling in with your own details. You will have three paragraphs of discussion, each on one of your points, plus an introductory and a concluding paragraph. Your conclusion should make a final statement on the passions you have chosen to write about.

Use your own specific words and phrases to explain your subject—lively verbs (Russell uses *sacrificed, blown*), vivid adjectives (Russell uses *mystic, shivering*), and specific nouns (Russell uses *anguish, abyss*). Explain your subject as fully as necessary for your reader to understand what you're saying. Try following Russell's lead on coherence. Repeat your key words, sometimes using synonyms, pronouns, or related words.

When you've finished writing, reread your essay. Does it follow the model? Have you explained your subject adequately? Have you used *specific* words and phrases? Do all parts of your essay follow your thesis? Have you used coherence devices? How is your spelling? your punctuation? Do you see any other errors you can correct? After thoroughly revising your essay, rewrite it, giving it a final proofreading. That means reading each word and punctuation mark separately—reading for *errors,* not meaning.

2

Shearing Sheep in Patagonia
GEORGE GAYLORD SIMPSON

George Gaylord Simpson, an educator and vertebrate paleontologist, led an archaeological expedition to Patagonia in 1930 to collect fossil remains of the unique animals that once lived in that bleak and barren land. (Politically a part of Argentina, Patagonia is the extreme southern tip of South America.) In *Attending Marvels* Simpson records his impressions of the people and the land, which at one time he describes as "one of the most magnificent things I have ever seen . . . a treeless jungle of badlands, peaks, ridges, and minor valleys" (p. xv). At another time the incredible wind is described as one "that may literally knock a man down and hold him down; people cling to clumps of brush to keep from being blown away, and crawl forward on hands and knees; automobiles can proceed only in low gear; a plane takes off from an airport and hangs suspended in the air for nearly four hours, unable to move forward" (p. xiv). The story below reports an experience among the people of Patagonia, whom Simpson greatly respects but who, in his words, are "set apart from all others."

Vocabulary Preview

line
1, 12 estanciero, estancia — Spanish words for rancher and ranch
1 Puerto Deseado — Patagonian city at the mouth of the Deseado River

16	Carmen de Patagones	city in northern part of Patagonia
16	Magallanes	Magellan Strait
23	Gobernación	Spanish word for government

Essay Preview: Questions to Answer as You Read

1. What kind of man is José?
2. Why did José willingly report back to the jail?
3. What is Simpson telling the reader about life in Patagonia?

Shearing Sheep in Patagonia

1   There was once an estanciero who lived near Puerto Deseado and who had a ranch hand who may be called José. This José was a pretty good sort, take him all in all, but he had his bad moments. One spring day he happened to have a bad moment just at the time when he also happened to have a knife in his hand and when someone who had once annoyed him was nearby.

2   After the funeral, the Majesty of the Law reached out from Deseado and collared poor José in spite of his kind heart. He was locked up in a cell and given a long time to get over his bad moments while he awaited trial. Out on the estancia the sheep were being sheared, but somehow things did not go well. The estanciero began to miss José very much—I almost forgot to say that in addition to having a kind heart José was a first-class sheep man and that from Carmen de Patagones down to Magallanes there was not his equal in shearing; he had a touch around the ears and tail that was a real pleasure to watch.

3   So the forlorn estanciero went in to Puerto Deseado and went to see the Majesty of the Law.

4   "Do you realize," he said, "that here I am right in the middle of spring shearing and that you have the very best sheep shearer in all Santa Cruz Gobernación in your lousy lock-up?"

16   Shearing Sheep in Patagonia

"Well," said the Majesty of the Law, "I can quite see your point of view, but you know there was that little unpleasantness about the knife, and the widow seems to feel that I should do something about it."

"Let's put it this way, then. Suppose you turn José over to me temporarily. As soon as we are through shearing I will send him back to you."

Thus it was agreed, and José worked long and faithfully, with some particularly fancy work around the tails and no bad moments. When the work was all done the estanciero said to him:

"Now, José, here is all the money that I owe you. It is a great deal and I am sorry to part with it, but after all you have earned it. And now they are waiting for you in Puerto Deseado, where the Majesty of the Law is planning to hang you. I promised him that you would be back, so just give me your word that you will report at the jail there, and then skip along like a good fellow. Goodbye!"

So of course José went to Puerto Deseado and reported at the jail where he was immediately locked up, he and all the money he had earned shearing sheep so well. The next day he asked to see the Majesty of the Law.

On the second day, José turned up healthy but broke at the estancia, where he asked for work and was given it.

"Oh well," the Majesty of the Law was saying at about the same time, "it was just a bad moment after all, poor chap." And he paid cash for a very shiny new automobile.

That is a true story.

Questions for Discussion

1. In the last sentence we are told that this story is true. *What is the effect of this statement on your reading of the story? How do you suppose that Simpson, a stranger in Patagonia, came to know about this occurrence in Puerto Deseado?*

   While some narratives report personally observed events, this one more likely reports the story second-hand. Someone probably related it to Simpson, perhaps introducing it by asking the familiar "Have you ever heard the one about . . .?"

2. Even though the story may be secondhand—that is, the narrator wasn't participating or watching it happen—it has the vivid freshness of a firsthand account. *What contributes to this freshness?*

The wealth of detail is one factor. *Consider Simpson's use of proper names: when does he use them? For what important characters does he* not *use them? What effect is achieved by not referring to these people by name?*

Freshness is also gained by the use of dialogue. While these are most likely not the original words of the participants, they are characteristic of the people and fitting to the situation. Notice how a narrator works quotations into his story—by making clear who the speaker is, enclosing the words in quotation marks, and wording the speech as the speaker would have said it: *I* speaking to *you* now. Therefore pronouns are first person (*I, we*) and second person (*you*). Also, the verb time is present ("I *am* right in the middle of spring shearing"). *Find examples of pronouns and verbs in the quoted dialogue.*

3. *In the preliminary questions you were asked to find evidence of why José willingly went back to jail. Now that you've read the story, what do you think?* The estanciero did not accompany José to the jail, just paid him and sent him across country on his own. And José actually went. *Why? Was it a sense of honor that impelled him? a sense of justice? a sense of fate?*

Well, when you consider the ending of the story, you can't help thinking that it wasn't because of any of these noble virtues that José went, but rather that somehow he knew all along he'd be returning soon to the estancia.

4. While Simpson's narrative has plenty of specific details about José's affair, there are two gaps in the story, where something happened that was not reported. *What happened between paragraphs 1 and 2 and between paragraphs 9 and 10? Why do you suppose Simpson left out these two crucial bits of information?*

18 Shearing Sheep in Patagonia

5. *What is Simpson's attitude toward this story? Note the sentence that begins on line 4, and then the first two sentences of paragraph 2.*

Clearly the story is not meant to be taken too seriously. Find other evidence of this light-hearted tone reflecting the author's attitude toward the subject.

6. *If the tone of the essay is mildly humorous, then what would you say is Simpson's purpose for telling this story? There is no statement of thesis, is there?*

We have simply a straight narrative, beginning like the traditional "once upon a time" story and concluding with the popular happy ending. *So what's the purpose?*

7. Even if the purpose is just to entertain, the story means something. There is an underlying theme or thesis, whether it's expressed or not. *What would you say it is?* At times like these we understand why essays usually have a stated thesis, because there's no doubt about what idea the writer wanted to convey. *If you were writing a thesis for this essay, what would it be, and where would you put it?*

One way of wording the thesis might be: "The wise man in Patagonia survives by knowing how to play the game." If this sentence were included in the narrative, it might go at the end.

Sentence Patterning

Simpson uses dialogue effectively in this story, reporting in quotation marks the actual words—or what might have been the actual words—of the participants. Doing so gives a sense of immediacy to a narrative and makes the reader feel as if he or she is on the scene too. One requirement of dialogue is that it must be written in the words of the *speaker,* not of the narrator, nor of some combination of the two. Speakers refer to themselves as *I* or *we* and to their audience as *you,* whereas a narrator in an indirect method of reporting speech would use *he, she,* or *they* (or a name) for both speaker and the speaker's audience. A speaker exists in the present and generally uses present-time verbs (unless referring to a past or future action), but narrators usually use *past*-time verbs—to report speech that already happened. See how these points are carried out in the sentence below. Within the quotation marks, this sentence picks up again the pattern of coordination practiced in Chapter 1, "What I Have Lived For."

SENTENCE

"Well," said the Majesty of the Law, "I can quite see your point of view, but you know there was that little unpleasantness about the knife, and the widow seems to feel that I should do something about it."

Copy the sentence exactly as it is written. Study its pattern and the example; finally write your own sentence in imitation. In place of *but* and *and* you can use any of the coordinating conjunctions: *and, but, or, nor, for, so, yet.*

PATTERN

"_____," said _____," _____
_____, but _____
_____, and _____."

EXAMPLE

"On the other hand," said the Chief of Police, "your driving record is far from impressive, and your car is not in legal driving condition, so we have no recourse but to take your driver's license."

WRITING ASSIGNMENT

Tell a story, either first- or secondhand, about something you saw happen or something you heard about. It must be something you know enough about in order to recount it in detail. Try to think of an incident involving people, one that makes some kind of a statement about people—what they're like, how they react to their environment. Once you've decided on an incident, prod your mind to remember details. Ask:

What happened?	What was said?
How did it happen?	Why did it happen?
When did it happen?	What were the results?
Where did it happen?	Why do I remember it?
Who was involved?	How do I feel about it?

When you can't think of any more questions, go back to the beginning and ask questions in greater detail:

What did I omit from "What happened?"?
Any more details on how it happened?
What time of day, or when in relation to other events?
Where—specific place names; what is important about the place?

And so on. After you've collected details about the incident, organize them chronologically. Delete the ones that you can't use, and add more where you need them. Write a tentative thesis that gives a point to the whole narrative. Then start to write.

Use some dialogue. While you may have to make this up, write what you think was said, in the way the speaker would have said it. Slang and dialect are appropriate; punctuation, however, follows the usual conventions. As you write your dialogue, observe in the model essay how the quotations are managed. Pronouns will be first person *I* speaking to second person *you* in present-time verbs (except when the speaker is relating a past or future event). Quotation marks will follow conventional usage, as illustrated in the pattern sentence.

Name the participants in your narrative unless you have a good reason not to. Name places, and use specific details to explain events.

Begin with the story format Simpson used, if you want to, but somewhere in your introduction you must introduce the main participants and the setting. From there go on to tell the story. Know before you start what the meaning, or controlling idea, of your essay is; then choose your words and details accordingly. Simpson, for example, in showing how resourceful an uneducated Patagonian sheepshearer can be, includes details that show shearing expertise to be more important in Patagonia of the 1920s than controlling "bad moments." When you get to the end of your essay, express your central idea in a final statement, or, as Simpson does, leave it unexpressed. If you choose for stylistic reasons not to express your thesis in your essay, write it on another sheet of paper for your teacher's benefit. In academic writing it's generally better for students to state their thesis so as not to keep their reader (who's usually the teacher) guessing.

After you've completed your first draft, read it over. Are your unquoted verbs in *past* time? Are those in dialogue written in present time? Is your punctuation correct? Have you included enough details? some proper names? What is the tone of your essay—serious or light? It shouldn't be both, and whichever it is should be clear from the beginning.

When you're satisfied with your narrative, make a clean copy and proofread it.

3

The Beginning of a Word

J. WALLACE HAMILTON

J. Wallace Hamilton was a twentieth-century Christian minister who drew crowds of people to hear his simple, direct preaching at his Pasadena (Florida) Community Church. In addition to his sermons he wrote a number of books, one of which is entitled *Serendipity*. The following excerpt comes from its opening pages, where Hamilton begins to acquaint his reader with a word that in 1965, the date of publication, was somewhat unfamiliar. The essay below defines it.

Vocabulary Preview

line		
7	derivation	origination; source
17	sagacity	wisdom; sound judgment; intelligence
17	quest	a seeking; a search; a journey in search of adventure
32	pasteurization	a method of destroying bacteria in milk, beer, and a few other liquids by heating them to a certain temperature for a given period of time
35	itinerant	traveling from place to place, usually in order to do some kind of work
42	vacuum tube	an electron tube that has as much air removed as possible to permit free movement of electrons, used as an amplifier and for other electronic functions

49 saltpeter   potassium nitrate, a transparent white crystalline compound used in fertilizers, gunpowder, and as a chemical agent

Essay Preview: Questions to Answer as You Read

1. What is the origin of the word "serendipity"?
2. What are three medical examples of serendipity?
3. How is the discovery of glass said to be serendipitous?

The Beginning of a Word

Serendipity! Most people now are somewhat acquainted with this unusual word. It's an uncommon word for a very common experience. It means "the gift of finding valuable or agreeable things not sought for." It's a word used to describe that strange process of indirection, the unexpected that happens when one is pursuing something else.

Perhaps its definition is best provided by its derivation. It was Sir Horace Walpole who coined the word in 1754, basing it on a Persian fairy tale, *Three Princes of Serendip*. Serendip was the ancient or Arabic name for the island now called Ceylon. The legend was that every time the princes of Serendip went on a journey something unexpected happened; quite by coincidence they found valuable things not sought for. Sir Horace called it *serendipity*. In a letter to Horace Mann, January 8, 1754, he said he formed the word "because as their highnesses traveled they were always making discoveries by accident or sagacity of things they were not in quest of."

Certainly there ought to be a word for that, because life is full of it. "Columbus," as Emerson said, "looking for a direct route to Asia, stubbed his toe on America"; Edison, looking for an electric light, found a phonograph; a chemist, holding over the fire a test tube with a few grains of rice in it, happened to drop the tube, and when he picked it up the rice had exploded: puffed rice—serendipity!—seeking one thing and incidentally finding another. . . .

Certainly the history of medicine is filled with serendipitous events. We could begin with Louis Pasteur, although long before his time medical history had recorded many fortunate surprises. It was Pasteur who said, "Chance favors the prepared mind," and he, himself, was his own best illustration. Looking for a way to keep wine from turning sour, by chance he found the process of pasteurization. What a lifesaver that has been!

5   The discovery of anesthetics came, in part, by accident. Dr. Crawford Long of Jefferson, Georgia, heard an itinerant lecturer speak on laughing gas which, when inhaled, made people laugh-happy. Having had some experience with ether, Dr. Long tried it out; he put a man to sleep—even as the Lord did with Adam in the Eden story. Oliver Wendell Holmes named it "anesthesia." Wilhelm Roentgen, a professor in a Bavarian university, after class one day was working with the vacuum tube for improved photography, and leaning wearily on the table saw some unusual fluorescent action that started him down a two-year trail to the X ray. . . .

6   Glass is a serendipity. According to the old story which can never be fully verified, some Phoenician sailors anchored their ship off the North African coast. Unable to find stones on which to set their cooking pots, they took lumps of saltpeter from the cargo of their ship and set their kettles on them. In the heat of the fire the saltpeter melted, mingled with the sand, and when it cooled they had a hard, clear, transparent substance—glass. So runs the old story which the encyclopedia says should not be discarded as wholly fiction. . . .

7   So we've come far enough at least to put this down: in many of the most exciting discoveries of human history all the way from grandfather's clock to the most epochmaking breakthrough of the ages—the process of indirection can be traced clearly: something was discovered while the discoverers were pursuing something else.

Questions for Discussion

1. *Define "serendipity" in a single sentence and with your own words.*
2. Hamilton says that serendipity is a common occurrence. *Think of a serendipitous event in your own life and write*

about it in a short paragraph like one of Hamilton's. Would your paragraph make a suitable addition to his essay? Where might you place it in his essay?

3. *What is the effect of the numerous examples that illustrate serendipity? If the word was new to you when you began reading the essay, would you now feel at ease using it in your own speech or writing?*

4. *Note the specific mention of proper names and other details and the use of direct quotations where they're appropriate. What is the effect of specific details on you as a reader? What would be the difference if the second sentence in paragraph 5, instead of beginning "Dr. Crawford Long . . . ," began "A certain man from the South . . ."?* One characteristic of general, non-specific writing is that it is BORING. Next time you write, you might ask, "Am I boring my reader?" If you suspect that you are, revise the writing by substituting specific words and details for some of your general words and phrases.

5. Hamilton organizes his definition of serendipity by introducing the word and then piling up numerous examples. Broken down, his essay looks something like this outline:

    paragraph
    _____   I. Introduction: meaning of word
    _____ II. Derivation of word
    _____ III. Three short examples
    _____ IV. Examples in medical field
    _____   V. One long example
    _____ VI. Summary

    Identify the paragraphs that correspond to parts I through VI of the outline.

6. It appears that Hamilton had two purposes for writing this essay: to define serendipity and to show how prevalent the experience is. *Reread his conclusion and see how these two purposes are intertwined.* This is his summary or restatement of his thesis. It is a broadening of the early statement in paragraph 1: "Serendipity! . . . It's an uncommon word for a very common experience."

7. *Notice how each paragraph is linked to the thesis by repeating the key words. At the beginning of each paragraph, underline words that repeat, are synonyms for, or represent (as pronouns) the three key words in the thesis statement:* serendipity, word, experience. *For example, in the first sentence of paragraph 2 you would underline* its, *a pronoun referring back to* serendipity. *Proceed with the remaining paragraphs.*

   Paragraph 5 does not have a sentence keyed to the thesis. Why not? *What is this paragraph keyed to? Recall your placement of it in the outline.* Notice that other paragraphs too are connected not only to the thesis but to one another. Paragraph 5 goes on with medical examples begun in paragraph 4. Paragraphs 3 and 4 are connected by the repetition of an opening word. Paragraph 3 connects to paragraph 2 with the pronouns *that* and *it,* referring to *serendipity,* which is mentioned in paragraph 2 as well as in the thesis.

8. Is there any evidence in the essay that Hamilton as a Christian minister was writing strictly for a Christian audience? Give examples from the essay to support your answer.

9. In paragraph 4 Hamilton quotes Louis Pasteur as saying "Chance favors the prepared mind." *What does this statement mean in relation to serendipity? What does it say about education?*

Sentence Patterning

Two common errors in writing are the comma splice and the run-on (or fused) sentence. Actually they're the same error: two independent clauses with only a comma or no punctuation between them. To be correct they need a coordinating conjunction or a semicolon. In Chapters 1 and 2 we practiced using the coordinating conjunction. The pattern sentence for this assignment gives practice writing compound sentences that have semicolons (another practice of this pattern accompanies "Spelling Is Nonsense," p. 30).

In the sentence below, observe that the portion that comes before the semicolon could be written as a sentence, as could the part that follows it. In other words, the semicolon *could* be replaced by a period, making two sentences. Hamilton chose to include both portions in the same sentence because they express closely related ideas.

SENTENCE

> The legend was that every time the princes of Serendip went on a journey something unexpected happened; quite by coincidence they found valuable things not sought for.

Just to get the feeling of writing this kind of compound sentence, *copy* it; write it word for word on a piece of paper. Here's the pattern it follows and an example of another sentence written on this pattern:

PATTERN

———————————————————————— ; ————————————
———————————————————————— .

EXAMPLE

> My friend Mark is the best example I know of a sarcastic person; every time he opens his mouth he lets out words of biting sarcasm.

Now write a sentence of your own that observes the pattern of two independent clauses with a semicolon between them. As a test, read each clause separately: could each one be a sentence?

WRITING ASSIGNMENT

In this writing assignment you are to define a word, as Hamilton does, by giving several examples of the thing the word stands for. That is, don't give examples of how the word is used in sentences; instead, show what the word means by giving examples of its meaning. Hamilton presents examples of serendipity; if you were to write on prescience, you would give examples of it. Here are some words that may or may not be familiar to you. Choose one, find out what it means, and then see if you can think of some examples. Or, read the list slowly, checking definitions and trying to recall examples for each word; then choose the one that you can illustrate best:

rhythm	vanity
euphemism	hypocrisy
pathos	eccentricity
prescience	din
sarcasm	equivocation

Begin, as Hamilton does, with a definition—not quoting from a dictionary, but using your own words (after you've consulted the dictionary). Also in your introduction make a statement of thesis: what's the point you're making? With Hamilton the point is that serendipity is an uncommon word for a common experience.

In your second paragraph you may discuss derivation of the word or go right on to your examples. Hamilton uses examples in several different ways: three short ones, then several on one subject, then a long one. You may want to use some combination of these methods. Just keep in mind that you want to present the *best* examples you can think of and *enough* examples to illustrate the meaning of your word so that it's clear to your reader when you finish.

Begin your paragraphs with transitional sentences that link the paragraphs to the thesis by means of repeating key words. These opening sentences will also serve as topic sentences, suggesting the central idea of the paragraph. Notice that the first sentences of paragraphs 4 and 6 are good examples of topic sentences, with key words repeated. End with a restatement of your thesis that also repeats your definition. Reread Hamilton's final paragraph as one example of how this can be done.

After you've finished writing your rough draft, check your connections. Are your examples clearly related to your thesis? Are all your paragraphs connected to your thesis and to each other? Reread your examples to see if you've explained them clearly enough. Have you included all the details your reader will need? (You can assume that your reader is an intelligent human being, but don't assume knowledge of your thoughts and subject.) Have you used specific words and phrases that bring your examples to life? Is your thesis stated clearly so that it accurately indicates the point of your essay?

Finally, check for correctness in grammar, spelling, and punctuation. If you know that you often make a particular kind of error, check especially for that. See if you have any comma-spliced or run-on sentences: two independent clauses with only a comma or no punctuation between them. If you find any sentences that you suspect, try putting a period between the two clauses. If you make two complete sentences by doing so, then you can use a semicolon or keep the period. Another thing to check is the endings of your words to make sure you haven't omitted a necessary *-s* or *-ed*. Carefully read the entire essay through several times. When you're satisfied with your revisions, make a clean copy and proofread it, looking at every word and punctuation mark.

4

Spelling Is Nonsense

DONALD E. P. SMITH, EDITOR

Donald E. P. Smith is the editor of *Learning to Learn*, a study skills textbook written for college students by several teachers experienced in teaching study skills and reading. The selection below is one small section of this book and presents a technique for improving spelling as well as some opinions about spelling.

Vocabulary Preview

line
8	imbecile	in psychology terms, a mentally retarded person with an I.Q. ranging from 30 to 50
20	nonsensible	not able to be perceived by the senses or the intellect
23	rote	a fixed, mechanical way of doing something; by memory alone, without understanding
26	obliterating	blotting out; erasing

Essay Preview: Questions to Answer as You Read

1. What two kinds of words should people learn how to spell?
2. What parts of the body other than the brain are used in the learning process presented here?
3. Describe the format of the instructions.

Spelling Is Nonsense

1. For some unaccountable reason, the executive, the parent, the man in the street—sometimes even college professors—judge a man's intelligence by his ability to spell. Such a practice is grossly unjust. The relationship between spelling ability and brightness is so small as to be negligible. And when conditions for learning words are optimum, even this small relationship disappears.

2. To press the point further, some children classified as imbeciles excel in spelling. The child need not know what the word imbecile means to be able to spell it!

3. One's intelligence indicates one's ability to deal with ideas, with meanings, in short, with things sensible. Now, no matter how sensible a man is, he won't be able to determine the spelling of *enough* unless he is told. True, some spelling words follow rules; the thinking man is able to spell *sleigh* by applying the crutch, "*i* before *e,* except after *c,* or pronounced as *a* as in *neighbor* or *weigh.*" But then what should he do with *either, neither, height, deity, leisure, heir, weird,* and *seive,* not to mention *heigh-ho!*

4. Materials which are nonsensible are called nonsense materials, as noted earlier. If mastery of such materials does not yield to cold logic, how will it occur? Once more we return to the problem of rote learning, or brute memory. We must develop an association between the sound of a word and its picture. Such an association is difficult for some people to establish. Tension may result in obliterating traces, or attention to a word may be inadequate so that the spelling is not seen clearly or the sound not heard correctly to begin with.

5. One way to remedy this problem is to increase attention by increasing the strength of stimulation. Greater input = greater number of associations. The procedure is as follows:

1. Limit your words to be learned to two kinds:
   a. Those which you understand. In general, the more meaning a word has, the easier it is to learn.
   b. Those which appear to be your personal demons. Most

people who consider themselves poor spellers consistently err on only 100 words. Find those words in your old theme papers.
2. Write the word in large script.
A discharge from blood vessels caused by injury:

hemorrhage

3. Trace the word with your index finger three times *saying the word (not* the letters) aloud as you trace. Begin tracing and saying simultaneously. (Do this now with the word *hemorrhage.*)
4. Next, close your eyes and try to visualize the word in your "mind's eye." (Do this now. Some people are unable to visualize. If you are one of those, skip this step.)
5. Next, trace the word on the desk, saying it aloud as you trace it. (Do this now. If you are unable to see part of the word or to trace it, repeat steps 3 and 4.)
6. Now, write the word normally. (Do this now.)
7. Compare the word you have just written with that in large script. Find any errors?
8. If there is an error, repeat the whole procedure, paying particular attention to the trouble spot.

Now learning will be relatively complete, and retention will be high. You have provided multiple sensory input: vision, hearing, touch, muscular sensations (kinesthesis), all in the context of meaning.

Now try these:
A physician who specializes in vision:

ophthalmologist

Sleeping sickness:

encephalitis

A specialist in behavior:

psychologist

Questions for Discussion

1. *Think about the writer's purpose in this essay.*
   a. *Is it to undercut some fallacies about spelling?*
   b. *Is it to point out some techniques that don't work for learning to spell?*
   c. *Is it to convince the reader that "Spelling is Nonsense"?*

   Considering the major thrust of the essay and the fact that it appears in a book on study and reading skills, what would you say is the ultimate purpose?

   While the writer wants you to know that much of our thinking about spelling is faulty and illogical, his ultimate purpose must surely be to present a method that he thinks works. We infer this because he devotes half of the essay to detailing that method.

2. *What does the title mean? Does "Spelling Is Nonsense" mean that we shouldn't bother about spelling, that it isn't important?*

   Paragraphs 3 and 4 explain the title by clarifying the terms *sensible* and *nonsensible*. The mind perceives ideas or meanings, but much of our English spelling defies understanding. (Actually, some of the rules are more useful than implied here.) Therefore, spelling is "nonsensible," not able to be understood by ordinary means, and we must resort to methods other than cold logic for learning it.

3. *What learning tools does the suggested method use if not logic? What do paragraphs 5 and 6 tell you? Do you think this method will work for learning difficult words?*

4. *What kinds of words does Smith say we should learn? How can you find out what your "demons" are?*

5. *Did you try Smith's method as you read the essay? If not, try it now, exactly as explained. Don't omit or shorten any steps. When you have tried out the method on* hemorrhage, *practice it on* ophthalmologist, en-

cephalitis, *and* psychologist. *These are really hard words, and not often used, so next practice the method on a few of your own spelling demons.*

Now what do you think about the effectiveness of the method? Does it work for you?

6. Take a look at how the essay is put together. Paragraph 5 outlines the process and paragraph 7 gives additional practice, while paragraphs 1 through 4 lead up to the process. In outline form, the essay looks something like this:

paragraph
_____	I. Fallacy about spelling
_____	II. Spelling not sensible
_____	III. Nonsensible method needed
_____	IV. Thesis statement
____5____	V. Method
_____	VI. Summary
____7____	VII. Practice

At the left, parts V and VII are labeled with their corresponding paragraphs. *Identify the others.*

7. *Which paragraph states the thesis?*

The thesis statement in this essay serves as a pivot between the introductory first half and the instructional second half. After using four paragraphs to present the problem, the writer begins paragraph 5, "One way to remedy this problem . . . ," and then presents the solution. Thus the beginning half and the second half both are contained in this pivotal sentence.

8. The supporting example in paragraph 3 has its own problems. *Can you identify two weaknesses in the two last sentences of this paragraph?*

The first problem is with the wording of the *i*-before-*e* rule. Another way of phrasing the rule is "*i* before *e* except after *c* when the sound is long *ee*," and this phrasing allows for only a few exceptions. With it said in this way, *height* is no longer an exception, nor is *heir* or *deity*. Furthermore, one of the so-called exceptions in this essay is in fact a misspelling, and that's the second weakness in this paragraph. The misspelled word is copied in this book exactly as it was printed in *Learning to Learn*. Which word is it? You may need to use your dictionary.

Sentence Patterning

The semicolon in English is a punctuation mark that is frequently either overused or not used when it's needed. Our sentence for this imitation is one with a semicolon (the sentence has been edited for this exercise):

SENTENCE

> Some spelling words follow rules; the thinking man is able to spell *sleigh* by applying the *i*-before-*e* rule as a crutch.

Copy the sentence exactly as it is, watching spelling and punctuation. In modern written English, the semicolon has almost the force of a period, separating two independent clauses that the writer wants contained in the same sentence because of the close relationship of ideas. Grammatically, the writer *could* use a period between the two clauses and make two sentences. Thus we could write the sentence above as follows:

> Some spelling words follow rules. The thinking man is able to spell *sleigh* by applying the *i*-before-*e* rule as a crutch.

Here the meaning is the same but the separation is greater.

Use a semicolon, therefore, between two independent clauses not connected with a conjunction—when you could use a period if you wanted that much separation. *Don't* use the semicolon when you could use a comma, and don't confuse it with the colon (see Chapter 6, "Good and Bad," for a sentence pattern using the colon). As indicated in Chapter 3, "The Beginning of a

Word," using a comma where a period or semicolon is needed makes a comma splice.

Observe the sentence pattern below and study the example of a sentence written on this pattern. Then write your own imitative sentence.

PATTERN

_____ ; _____
_____.

EXAMPLE

A ditto machine is not always a willing servant; in the hands of an unskilled operator it can be an uncooperative little beast.

WRITING ASSIGNMENT

"Spelling Is Nonsense" is an essay that tells the reader how to do something. The instructions are directed explicitly to the reader through use of imperative verbs (with *you* understood: *limit, write, trace,* etc.) and the second person pronoun *you*. The instructions also, as you've probably noticed, are written in the form of a numbered list. The paragraphs preceding the instructions explain the need for this process, and the final paragraph makes a suitable conclusion. So the structure of the essay is rather simple. A shortened form of the outline in Question 6 might look like this:

    I. Explanation of need
   II. Introduction of process
  III. Steps in the process
  IV. Conclusion

This is the outline you are to follow in writing this assignment. Your explanation of the need may be a little shorter than the one about spelling—one or two paragraphs perhaps, instead of four. Follow this explanation with your thesis sentence and then the process in a list of numbered steps. Conclude with a suitable ending, referring again to the value of the process. Do note that the listed steps are written as *complete sentences,* using imperative verbs, with the subject, *you,* understood.

You probably know better than anyone else what a good subject for you might be—something you know how to do well enough that you can explain it to someone else. The following topics, however, might lead you to an idea. How to:

Do the laundry	Repair a cuckoo clock
Iron a shirt	Strip varnish from a
Fill a car with gas	wood surface
Take a good picture	Make French toast
Develop photographic film	Use a ditto machine

Once you've decided on a topic, think through—and jot down—all the steps for completing this process. When you feel you've covered everything, read through the steps you've written down and picture yourself doing them. Have you omitted anything that a novice will need to know? If so, jot it down. Are your steps arranged sequentially—in the exact order in which they should be done? If not, rearrange them now, while they're still in note form. Before you write, you'll also need to decide how your reader would be helped by learning this process. This information will make up the beginning part of your essay. Then write a thesis sentence that will serve as a pivot between your explanation and your outline of the process. It will refer to both parts. When you're satisfied with the phrasing of your thesis, you're ready to start writing.

While you are writing, keep your reader in mind at all times. In the first part you need to convince the reader that he or she can benefit by learning this process. What will be convincing? Then as you're telling the reader how to do this thing, you need to be constantly aware of the reader there with you, trying to follow your instructions. What difficulties might he or she have? What further explanations are needed? What step are you omitting because doing it is so natural for you? Remember that *you* are the expert now, sharing your expertise with someone you want to make an expert too.

When you finish writing, the most important point to check is whether your instructions are *complete*. If not, make necessary additions. Also, are your instructions *clear?* If not, you'll need to adjust your writing accordingly. Another thing to check is whether you've included *unnecessary details.* It's not necessary, for example, when telling someone how to make French toast to instruct that person to "walk over to the refrigerator and take out two eggs." A sensible person will know where the eggs are kept and how to get there. Don't insult your reader with unnecessary details, yet don't frustrate him with insufficient ones either.

Check also to see that you've written complete sentences—not fragments—in detailing your instructions. You should have a period at the end of each step. Reread the rest of your essay too for sentence completeness and clarity. Make sure that two independent clauses in the same sentences are joined with either a conjunction or a semicolon. Check "little" things like spelling and punctuation, because when a number of little things go wrong they detract from the idea presented in the paper. Sometimes the meaning is even obscured.

When you've finished revising your paper, write a clean draft, proofread it, and turn it in.

5

The Great Process

TOM SCHWABE

Tom Schwabe wrote the following essay in response to an assignment in his freshman composition class. He was to analyze his own process of writing and describe it in an essay. Tom, an architecture major, chose to write for an audience of fellow students who might be interested in this kind of idea-sharing.

Vocabulary Preview

line		
29	comprise(s)	to include; consist of; make up
62	iterative	repetitious; done again repeatedly
65	incorporate	to combine with something else, making a single whole
84	intimidating	inspiring fear; making one timid

Essay Preview: Questions to Answer as You Read

1. What steps does Schwabe follow as he writes?
2. Are these steps separate and distinct?
3. What does Schwabe do when he's trying to generate ideas for writing?

The Great Process

1   Are you having trouble with your essay writing? Do you have a certain writing process you follow each time you write? If the respective answers to these questions were *yes* and *no,* you certainly aren't the only banana in the bunch.

The Great Process

You probably wonder, as I myself do, how I could write like or be as successful as writers like Twain, Steinbeck, Poe, Skwire*, or Chitwood*. One thing all known writers have in common is that they follow their own fixed process for writing. Now I am just another Joe-Amateur writer, but maybe I can help you along by showing you my process for an example. One easy method of writing that I and others use is to break the process into prewriting, writing, and revision steps. This method might not get you or me a bestseller, but it sure helps when writing academic papers.

2   The prewriting phase is one you should pay attention to all through your essay writing. It could involve making an outline or, like me, jotting down ideas. I usually think about a writing assignment while riding the bus, playing a sport, or sitting by myself with nothing on my hands but time. For me it's not boring to just sit in my backyard and stare into space, so a lot of times while I sit I think of ideas for an essay. I jot down main ideas instead of using an outline, since most times I write spontaneously, thinking of most of my ideas while I write. As long as I take my time when thinking and writing, occasionally referring back to my original ideas to see if I am doing what I set out to do, I can pretty well accomplish the task at hand. So prewriting for me involves thinking about ideas before I start and while I am writing.

3   The second phase of writing, the actual writing part, usually comprises the bulk of the process. As stated before, if you use enough time in the prewriting phase, this step shouldn't be as tough as your first impression of it was. Many times I think of additional ideas as I write, and I integrate them into the paragraph. Or if the idea isn't related to the paragraph, I jot down the idea for future reference. If I am stuck and can't think of any more ideas, I stop writing and do something else.

4   Writing for me involves pausing momentarily to think of another idea, and while I think I might play a little basketball or kick a Nerf ball against the wall of my room. Or, for

---

*Authors of Schwabe's composition textbook: David Skwire and Frances Chitwood, *Student's Book of College English,* 3rd ed. (New York: Macmillan, 1981).

instance, right now I'm outside doing a combination of spontaneous writing and staring into space. I pause and pet my dog or just watch the trees blow or the little kids fight next door. If it's too cold or dark to write outside, I write in my room. My parents used to wonder what was going on whenever I wrote since they could hear the music fluctuating from loud to soft levels. They now know from experience that when they hardly hear a thing coming from my room I've got a good idea going. And when they see or hear the ceiling rattle, they know that it is the result of my frequent pauses when I turn up the music and kick my Nerf around.

5   I know I am not the model writer who makes an outline and goes from there, but it works better for me to think of ideas while I go. For me the process of writing includes both prewriting and revision along with the actual writing. Composing is easier if I use enough time before and while writing to think of what I am going to say and to sometimes revise as I go along.

6   Revision is a tedious task that many people take too lightly. It is the process of rereading what you have written to see if the writing is clear and correct. Revising an essay is like designing a building; they both are feedback and iterative processes. Feedback involves the generating of new ideas along the way, causing the writer or designer to review previous work and incorporate the idea if it is appropriate. And iteration is the process in which the designer or writer runs through the work over and over at various times along the way. Successive iterations most times give a satisfactory piece of work.

7   So the bulk of my revision occurs while writing. I refer back to previous sentences often and sometimes even to entire paragraphs to see where I left off. After layoffs, I have to remind myself of the purpose of the paper, and sometimes I don't do that. Even when I know the purpose, there's a good possibility I'll leave out a comma or a letter, small items but necessary ones. After I've finished the essay, I read the entire essay for overlooked mistakes. And I reread the final copy also to see if I made any mistakes while recopying.

8   The process of writing can be a long task for me; however, taking my time with the prewriting, writing, and revision

steps makes it seem easier. It's much easier for me to write if I'm not rushed, so I start early and spread the process into several days. Using this method makes the process of writing less intimidating and easier to accomplish.

Questions for Discussion

1. *What three steps does Schwabe observe as he writes? Are these steps separate and distinct?*

   While it is common to describe the writing process in terms of prewriting, writing, and revision, these three steps generally overlap, as Schwabe explains. *Think about your own writing. Does your prewriting—your generation of ideas—continue while you are writing? Do you revise as you write?*

2. *How would you describe the tone of Schwabe's essay? How serious is he about his subject? Why does he include Skwire and Chitwood with Twain, Steinbeck, and Poe as successful writers?*

   By naming Skwire and Chitwood along with writers of international note, Schwabe seems to be saying that he's going to have a little fun with this essay and the reader is welcome to join him (no offense to Skwire and Chitwood intended). *Find other instances of a less-than-serious treatment of the subject.*

3. While Schwabe has given his essay a somewhat breezy, carefree tone, he nevertheless is serious about carefully describing his subject for the interested reader. *Find some sentences that indicate this intent.*

4. As indicated by the title, this essay describes a *process*. Process writing sometimes tells how something is done ("Blubber on Ice," p. 83), sometimes "how I do something," and sometimes "how you, the reader, can do something" ("Spelling Is Nonsense," p. 30). Schwabe combines the last two types: telling the reader how to do something by describing how he does it. He brings "you" (the reader) into the essay in his very first sentence, and he introduces the "I" (himself) in his third sentence. *Find other instances of the "you" and of the "I."*

5. An introduction to an essay accomplishes several tasks. One is to establish a relationship with the reader, as discussed in Question 4. In his introductory paragraph, Schwabe establishes that he is a student writing to another student about a subject that concerns both. An introduction also sets the tone for the essay, as discussed in Questions 2 and 3. Another thing it does is present the subject and restrict this subject to a particular aspect, which is expressed in the thesis statement. *What is the subject of the essay? What is the thesis?*

    Subjects and thesis statements are not the same thing. Subjects can be expressed in a phrase, a fragment of a sentence, like "the writing process," which is the subject of this essay. A thesis statement, on the other hand, makes a *predication*—an assertion or firm statement—about the subject. The thesis *must be a sentence,* and it answers the question "so what?" So what about the writing process? "Maybe I can help you along by showing you my process; it consists of three steps: prewriting, writing, and revision." This is Schwabe's thesis, which he expands into two sentences in his introduction. Divided into subject and predication, it might look like this:

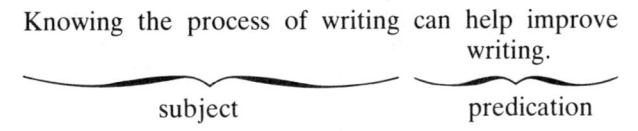

    $$\underbrace{\text{Knowing the process of writing can}}_{\text{subject}} \underbrace{\text{help improve writing.}}_{\text{predication}}$$

    The predication makes the *point.*

6. *How is Schwabe's essay organized?* The organization of process essays is usually easy and obvious: according to the steps in the process. So Schwabe writes about prewriting, writing, and revision, making clear throughout that the categories overlap.

Sentence Patterning

Transitional words and phrases (like *however, for example, therefore*) are sometimes used in sentences like those you practiced in Chapters 3 and 4, in which you used a semicolon to separate two independent clauses. These words can be used at the *beginning* of the second clause, as an *interruption* somewhere in the clause, or even at the *end* of the clause. This feature of being movable is one way of distinguishing these words (which are adverbs) from conjunctions, which are not movable. To see how adverbs can be moved, try inserting *however* in the sentence below at each of the positions marked with a ∧ .

> Howard wanted to sing in the choir; ∧ he had to work ∧ during the auditions ∧ .

It works, doesn't it? *However,* set off with commas, can be used in each of these positions. Now try the same thing with *but,* a conjunction.

> Howard wanted to sing in the choir; ∧ he had to work ∧ during the auditions ∧ .

It's obvious that *but* can be used in only one position—at the beginning of its clause. Conjunctions are not movable; adverbs are.

As you remember from Chapters 3 and 4, sentences made up of two independent clauses not joined by a conjunction must be connected with a semicolon. This is true even when the second clause begins with a transitional adverb, like *however* or *then.* The sentence below is an example of this type of sentence. It has two independent clauses (either one of which could be a sentence) connected by a semicolon, with a transitional adverb introducing the second clause.

SENTENCE

> The process of writing can be a long task for me<u>;
> however,</u> taking my time with the prewriting, writing, and revision steps makes it seem easier.

Copy the sentence exactly as it is, word for word. Here is the pattern to study before you write your own sentence:

PATTERN

_____; however,
_____.

Here is an example of a sentence written on the pattern:

EXAMPLE

At the beginning of a new writing project I always have to sharpen my pencils<u>; however,</u> sharp pencils don't guarantee sharp ideas.

Now write your own sentence, beginning your second clause with a transitional adverb from the following list:

Example	*Contrast*	*Addition*
for example	however	also
for instance	nevertheless	finally
	on the other hand	furthermore
Result	instead	in addition
accordingly	otherwise	indeed
consequently		in fact
therefore		likewise
thus		meanwhile
		moreover
		then

WRITING ASSIGNMENT

Analyze your own process of writing and describe it in an essay similar to Schwabe's. In order to know how you write you may need to write something first, looking over your shoulder, so to speak, all the while to see what's happening.

The tripartite description used by Schwabe is one way of carrying out this assignment, but only one way. Another way was described by James Britton, a British teacher and researcher of writing. He divides the process into *conception,* at which time you receive the assignment and know what your subject is; *incubation,* during which you explore the subject and plan your writing; and *production,* when the actual writing is carried out. Some people think only in terms of production, and this is a mistake—unless they have no preliminary stages.

Some people do begin writing without first thinking about the idea; they get the assignment and start to write. This is sometimes called "free writing"—just writing as ideas occur—but it's actually just one kind of incubation. These writers generally need to rearrange their ideas after they're written down, and they must do considerable rewriting and other additional writing before achieving a finished product. Other people need an outline before they begin. Some people must first clean off the desk, sharpen the pencils, and perform other perfunctory preparatory tasks in order to establish the mood for writing. Some people go for walks while exploring ideas, others run, some drive, some sit at a desk and stare out a window. Some writers must use pencils, some use pens, and some type; some of the luckier ones use word processors.

The point is that everybody has an individual way of writing, and your assignment is to find out what *your* process is and then write it down. Like Tom Schwabe, you might like to think of an audience that consists of other student writers as well as your teacher. How you go about this assignment depends on how you write. You may be able to sit down at a desk and just think through the process, making notes as ideas occur to you. Or you may need to write something in order to recall the process. In that case, have a separate sheet of paper handy where you can jot down notes as you go.

Once you have some notes about the process, you can begin to organize them. Try to group the things you do into categories. These categories will be the subsections of your paper. Then write a sentence that makes a point about how you write. That will be your thesis. Now see if you can find a "hook"—something to interest a potential reader of your essay. Schwabe's hook is to question his readers about writing problems, then reassure them that everyone has these problems. Other hooks might be a quotation, a narrative example, or a challenging statement.

At this point, depending on your style, you may have some notes in front of you, some hastily written paragraphs, or a few disconnected ideas in your head. When you're ready, write your essay, ending with a suitable conclusion, one that makes your point for the last time.

When you finish writing, your essay will probably be pretty rough. You may have thought of additional things to say as you went along. You may have recalled an essential step after you finished. You may still be missing something important. So why not let your essay rest for a day or two, then go back to it with a fresh mind and begin making changes. You may find a lot of repetition and wordiness. (Tom's is reduced considerably from earlier drafts.) You will probably need to add details, explain some things, sharpen some words and sentences, correct some errors. Do whatever is necessary to make your essay suitable for public presentation. (Whether or not anyone but your teacher sees your writing, this is always a good goal.)

6

Good and Bad

PAUL ROBERTS

Paul Roberts was an educator, linguist, and author who taught English and linguistics (the study of language) at San Jose State College and Cornell University. He was also Director of Language at the Rome (Italy) Center for American Studies. He wrote several books about linguistics for high school and college students. The essay below is excerpted from one of these books, *Understanding English,* and expresses his ideas about what good English is.

Vocabulary Preview

line		
19	jargon	the specialized vocabulary of people in the same work, generally unintelligible to outsiders; also used to refer to any unintelligible speech
20	ennobling	giving dignity to
31	hypothesis	an unproved explanation; something taken to be true as a basis for further investigation
34	converse(ly)	opposite
49	clarity	clearness
50	obscurity	the quality of being not easily understood or seen
50	precision	exactness, accuracy
50	vagueness	lack of precision or clarity
53	presumption	belief based on reasonable evidence
55	connote	to suggest or imply in addition to the usual meaning

64	evoke(s)	to call forth
64	disdain	contempt

Essay Preview: Questions to Answer as You Read

1. According to Roberts, what is "good" English?
2. What does Roberts jokingly identify as the "noblest, loveliest, purest English"? Why does he choose this variety of language?
3. What does Roberts say it means if we admire the speech of someone else?

Good and Bad

1   Speech communities, then, are formed by many features: age, geography, education, occupation, social position. Young people speak differently from old people, Kansans differently from Virginians, Yale graduates differently from Dannemora graduates. Now let us pose a delicate question: aren't some of these speech communities better than others? That is, isn't better language heard in some than in others?

2   Well, yes, of course. One speech community is always better than all the rest. This is the group in which one happens to find oneself. The writer would answer unhesitatingly that the noblest, loveliest, purest English is that heard in the Men's Faculty Club of San Jose State College, San Jose, California. He would admit, of course, that the speech of some of the younger members leaves something to be desired; that certain recent immigrants from Harvard, Michigan, and other foreign parts need to work on the laughable oddities lingering in their speech; and that members of certain departments tend to introduce a lot of queer terms that can only be described as jargon. But in general the English of the Faculty Club is ennobling and sweet.

3   As a practical matter, good English is whatever English is spoken by the group in which one moves contentedly and at ease. To the bum on Main Street in Los Angeles, good English is the language of other L.A. bums. Should he wander

onto the campus of UCLA, he would find the talk there unpleasant, confusing, and comical. He might agree, if pressed, that the college man speaks "correctly" and he doesn't. But in his heart he knows better. He wouldn't talk like them college jerks if you paid him.

4   If you admire the language of other speech communities more than you do your own, the reasonable hypothesis is that you are dissatisfied with the community itself. It is not precisely other speech that attracts you but the people who use the speech. Conversely, if some language strikes you as unpleasant or foolish or rough, it is presumably because the speakers themselves seem so.

5   To many people, the sentence "Where is he at?" sounds bad. It is bad, they would say, in and of itself. The sounds are bad. But this is very hard to prove. If "Where is he at?" is bad because it has bad sound combinations, then presumably "Where is the cat?" or "Where is my hat?" are just as bad, yet no one thinks them so. Well, then, "Where is he at?" is bad because it uses too many words. One gets the same meaning from "Where is he?" so why add the *at?* True. Then "He going with us?" is a better sentence than "Is he going with us?" You don't really need the *is,* so why put it in?

6   Certainly there are some features of language to which we can apply the terms *good* and *bad, better* and *worse.* Clarity is usually better than obscurity; precision is better than vagueness. But these are not often what we have in mind when we speak of good and bad English. If we like the speech of upperclass Englishmen, the presumption is that we admire upperclass Englishmen—their characters, culture, habits of mind. Their sounds and words simply come to connote the people themselves and become admirable therefore. If we knew the same sounds and words from people who were distasteful to us, we would find the speech ugly.

7   This is not to say that correctness and incorrectness do not exist in speech. They obviously do, but they are relative to the speech community—or communities—in which one operates. As a practical matter, correct speech is that which sounds normal or natural to one's comrades. Incorrect speech is that which evokes in them discomfort or hostility or disdain.

Questions for Discussion

1. Roberts is joking in his second paragraph when he says that the variety of English spoken in the Men's Faculty Club at San Jose State College is the one that is "noblest, loveliest, and purest." But he's also serious. *What point is he making?*
2. The biographical note that begins this chapter says that Roberts wrote books for high school and college students. *Would you say that this excerpt from* Understanding English *was written for this audience? Why do you say so?*
3. *What does paragraph 2 tell us about Roberts' relation to his subject? How does the biographical note support his point?*
4. *What would you say was Roberts' purpose for writing? What did he hope to achieve with his audience?*
5. Roberts, a linguist who spent many years studying language and how it is used, in this essay clearly wants to persuade you, a layman in the subject, to his way of thinking about correctness in speech and writing. He does it by upsetting the usual ideas of what good English is. Here's an outline of his essay:

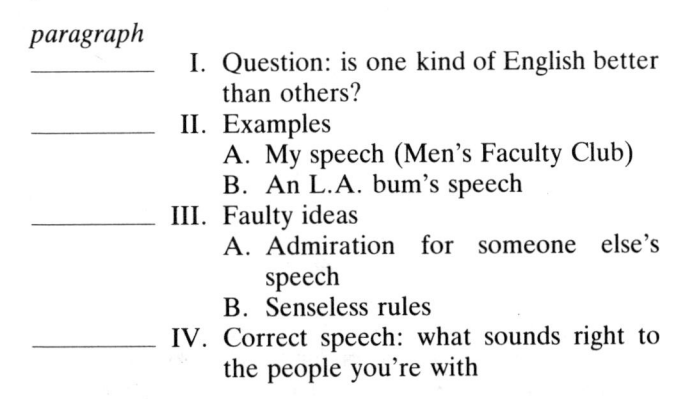

    paragraph

    _____ I. Question: is one kind of English better than others?
    _____ II. Examples
        A. My speech (Men's Faculty Club)
        B. An L.A. bum's speech
    _____ III. Faulty ideas
        A. Admiration for someone else's speech
        B. Senseless rules
    _____ IV. Correct speech: what sounds right to the people you're with

    Identify the corresponding paragraphs for each of these outline parts.

52   Good and Bad

6. *Do you agree with what Roberts says is correct speech? Why or why not?*
7. In the last paragraph Roberts notes parenthetically "or communities," implying that we may live in more than one speech community. *How many speech communities do you live and work in? (Use Roberts' opening sentence as a guide.)*

One speech community that you as a student cannot overlook is the academic community. You have no doubt become aware that the language you use when speaking with your peers is not the appropriate language for writing your class papers. When you enter the classroom, you switch speech communities. You may also have learned that the variety of language you used for writing your papers as a sophomore in high school is not entirely acceptable to your college English teacher. Your college composition class as another speech community is different from your high school class. Furthermore, you will continue to enter new speech communities—graduate school, your profession, new social groups, etc.

As you consider the various speech communities of which you are a part, think again about the point that Roberts concludes with: "correct speech is that which sounds normal or natural to one's comrades." Your street language is more correct on the street than your academic language is, just as standard written English is more appropriate for your college papers than the language you use with your friends.

Sentence Patterning

One of the least used punctuation marks in written English is the colon, and because it's used so infrequently many people aren't sure about how to use it. Sometimes it's confused with the semicolon, which looks similar to the colon and has a similar name—though a very different use. As we discussed in Chapter 4, the *semicolon* most commonly stands between two independent clauses and could be replaced by a period. A *colon,* however, usually comes between an independent clause and a list—two, three, or more parallel sentence elements. If the colon were to be replaced with a period, the list would become a sentence fragment. In diagram form, the two sentence patterns look like this:

SEMICOLON

    [independent clause] ; [independent clause] .

COLON

    [independent clause] : _____, _____, and _____.

The opening sentence in "Good and Bad" follows the basic colon pattern, starting with an independent clause and ending with a list of five items. Study the sentence as it appears below, together with the diagramed pattern, and then copy the sentence exactly. Observe how the example follows the pattern. Finally, write your own sentence in imitation of the original.

SENTENCE

    Speech communities are formed by many features: age, geography, education, occupation, social position.

PATTERN

    _____ _____: _____, _____, _____, _____, _____.

EXAMPLE

    A person is said to gain many benefits from a college education: knowledge, a job, mobility, a social life, and even a spouse. (The last item of a list is usually preceded by a conjunction, as shown in the example sentence.)

WRITING ASSIGNMENT

Roberts presents his problem in the form of a question ("Aren't some . . . speech communities better than others?")—a question to which the common answer might be "yes." In his second paragraph he seems at first to be agreeing with that "yes" answer; however, he soon makes clear what he means when he says that some speech communities are better than others. Then in the rest of his essay he shows why the answer is "no." This writing assignment asks you to persuade your reader in the same way Roberts does, following his pattern of development. Begin by deciding on a question, perhaps one of these:

> Should everyone get a college degree?
> Is television a waste of time?
> Is cleanliness really "next to godliness"?
> Is rural morality better than urban morality?

Each question of course is asking for a value judgment, assuming a "yes" answer. When you first pose your question, your audience will be thinking "yes": everyone should get a college degree; television is a waste of time; we all know that some ways of speaking are better than others. Anticipating these "yes" answers, you will be challenged to convince your reader that the answer is "no": not everyone should get a college degree; television is not a waste of time; some speech communities are not intrinsically better than others. Let's take another look at how Roberts convinced you that there are many ways of speaking correctly.

He begins by clarifying his term "speech communities," and you may need to define or clarify also. What do you mean by cleanliness, or by morality? Then he asks his question, which serves as his thesis until he answers the question. In the next two paragraphs he uses examples in support of his point, showing that correctness is determined by the persons one associates with. If you were trying to show that television is not a waste of time, you might, in one paragraph, show that it provides information on the latest world events and, in another paragraph, discuss how it can educate viewers on the wonders of the natural world.

Then Roberts deals with some faulty ideas about correctness in language. In paragraph 4 he says that if you admire the language of other people it's only because you're dissatisfied with the people you associate with. And in paragraph 5 he declares that some of our arbitrary rules on correctness are silly and senseless. In your essay you too can deal with the mistaken ideas people usually have about your subject. For example, the idea that a college education guarantees a higher income and a better life is contrary to fact. Or, people who think that the morals of those who live in the country are as clean and pure as the air they breathe have never lived there themselves. You should have at least one paragraph dealing with these opposing ideas—two, like Roberts, if you can manage them.

From there you might write one more paragraph supporting your view, and then you might proceed directly to your conclusion, which summarizes your main points and answers the question you started with. This answer will state your thesis. Your essay should have a structure something like this:

   I. Question
  II. Examples
      A. First example
      B. Second example
 III. Faulty ideas
      A. First faulty idea
      B. Second faulty idea
  IV. Summary, answer to question (statement of thesis)

Since this will be a persuasive essay, you need to decide who your audience will be. Then, as you write, keep in mind what you need to do to convince that audience. What evidence will succeed? What choice of words and details will work? Also consider who *you* are in relation to your subject. Roberts is a grammarian writing about grammar, so even if we might want to disagree we may concede anyway because he's an "expert" on the subject. You might write about television from the perspective of an "expert" television freak.

When you've finished writing, reread and revise. Do you think your essay will persuade anyone? How might you be more convincing? What's good about your essay? How can you improve on that? Work with your sentences to see that they express your ideas clearly and concisely. Make a final check for errors. Then rewrite, making a clean draft to turn in.

7

Mr. McElroy

MAYA ANGELOU

Maya Angelou has degrees from Smith College, Mills College, and Lawrence University. She is the author of several books and in 1976 was Woman of the Year in Communications. In this excerpt from her book *I Know Why the Caged Bird Sings*, she remembers one of the people she knew as she was growing up in Arkansas back in the 1930s.

Vocabulary Preview

line		
1	rambling	growing or spreading in all directions; aimless
14	Bailey	the narrator's brother
17	Momma	the narrator's grandmother
20	disenchanted	set free from an attraction or a magic spell
20	perch	resting place of a bird, generally elevated, affording a good view
22	patent medicine	a medical preparation sold without a prescription
22	tonic(s)	medicine that invigorates, refreshes, or restores
23	Stamps	the town in Arkansas where the narrator grew up
30	Panama	a straw hat
41	anachronism	something out of its proper time in history

57

Mr. McElroy

Essay Preview: Questions to Answer as You Read
1. Who is Mr. McElroy?
2. Does the narrator admire Mr. McElroy?
3. What is the point of this description?

Mr. McElroy

1   Mr. McElroy, who lived in the big rambling house next to the Store, was very tall and broad, and although the years had eaten away the flesh from his shoulders, they had not, at the time of my knowing him, gotten to his high stomach, or his hands or feet.

2   He was the only Negro I knew, except for the school principal and the visiting teachers, who wore matching pants and jackets. When I learned that men's clothes were sold like that and called suits, I remember thinking that somebody had been very bright, for it made men look less manly, less threatening and a little more like women.

3   Mr. McElroy never laughed, and seldom smiled, and to his credit was the fact that he liked to talk to Uncle Willie. He never went to church, which Bailey and I thought also proved he was a very courageous person. How great it would be to grow up like that, to be able to stare religion down, especially living next door to a woman like Momma.

4   I watched him with the excitement of expecting him to do anything at any time. I never tired of this, or became disappointed or disenchanted with him, although from the perch of age, I see him now as a very simple and uninteresting man who sold patent medicine and tonics to the less sophisticated people in towns (villages) surrounding the metropolis of Stamps.

5   There seemed to be an understanding between Mr. McElroy and Grandmother. This was obvious to us because he never chased us off his land. In summer's late sunshine I often sat under the chinaberry tree in his yard, surrounded by the bitter aroma of its fruit and lulled by the drone of flies that fed on the berries. He sat in a slotted swing on his porch,

rocking in his brown three-piece, his wide Panama nodding in time with the whir of insects.

6   One greeting a day was all that could be expected from Mr. McElroy. After his "Good morning, child," or "Good afternoon, child," he never said a word, even if I met him again on the road in front of his house or down by the well, or ran into him behind the house escaping a game of hide-and-seek.

7   He remained a mystery in my childhood. A man who owned his land and the big many-windowed house with a porch that clung to its sides all around the house. An independent Black man. A near anachronism in Stamps.

Questions for Discussion

1. Maya Angelou describes Mr. McElroy with specific details. In the first paragraph, for example, we get the picture of a man narrow at the top and big around the middle. In paragraph 2 we learn that he wore suits, which apparently set him apart from other men in the town. *Looking at the successive paragraphs, three through six, summarize what additional facts we learn about him.*

2. Angelou also describes Mr. McElroy through her own personal reactions to him. In paragraph 2, for example, we learn what impression his suit made on her. *Find other reactions of the child Angelou to the next-door neighbor.*

3. The organization of this essay is the piling up of details about the man until the final paragraph, where Angelou makes her point. *Identify her point.*

4. Actually, Angelou makes *two* points about McElroy. One was how she saw him as a child, a mystery, and the second was from her perspective as an adult: an anachronism, a man out of time, an independent Black man at a time when Black men were in an economically inferior position.

    Do you think Angelou was wise in waiting till the end to reveal her point? Can you see an advantage to holding off?

Mr. McElroy

5. For the most part, Angelou describes Mr. McElroy as she remembers him from childhood. We have seen one exception in paragraph 7. *Can you find another instance of Angelou reacting as an adult?*

6. Angelou ends her essay with three sentence fragments. The first one, beginning "A man who owned . . .," is long, but it's still a fragment, because there's no verb to finish out the idea begun with "A man." The next two—"An independent Black man" and "A near anachronism in Stamps"—are shorter but do essentially the same thing as the first. They are all *appositives*—the three nouns *man, man,* and *anachronism* all rename *He* in the preceding sentence, all refer to Mr. McElroy, and all say something more about him. Now, appositives are useful devices in writing, but usually they are set off with commas or dashes. Here Angelou uses periods, thus creating the fragments.

What do you think about this use of periods? Would the essay have been better if Angelou had written her final paragraph this way:

> He remained a mystery in my childhood—a man who owned his land and the big many-windowed house with a porch that clung to its sides all around the house, an independent Black man, a near anachronism in Stamps.

Let's face it: professional writers have a few more options than student writers. You are better off avoiding fragments, because doing so shows you know one when you see one. (There's more on fragments in "The New Ambidexters," p. 147.)

Sentence Patterning

Angelou's first sentence contains a *who* clause set off with commas. In "Blubber on Ice," p. 83, we will be looking at *who* clauses with *no* commas, but here we'll practice a sentence that has them. The problem, of course, is knowing when to use the commas. For our patterning we'll imitate only the first part of the sentence, as follows:

SENTENCE

> Mr. McElroy, who lived in the big rambling house next to the Store, was very tall and broad.

Before dealing with the problem of *when* to use the commas, let's first observe that there are *two* of them. When you use a comma at the end of the *who* clause (after *Store*), you must also use one at the beginning (before *who*). The clause, in other words, is enclosed, or set off, from the rest of the sentence. It's treated as an interruption. Angelou thus is saying, "Mr. McElroy was very tall and broad," an idea which she interrupts by adding the information that he "lived in the big rambling house next to the Store."

Now, since the clause is an interruption, it must take commas. If the clause were *not* an interruption—if it *identified* Mr. McElroy—it would take no commas. But it does *not* identify him; his name does that. So, that's how you decide whether to use commas. Ask yourself if the clause identifies the person or thing represented by the word the clause modifies; if it tells *which one,* use *no commas.* But if the information conveyed by the clause is not essential—maybe useful, interesting, helpful, but not essential—the clause is set off, enclosed, with commas. This is the kind of sentence we're writing in this assignment.

Read the sentence again, copy it exactly, then study the pattern below; finally write a sentence of your own that imitates the original. You'll need to make sure that the information in the clause does not identify the person or thing it modifies. The easiest way to make sure is to start with a proper name, since anything that follows obviously is not needed to identify that person.

Mr. McElroy

PATTERN

_____[name]_____, who _____
_____, _____
_____.

EXAMPLE

Professor Campbell, <u>who teaches my nineteenth-century English literature class</u>, is an accomplished organist and composer.

WRITING ASSIGNMENT

Think of someone you *once* knew, and write a description of that person. To get the ideas and memories flowing, try free writing. Just think of that person and begin to write anything that you remember: appearance, personality, activities, how you felt about him or her, how old you were at the time, where you knew that person, etc. Don't think about organizing your thoughts now, and don't worry about spelling, grammar, or punctuation. What you're doing now is getting ideas out of your head and onto paper, where you can work with them later. Keep writing until you've exhausted your memory.

Now think about a point. What does this person mean to you? Why did you choose to write about this person? With Maya Angelou, the point was that Mr. McElroy was a mystery; that's why she remembered him. Express your point in a sentence; it'll be your thesis.

Then start to rearrange and revise your free writing. As Angelou did, first describe your subject physically, noting not everything but only outstanding characteristics. Angelou, for example, reports McElroy's size and clothing. Then you can follow your physical description with several details about your subject's personality and/or activities. In your last paragraph, express your point. Your basic outline will look something like this:

I. Physical description
II. Personality and/or activities
III. Thesis—point

Make sure your point and details are related to one another. Angelou, for example, gives several details to illustrate why she didn't understand Mr. McElroy, so that when she gets to that point in paragraph 7 it is clear. But she goes one step further: she explains the point from her adult perspective—that Mr. McElroy was a mystery because he was a man out of time, an anachronism. You might want to end your essay with two points also: one from your perspective at the time you knew the person and a second seen from where you stand now. If your ending is something like Angelou's—several appositives that summarize your point—try writing the appositives as fragments. We have seen that fragments, when you know what you're doing, are an effective option of written style.

Make your details specific. Allow your reader to picture this person you're describing. Can't you just see Mr. McElroy on his front porch, rocking in his slotted swing, wearing his brown three-piece suit and straw hat, dozing to the whirring sound of the flies? Aim for this kind of detail. In addition, be specific about your reactions to your person. We know that Angelou respected Mr. McElroy's daring in staying away from church, because she says so in paragraph 3. She also tells us in other ways how she felt about the man. In writing your description, you yourself need to understand how you feel about the person you're describing. Then you need to let the reader in on your reactions.

When you've finished writing, reread your essay. Does your person seem real, alive on the page? Is it clear why you're writing about this person, how you feel about her or him? Do you need more specific details, more specific words? Do you have errors that you can correct?

Turn in a clean, finished draft to your teacher.

8

Summary of "Take This Fish"

L. DANIEL ROSIN

Dan Rosin wrote the following summary in response to an assignment in his college composition course. The essay it summarizes, "Take This Fish and Look at It" by Samuel H. Scudder, follows the summary. Read the summary first and then Scudder's essay.

Vocabulary Preview

line
1	entomologist	one who studies insects
16	symmetrical	having similar form or arrangement on either side of a central dividing line

Essay Preview: Questions to Answer as You Read

1. What is a haemulon?
2. What is the "most obvious aspect" of a fish?
3. According to Rosin, what is the point or purpose of Scudder's essay?

Summary of "Take This Fish"

1   Samuel Scudder, the learned entomologist, wrote "Take This Fish and Look at It" in an attempt to show the importance of observation.

2   When Scudder was a student, he mentioned to Professor

64

Agassiz that he would like to become a natural historian. Agassiz gave him a small fish, a haemulon, and told him to examine it carefully. After ten minutes Scudder felt he had noticed everything about the fish, and he looked for Agassiz so he could report his findings. Not finding Agassiz, he reluctantly went back to his fish. It was only after several hours of desperately looking for something about the fish that he finally was able to talk to the professor. Agassiz listened to Scudder's short report and told Scudder he had missed the most obvious aspect of the fish.

3   The next morning, Scudder did discover the missing aspect—that fish have symmetrical sides and paired organs. Agassiz was pleased, but he told his new student to continue to observe the fish. On the fourth day, Agassiz added another fish of the haemulon family to the first, and he told Scudder to compare them. More fish were added until over a period of eight months Scudder had compared the whole family.

4   As Scudder looked back on this experience he realized the importance of close observation to his career as an entomologist.

Vocabulary Preview (for Scudder's essay)

line

5	antecedents	one's ancestors and past life
27	entomology	the study of insects
28	ichthyology	the scientific study of fishes
32	aversion	an intense dislike
47	mute	silent; not speaking
61	interdicted	prohibited with authority; denied the privilege of doing something
75	operculum	a lid or flap covering an opening; in some fishes, a gill cover
76	lateral	toward the side; sideways
76	spinous	having spines or similar projections
85	piqued	provoked to anger or resentment; offended
85	mortified	humiliated
97	disconcerting	upsetting

109	discourse(d)	to speak at some length; carry on conversation
123	legacy	money or property left to someone by will; anything handed down by a predecessor
124	inestimable	too valuable to be measured
128	hydra-headed	many-headed
129	crawfish(es)	(crayfish) a fresh water creature resembling a lobster but smaller

Take This Fish and Look at It

SAMUEL H. SCUDDER

1   It was more than fifteen years ago that I entered the laboratory of Professor Agassiz, and told him I had enrolled my name in the Scientific School as a student of natural history. He asked me a few questions about my object in coming, my antecedents generally, the mode in which I afterwards proposed to use the knowledge I might acquire, and finally, whether I wished to study any special branch. To the latter I replied that, while I wished to be well grounded in all departments of zoology, I purposed to devote myself specifically to insects.

2   "When do you wish to begin?" he asked.

3   "Now," I replied.

4   This seemed to please him, and with an energetic "Very well!" he reached from a shelf a huge jar of specimens in yellow alcohol. "Take this fish," he said, "and look at it; we call it a haemulon; by and by I will ask what you have seen."

5   With that he left me, but in a moment returned with explicit instructions as to the care of the object entrusted to me.

6   "No man is fit to be a naturalist," said he, "who does not know how to take care of specimens."

7   I was to keep the fish before me in a tin tray, and occasionally moisten the surface with alcohol from the jar, always taking care to replace the stopper tightly. Those were not the days of ground-glass stoppers and elegantly shaped exhibition jars; all the old students will recall the huge neckless glass

bottles with their leaky, wax-besmeared corks, half eaten by insects, and begrimed with cellar dust. Entomology was a cleaner science than ichthyology, but the example of the Professor, who had unhesitatingly plunged to the bottom of the jar to produce the fish, was infectious; and though this alcohol had a "very ancient and fishlike smell," I really dared not show any aversion within these sacred precincts, and treated the alcohol as though it were pure water. Still I was conscious of a passing feeling of disappointment, for gazing at a fish did not commend itself to an ardent entomologist. My friends at home, too, were annoyed when they discovered that no amount of eau-de-Cologne would drown the perfume which haunted me like a shadow.

8   In ten minutes I had seen all that could be seen in that fish, and started in search of the Professor—who had, however, left the Museum; and when I returned, after lingering over some of the odd animals stored in the upper apartment, my specimen was dry all over. I dashed the fluid over the fish as if to resuscitate the beast from a fainting fit, and looked with anxiety for a return of the normal sloppy appearance. This little excitement over, nothing was to be done but to return to a steadfast gaze at my mute companion. Half an hour passed—an hour—another hour; the fish began to look loathsome. I turned it over and around; looked it in the face—ghastly; from behind, beneath, above, sideways, at a three-quarters' view—just as ghastly. I was in despair; at an early hour I concluded that lunch was necessary; so, with infinite relief, the fish was carefully replaced in the jar, and for an hour I was free.

9   On my return, I learned that Professor Agassiz had been at the Museum, but had gone, and would not return for several hours. My fellow-students were too busy to be disturbed by continued conversation. Slowly I drew forth that hideous fish, and with a feeling of desperation again looked at it. I might not use a magnifying-glass; instruments of all kinds were interdicted. My two hands, my two eyes, and the fish; it seemed a most limited field. I pushed my finger down its throat to feel how sharp the teeth were. I began to count the scales in the different rows, until I was convinced that was nonsense. At last a happy thought struck me—I would

draw the fish; and now with surprise I began to discover new features in the creature. Just then the Professor returned.

10   "That's right," said he "a pencil is one of the best of eyes. I am glad to notice, too, that you keep your specimen wet, and your bottle corked."

11   With these encouraging words, he added:

12   "Well, what is it like?"

13   He listened attentively to my brief rehearsal of the structure of parts whose names were still unknown to me: the fringed gill-arches and movable operculum; the pores of the head, fleshy lips and lidless eyes, the lateral line, the spinous fins and forked tail, the compressed and arched body. When I finished, he waited as if expecting more, and then, with an air of disappointment:

14   "You have not looked very carefully; why," he continued more earnestly, "you haven't even seen one of the most conspicuous features of the animal, which is plainly before your eyes as the fish itself; look again, look again!" and he left me to my misery.

15   I was piqued; I was mortified. Still more of that wretched fish! But now I set myself to my task with a will, and discovered one new thing after another, until I saw how just the Professor's criticism had been. The afternoon passed quickly; and when, towards its close, the Professor inquired:

16   "Do you see it yet?"

17   "No," I replied, "I am certain I do not, but I see how little I saw before."

18   "That is next best," said he, earnestly, "but I won't hear you now; put away your fish and go home; perhaps you will be ready with a better answer in the morning. I will examine you before you look at the fish."

19   This was disconcerting. Not only must I think of my fish all night, studying, with the object before me, what this unknown but most visible feature might be; but also, without reviewing my discoveries, I must give an exact account of them the next day. I had a bad memory; so I walked home by the Charles River in a distracted state, with my two perplexities.

20   The cordial greeting from the Professor the next morning was reassuring; here was a man who seemed to be quite as anxious as I that I should see for myself what he saw.

21 "Do you perhaps mean," I asked, "that the fish has symmetrical sides with paired organs?"

22 His thoroughly pleased "Of course! of course!" repaid the wakeful hours of the previous night. After he had discoursed most happily and enthusiastically—as he always did—upon the importance of this point, I ventured to ask what I should do next.

23 "Oh, look at your fish!" he said, and left me again to my own devices. In a little more than an hour he returned, and heard my new catalogue.

24 "That is good, that is good!" he repeated; "but that is not all; go on"; and so for three long days he placed that fish before my eyes, forbidding me to look at anything else, or to use any artificial aid. "Look, look, look," was his repeated injunction.

25 This was the best entomological lesson I ever had—a lesson whose influence has extended to the details of every subsequent study; a legacy the Professor had left to me, as he has left it to so many others, of inestimable value, which we could not buy, with which we cannot part.

26 A year afterward, some of us were amusing ourselves with chalking outlandish beasts on the Museum blackboard. We drew prancing starfishes; frogs in mortal combat; hydra-headed worms; stately crawfishes, standing on their tails, bearing aloft umbrellas; and grotesque fishes with gaping mouths and staring eyes. The Professor came in shortly after, and was as amused as any at our experiments. He looked at the fishes.

27 "Haemulons, every one of them," he said; Mr. _____ drew them."

28 True; and to this day, if I attempt a fish, I can draw nothing but haemulons.

29 The fourth day, a second fish of the same group was placed beside the first, and I was bidden to point out the resemblances and differences between the two; another and another followed, until the entire family lay before me, and a whole legion of jars covered the table and surrounding shelves; the odor had become a pleasant perfume; and even now, the sight of an old, six-inch, worm-eaten cork brings fragrant memories.

70   Summary of "Take This Fish"

30   The whole group of haemulons was thus brought in review; and, whether engaged upon the dissection of the internal organs, the preparation and examination of the bony framework, or the description of the various parts, Agassiz's training in the method of observing facts and their orderly arrangement was ever accompanied by the urgent exhortation not to be content with them.

31   "Facts are stupid things," he would say, "until brought into connection with some general law."

32   At the end of eight months, it was almost with reluctance that I left these friends and turned to insects; but what I had gained by this outside experience has been of greater value than years of later investigation in my favorite groups.

Questions for Discussion

1. *What does Rosin say is the purpose, or point, of Scudder's "Take This Fish and Look at It"? What other information is included in Rosin's introductory paragraph?* Summaries in the academic setting ordinarily begin with an attribution—naming the work and its author—and a statement of the point or purpose of the work summarized. *How does Rosin work these into his opening sentence?*

2. Rosin's conclusion makes a final statement about the significance of the experience that Scudder reports. *Where in "Take This Fish" does he find this information?*

3. Rosin omitted many details found in Scudder's account. He left out all direct quotations and much of the narrative on the haemulon observations. Rosin tried to limit himself to the heart of the matter, selecting only those details that were essential for conveying the sense of Scudder's essay. *Do you think he omitted too much? What additional details would you have included?*

4. *Reread Rosin's summary, underlining all indications of the flow of time. You can begin with "When Scudder was a student" and should be able to underline five or six more.* These transitional phrases make it possible for

the reader to keep up with the changes in time despite the sharp reduction of the story.

The transitions in this summary are related to time because of the chronological nature of the essay summarized. Another summary might use other kinds of transitions. *If, for example, you were summarizing Bertrand Russell's "What I Have Lived For" (p. 5), what kind of transitions would you use?* In another summary your transitions might indicate comparative ideas, using words like "in contrast," "on the other hand," "similarly," or "in the same way." A summary of an essay explaining causal relations would use other transitions: "for this reason," "as a result," "because of such-and-such," and so on. In other words, the relationship between parts in the original writing should be reflected in the summary.

Sentence Patterning

Coordination is a familiar grammatical procedure that links together two sentence elements with one of these conjunctions: *and, but, or, for, nor, so, yet.* (Additional elements can be added, separated by commas, making a series of elements; see pp. 52 and 79.) Any sentence elements can be joined, so long as they are of the same kind, as illustrated below:

nouns	Those were not the days of ground-glass *stoppers* and elegantly shaped exhibition *jars*.
verbs	In a little more than an hour he *returned* and *heard* my new catalogue.
adverbs	I turned the fish *over* and *around*.
pronouns	*Another* and *another* followed.
clauses	*Take this fish,* and *look at it.*

These are only a few examples of the many coordinated elements in Scudder's essay.

For this patterning assignment we'll use a sentence from Rosin's summary that uses paired verbs. Coordination is an efficient tool in summaries because it com-

Summary of "Take This Fish"

presses ideas into fewer words. Here is Rosin's sentence and its pattern:

SENTENCE

Agassiz <u>listened</u> to Scudder's short report <u>and</u> <u>told</u> Scudder he had missed the most obvious aspect of the fish.

PATTERN

_____ [verb] _____ and _____ [verb] _____
_____.

Copy the sentence exactly. What makes this construction efficient is that the subject performs the action of *both* verbs and does not need to be repeated. Here is an example of another sentence written on this pattern:

EXAMPLE

Louisa <u>went</u> to class reluctantly <u>but</u> <u>left</u> her video cassette recorder to tape "Days of Our Lives."

Notice that the sentence has no comma before the conjunction. The comma is used only if the two parts joined are independent clauses.

Write a sentence of your own that follows the pattern. Then try expanding it by adding another verb, as shown in the following sentence:

EXAMPLE

Louisa <u>tore</u> herself away from the television set, <u>went</u> to class reluctantly, <u>but</u> <u>left</u> her video cassette recorder to tape "Days."

Observe the commas before *went* and before *but*. Here, with a series of three verbs, the commas are required.

WRITING ASSIGNMENT

Summary writing is an essential academic skill. It's needed for essay exams, research papers, notetaking, book and article reviews or reports, and many other writing jobs. It's also one way to ensure comprehension when studying. In this writing assignment you are to summarize "The Maker's Eye: Revising Your Own Manuscripts," found in this book beginning on p. 257.

First read the article through, making *no* notes or marks, seeking only for what Murray is saying in this article. After you've finished reading, write down in a single sentence what point you think he makes about revision. Then look for Murray's thesis statement and underline it. Does his thesis coincide with the sentence you wrote down? If not, make adjustments in your sentence or reconsider your selection of a thesis. Look at the essay again: is your view slanted towards one of his minor points?

Once you have a clear understanding of Murray's point, or purpose, for writing, read the essay again, now underlining the major points in support of the thesis—not necessarily complete sentences but more likely words and phrases here and there. Also underline transitional words that show how parts are connected. Omit specific details, examples, description, and unnecessary explanations. You may need to go through the essay twice in order to pick up everything you need.

Now begin writing your summary. Start with a sentence that names the author and title and states the main idea of the essay. Then write your summary, omitting nothing important and striving for overall coherence by indicating how parts are related. Try to be concise, using coordination to compress ideas. In your conclusion make a final statement that reflects the significance of the essay—not from your point of view but from Murray's. Throughout your summary do *not* insert your own opinions or thoughts; you are summarizing what *Murray* has to say on revision. Do not copy Murray's words and phrases. Use *your* words to express *his* ideas.

After you've written, read your summary for accuracy. Does it make the same point as Murray's essay? Have you omitted anything important? Does your summary read smoothly, with all parts clearly interrelated? Is it too long? A summary should be no more than one-fourth as long as the original. If yours is too long, see if you can cut out words rather than ideas. Then look for non-essential information and delete it. Write another draft (still a draft for revision) and let someone else read it critically. Can that person understand the sense of Murray's essay through reading your summary of it? Ask for critical comments. Weigh these criticisms, and if they're valid make changes accordingly.

Correct your spelling and punctuation errors, and look for other errors, especially those that you know commonly occur in your writing. Write a clean draft to turn in.

9

Echoes of Grief

DORIS LESSING

Doris Lessing, the daughter of a British army captain, was born in 1919 in Persia and grew up in Rhodesia. As a British novelist, she has published widely on the themes of racial justice and the place of women in a society dominated by white males. Two of her most distinguished books are *The Golden Notebook* and *Children of Violence*. In contrast is her small volume *Particularly Cats,* in which she describes her experiences with her furry friends. The excerpt below relates one of her earliest and most moving experiences, which occurred one wintry July when she was a child in southern Africa.

Vocabulary Preview

line
11	whitewash(ed)	to whiten with a mixture of lime, whiting, and water
14	maize	corn
17	interminable	without end; seeming to be without end
24	antiseptic	sterile; free from infection; preventing infection
34	permanganate	a salt of permanganic acid, usually dark purple; sometimes used as an antiseptic
43	besought	begged; past form of *beseech*

Essay Preview: Questions to Answer as You Read
1. What happens to the kitten?
2. How does the weather affect what happens to the kitten?

76   Echoes of Grief

3. How does the narrator as a child feel about cats? as an adult?

Echoes of Grief

After a certain age—and for some of us that can be very young—there are no new people, beasts, dreams, faces, events: it has all happened before, masked differently, wearing different clothes, another nationality, another colour; but the same, the same, and everything is an echo and a repetition; and there is no grief even that it is not a recurrence of something long out of memory that expresses itself in unbelievable anguish, days of tears, loneliness, knowledge of betrayal—and all for a small, thin, dying cat.

I was sick that winter. It was inconvenient because my big room was due to be whitewashed. I was put in the little room at the end of the house. The house, nearly but not quite on the crown of the hill, always seemed as if it might slide off into the maize fields below. This tiny room, not more than a slice off the end of the house, had a door, always open, and windows, always open, in spite of the windy cold of a July whose skies were an interminable light clear blue. The sky, full of sunshine; the field, sunlit. But cold, very cold. The cat, a bluish-grey Persian, arrived purring on my bed, and settled down to share my sickness, my food, my pillow, my sleep. When I woke in the mornings, my face turned to half-frozen linen; the outside of the fur blanket on the bed was cold; the smell of fresh whitewash from next door was cold and antiseptic; the wind lifting and laying the dust outside the door was cold—but in the crook of my arm, a light purring warmth, the cat, my friend.

At the back of the house a wooden tub was let into the earth, outside the bathroom, to catch the bathwater. No pipes carrying water to taps on that farm: water was fetched by ox-drawn cart when it was needed, from the well a couple of miles off. Through the months of the dry season the only water for the garden was the dirty bathwater. The cat fell into this tub when it was full of hot water. She screamed, was pulled out into a chill wind, washed in permanganate, for the tub was filthy and held leaves and dust as well as soapy water, was dried, and put into my bed to warm. But she sneezed and sneezed and then grew burning hot with fever. She had pneumonia. We dosed her with what there was in the house, but that was before antibiotics, and so she died. For a week she lay in my arms purring, purring, in a rough trembling hoarse little voice that became weaker, then was silent; licked my hand; opened enormous green eyes when I called her name and besought her to live; closed them, died, and was thrown into the deep shaft—over a hundred feet deep it was—which had gone dry, because the underground water streams had changed their course one year and left what we had believed was a reliable well a dry, cracked, rocky shaft that was soon half filled with rubbish, tin cans, and corpses.

4   That was it. Never again. And for years I matched cats in friends' houses, cats in shops, cats on farms, cats in the street, cats on walls, cats in memory, with that gentle blue-grey purring creature which for me was the cat, the Cat, never to be replaced.

5   And besides, for some years my life did not include extras, unnecessaries, adornments. Cats had no place in an existence spent always moving from place to place, room to room. A cat needs a place as much as it needs a person to make its own.

6   And so it was not till twenty-five years later that my life had room for a cat.

Questions for Discussion

1. *Without looking back at the essay, recall what you can of the setting. Describe (a) the weather, (b) the location of the house, (c) the room, (d) the bed. Now look again at paragraph 2 to see what details you overlooked. What is the weather like? (Why was it winter in July?) Where is the house set? What do you know about the sickroom? Describe the bed.*

2. Paragraph 1 establishes that Lessing is reaching back into her memory to narrate this story. *What triggers this reminiscence?*

Lessing begins the essay with a statement somewhat like that in Ecclesiastes in the Bible, that there is nothing new under the sun. There comes a time, she says, when a person has experienced everything, and whatever happens from then on has happened before. What triggers this reminiscence of a cat, however, is an occurrence of grief. Lessing's statement in lines 6 and 7 is her thesis: grief is a recurrence of another grief.

3. Lessing says that "after a certain age . . . there are no new people, beasts, dreams, faces, events." *Do you believe it is true that "it has all happened before"? Do you know of someone who has expressed a similar thought? Has this idea ever occurred to you?*

4. Lessing's essay has a rather simple organization. She starts with an introduction that presents her thesis—the point of the narration—and establishes her tone, a little sadness blended with wisdom. Paragraph 2 describes the setting, paragraph 3 retells the cat's accident, and the remaining paragraphs sum up the effects on the narrator. In bare outline form, the essay looks like this:

   I. Introduction—thesis
   II. Setting
   III. Incident
   IV. Effects on narrator

   Take the outline further and list sub-parts under Parts II and III.

5. The story has only two characters: the narrator and the cat. Other persons are included in the pronoun *we* but are not named. *What is the effect of having only two characters?*

6. *Note the shifting roles of the child and the cat. In paragraph 2 who is the comforter? in paragraph 3?*

7. *What is the narrator's attitude toward cats? How does her attitude change through the years? Support your answers with references from the essay.*

8. After narrating the incident from her childhood, Lessing comes back to her point: that grief, with all its pain-

ful effects, never goes away. *Find evidence in the last three paragraphs to support this point.*

Sentence Patterning

In this piece, Doris Lessing's writing style is characterized by extremely long sentences contrasted with extremely short ones. Note, for example, that the entire first paragraph is one sentence but that the first sentence of paragraph 2 is only five words long. This juxtaposition happens again with the last sentence of paragraph 3 and the first one of paragraph 4. The long sentences create a flow and tight coherence of ideas, while the very short sentences draw attention to themselves and emphasize the ideas they express. It's an effective stylistic option, one to try occasionally.

Another characteristic of Lessing's style here is the coordination of parallel ideas—divided by commas, sometimes with a coordinating conjunction and sometimes not. Near the end of paragraph 1, for instance, she links "unbelievable anguish, days of tears, loneliness, knowledge of betrayal"—four nouns (*anguish, days, loneliness, knowledge*) and their modifiers. In the middle of paragraph 2, referring to the cat, she says it "settled down to share my sickness, my food, my pillow, my sleep"—again four nouns in a parallel construction. Lessing uses this pattern frequently; read through the essay and look for more instances of it. (See p. 71 for other examples of coordinated sentence elements.)

In paragraph 4 Lessing uses the structure with a different twist: she repeats the same word, *cats,* and follows it with a prepositional phrase:

SENTENCE

For years I matched <u>cats in friends' houses</u>, <u>cats in shops</u>, <u>cats on farms</u>, <u>cats in the street</u>, <u>cats on walls</u>, <u>cats in memory</u>, with that gentle blue-grey purring creature.

The effect of repeating *cats,* of course, is emphasis, making for a strong ending.

Let's use this sentence for patterning. Copy it exactly as it appears above; then study the pattern and the example sentence below. Finally, write a sentence of your own that observes the pattern.

PATTERN

<u>   [key word plus prepositional phrase]   </u>, <u>   [key word plus prepositional phrase]   </u>, <u> [key word plus prepositional phrase] </u>, <u> [key word plus prepositional phrase] </u>, <u>   </u>.

EXAMPLE

As a result of my drawing class, I enjoy sketching <u>trees in the park</u>, <u>trees at home</u>, <u>trees during lunch hour</u>, <u>trees under a sunset</u>, at any time and place I can.

Repeat your key word four times and modify it each time with a prepositional phrase. Here's a list of some prepositions which may be useful:

at	down	on
about	during	over
above	except	since
across	for	through
before	from	to
behind	in	under
below	into	until
between	like	with
by	of	without

As you use these prepositions, make sure they are followed by an object:

in <u>shops</u>, on <u>farms</u>, across the <u>field</u>
in the <u>park</u>, at <u>home</u>, during <u>lunch hour</u>, under a <u>sunset</u>

WRITING ASSIGNMENT

Have you arrived at a view of life in which "there are no new people, beasts, dreams, faces, events," where "it has all happened before"? Perhaps not; nevertheless, we all can recall incidents that have had a profound influence on our lives. In the incident of the cat Lessing learned the experience of grief and its painful effects, so that all later sorrows merged with the first.

Think of such an incident in your life, one that has influenced you and remains very much a part of you. The memory may be a pleasant one or an unpleasant one, or even—like Lessing's—bittersweet, having something good and something bad. You're the best person to decide what that incident might be, but here are some suggestions to get your ideas started:

Learning:	Responsibility
	The need to control anger
	The effects of racial bias
	Respect for parents
	Unselfishness
	Respect for others' property
Getting:	A new brother or sister
	A pet of your own
	Your first F on a report card
	A gift you didn't like
Experiencing:	A frightening incident
	Hatred
	Selfishness (your own or someone else's)

After you think of a subject to write about, begin writing freely, without thinking or planning. Write down everything that occurs to you as you remember the incident you've selected. As you write, don't pause to think about grammar, spelling, or punctuation; just write, keeping your pen moving. Don't try to organize now; you'll do that later. If your ideas begin to slow down, ask yourself: who? what? where? when? why? and how? Ask as many times as necessary to fully explore the subject. After you've written everything you can remember, ask yourself why you remember this incident so well and what its significance is for you. Write this down as a tentative thesis statement. The reason you remember this incident is why it's significant: the point you'll make.

Now go back to your jottings and begin to organize them. Arrange the actions in chronological order and the descriptions of the setting in some kind of spatial order. Make notes of additional details if they occur to you.

When you're ready to write, begin with an introduction that presents your subject and the point of your essay. Your second paragraph should give the setting of your narrative. Use specific words and phrases, just as Lessing did ("a bluish-grey Persian," "half-frozen linen," "the fur blanket," "an interminable light clear blue"). In your third paragraph, present the events of your story as they occurred, again being specific in the words you choose and the details you include. Then come to a conclusion. Lessing used three short paragraphs, but you may be able to complete your essay in one. Make sure that your point—the effect of the incident—is clear at the end.

Now revise your work. See if you can make general words more specific ("Persian" rather than "cat") and can add specific details ("a bluish-grey Persian" rather than "a Persian"). Ask yourself if you've omitted any relevant details. Check the time of your verbs; they should reflect past actions. Check for comma-spliced and run-on sentences (see pp. 26 and 35 for an explanation of this problem); they're easy to write when you're carried away with a narrative. Look for spelling, punctuation, and other errors. Finally, rewrite, making a clean copy and proofreading to catch copying errors.

10

Blubber on Ice

ROBERT CUSHMAN MURPHY

Robert Cushman Murphy, a respected naturalist, wrote over 500 articles and nine books, one of which, *Oceanic Birds of South America,* is a classic in its field. But *Logbook for Grace,* from which the following excerpt is taken, was written at a much earlier period in his life. In 1912, he had just graduated from college and married his young fiancée, Grace, when he was commissioned to study the birds and animals of the South Atlantic. Leaving his bride behind, he sailed on the whaling brig *Daisy* for Antarctica. *Logbook* was adapted from the journal he kept throughout the voyage. This excerpt, "Blubber on Ice," reports one of the observations he made near the South Pole.

Vocabulary Preview

line		
1	sea elephant	a large seal that has a trunklike snout
3	seraglio	harem; a sultan's palace
6	aspire(s)	to have an ambition; to aim at
9	hauling out	a specialized term referring to the action described
17	Marquis of Queensberry rules	the basic rules for modern boxing
19	trounce	to beat; to defeat
22	rabidly	violently; in a rage
24	palate	the roof of the mouth
34	interloper	an intruder; someone who interferes in the affairs of others

83

Essay Preview: Questions to Answer as You Read
1. Why do bull sea elephants fight?
2. What makes a sea elephant battle so bloody?
3. How does a sea elephant battle usually end?

Blubber on Ice

1   To bull sea elephants, fighting is a profession, and the only known means of settling the wife problem. The average number in a seraglio may be about fifteen, but a truly successful gentleman gathers more. In the code of the bulls, the correct number of wives is just one more than you've got.

2   Each bull aspires to be beachmaster, even though no beachmaster is ever left in peace. Other bulls, possessed with the urge and personality to win ladies who don't care who is their husband, are forever swimming alongshore and hauling out in the other fellow's preserve.

3   The first stage of combat is bluff. Defender and challenger begin by roaring, gargling, strangling, retching, and seeming to be nauseated (or so it sounds). Next they rear up like a pair of rocking horses, even though they be still out of each other's reach. Crawling closer, they bump, raking rival necks and chests with their heavy canine teeth. When opportunity offers, they endeavor to clamp jaws and tear. Marquis of Queensberry rules are not observed!

4   One of the fighters may trounce the other quickly, or they may carry on until both collapse from exhaustion, to go at it again when they have sufficiently revived. It is rather slow-going for a heavyweight battle, and yet the bulls have a rabidly furious aspect because it appears to be normal for the arteries of the palate to rupture during the violent "gargling," so that the combatants are presently spewing out blood with every breath.

5   More rarely, there is plenty of ripped hide, or possibly a mangled snout, or even an eyeless socket. The captain says that one big bull in every hundred encountered looks as though he had been bounced through a stone crusher.

6   At any rate, the object of such a battle is to win, not to kill. When one bull retreats to sea, the other resumes control or takes over, as the case may be, and peace reigns until the next interloper lumbers ashore.

Questions for Discussion

1. One of the purposes of an introduction is to set the tone for a piece of writing. *In Murphy's first paragraph, what kind of tone does he set? Is it serious? humorous? cynical? angry? Consider phrases like "settling the wife problem," and "the correct number of wives is just one more than you've got." Why does Murphy choose to refer to the bull sea elephant as a "gentleman"?*

   What reason might Murphy have for treating these bloody battles so lightly? Find words elsewhere in the essay that carry out this lightly humorous tone.

2. Obviously from the tone, one of Murphy's purposes in writing this essay was to entertain. But we might also say, because of the wealth of details and the seeming accuracy of the description, that *he had another purpose. Identify it. His original audience, remember, was his new wife, although in the published version the audience was expanded to include any interested reader.*

3. We have seen how choice of words creates tone. Let's see also how it makes description come alive for the reader. In paragraph 3, the verbs "roaring, gargling, strangling, retching, and seeming to be nauseated" enable the reader to picture and almost hear the battle action. Then to see the creatures "like a pair of rocking horses" further sharpens the picture with simile. Later, we add blood to the scene as Murphy explains the ruptured arteries. These are a few examples. *Find other vivid words and specific details that help you see the battle scene as it is described.*

4. This essay describes a *process,* reporting the author's observations on *how* something is done: how bull sea elephants fight to acquire cows. In process writing, transitions are distinctive in that they aid the reader in fol-

lowing the steps. *In paragraph 3, underline all transitions that lead you chronologically through the battle.*

You probably underlined *the first stage,* perhaps the verb *begin,* certainly *next;* also *Crawling closer* helps, as does *When opportunity offers.* All of these words and phrases suggest time, the order of events.

5. While the events in paragraph 3 are ordered chronologically, not all of Murphy's paragraphs are so arranged. The first paragraph presents the situation, thesis, and tone, and the second expands on the situation, stating why bull sea elephants fight. Following the steps of the battle in paragraph 3, Murphy then presents some alternatives. That is, the actions of paragraph 3 are generally true of such conflicts; but from there, as described in paragraphs 4, 5, and 6, the battle may be carried on in several ways. One way is that it will end quickly, another that it may go on indefinitely. After the explanation for all the blood, which seems to turn up in all fights, Murphy continues with alternatives: possible outcomes. *Identify them; which one is the usual outcome?*

6. Murphy generalizes about what sea elephants do when they're inclined to collect mates. He does not describe a given event that happened at a particular time, but rather a *habitual* action. As a consequence, he uses present-time verbs. In paragraph 1, they are *is, may be, gathers, is, 've (have). Find other verbs throughout the essay and see if any denote a past action.*

Sentence Patterning

One way to pack ideas into sentences without adding main clauses is to use *participial phrases.* A participle is an adjective and as such modifies, or describes, a noun. Formed from verbs, participles take two basic forms: the *-ing* and the *-ed.* With additional words they make up participial phrases. In this patterning exercise we'll imitate a sentence that uses the *-ed* participle. (The *-ing* is practiced in "Ticaspleeze and Trees," p. 158.) Here's the pattern sentence, simplified a little from the way it appears on lines 7–10. Copy it as it is here.

SENTENCE

> Other bulls, possessed with the urge and personality to win ladies, are forever swimming alongshore and hauling out in the other fellow's preserve.

Notice that the participle *possessed* describes *bulls.* It is not the verb of the sentence. The two *-ing* words—*swimming* and *hauling*—plus the auxiliary *are* make up the verb. (To act as verbs, the *-ing* participles require a form of *be:* mainly *are, is, was, were,* or *have been.*)

The entire participial phrase is set off from the rest of the sentence with two commas because, even though it expresses useful information, it is an interruption in the flow of the sentence and is not essential for identifying who the bulls are. (This is the same reasoning as that expressed on pp. 60–62 in the discussion about *who* clauses.) After studying the pattern of the sentence, write one of your own in imitation.

PATTERN

_____, _____ed _____,
_____.

EXAMPLE

> A household cat, convinced of the need to defend the fence around its backyard, raises its fur and arches its back as a warning to any intruder.

WRITING ASSIGNMENT

Process essays take several forms. Sometimes the writer instructs the reader on how to do something, as in "Spelling Is Nonsense." Sometimes the writer describes how he or she does something, as in "The Great Process," in which a college freshman describes how he writes a paper. Still another kind of process essay is "Blubber on Ice," in which the writer describes a process he has observed. This is the kind of paper you are asked to write in this assignment. Below you'll find some suggested topics; you may choose to write on one of them, or they may lead you instead to other topic ideas that appeal to you more.

>How a cat cleans its fur
>How a dog settles down to sleep
>How two cats fight
>How a baby cries
>How a child tries to wheedle something from its mom or dad
>How people wait in line
>How a fire in a fireplace burns

Start off by collecting some details with the *who, what, where, when, why, how* questions. Notice that the discussion of each of the topics listed above will have a beginning, a middle, and an end. As with the sea elephant fight, however, there may be alternative endings; there may also be alternative beginnings. If there are alternatives, you should deal with them. At the same time, some part of the process should be common to most occurrences of the situation.

So you might start as Murphy did, presenting what the situation is, the reason for its occurrence, and the tone of your description. Essays of this type, of course, can be serious, but this time experiment with establishing a lighter, more humorous tone by choosing your words and details accordingly.

Once the setting is established, describe the action itself, as Murphy did in paragraph 3. Use vivid words and details. Then present some alternative paths of action as needed according to your topic, and finally the way or ways the action ends. Use Murphy's essay as your guide. Outlined, your essay may look like this:

>I. Thesis, setting, tone
>II. Reasons for the action
>III. Description of the action
>IV. Alternative actions
>V. Possible outcomes of the action

Note carefully that all of the listed topics describe *habitual* actions, actions that ordinarily occur under given circumstances. If you choose another topic, it should do the same. That is, you will not be describing a single event that happened at a particular time; instead, you will describe what usually happens under certain circumstances. You are generalizing—about how a cat cleans its fur, for example. Therefore, you'll be using *present*-time verbs, as Murphy did throughout his essay. Past-time verbs do not generalize about something that habitually happens; they close an action off at some time in the past.

When you've finished writing your rough draft, check all of your verbs to make sure they don't slip into describing a completed action. Also check your details; have you said enough so that the reader can picture (or hear) the action you're describing? Check your verbs and nouns to see if you can substitute something more vivid. Check for errors. Then, when you're satisfied that your reader will enjoy this description of an action, recopy it on clean paper, proofread the copy, and turn it in.

11

Why the Sky Looks Blue

SIR JAMES JEANS

Sir James Jeans was an English mathematician, a physicist, an astronomer, and a popular scientific writer. He taught at Trinity College at Cambridge and at Princeton University. He is best known for his books which explain physical and astronomical theories for the non-scientific person. In this excerpt from his book *The Stars and Their Courses,* he uses an analogy to explain a difficult concept. That is, he uses something we can see (waves of water) to describe something we can't see (waves of light).

Vocabulary Preview

line
1	pier	a platform built out over the water and supported by pillars, or columns; used as a landing place for boats
5	regiment	a large number of military troops
8	formidable	difficult to overcome
9	impinge	to strike; to hit
17	interpose(s)	to set between; to insert
22	prism	a transparent glass with usually triangular ends and rectangular sides, used for separating light into its various colors
28	constitute(s)	to make up; to be the elements of
34	constituent(s)	a necessary part or element

Essay Preview: Questions to Answer as You Read

1. What does Jeans compare large waves to?
2. To what does he compare the columns of a pier?
3. In your own words, why, according to Jeans, does the sky look blue?

Why the Sky Looks Blue

1   Imagine that we stand on an ordinary seaside pier, and watch the waves rolling in and striking against the iron columns of the pier. Large waves pay very little attention to the columns—they divide right and left and reunite after passing each column, much as a regiment of soldiers would if a tree stood in their road; it is almost as though the columns had not been there. But the short waves and ripples find the columns of a pier a much more formidable obstacle. When the short waves impinge on the columns, they are reflected back and spread as new ripples in all directions. To use the technical term, they are "scattered." The obstacle provided by the iron columns hardly affects the long waves at all, but scatters the short ripples.

2   We have been watching a sort of working model of the way in which sunlight struggles through the earth's atmosphere. Between us on earth and outer space the atmosphere interposes innumerable obstacles in the form of molecules of air, tiny droplets of water, and small particles of dust. These are represented by the columns of the pier.

3   The waves of the sea represent the sunlight. We know that sunlight is a blend of many colors—as we can prove for ourselves by passing it through a prism, or even through a jug of water, or as nature demonstrates to us when she passes it through the raindrops of a summer shower and produces a rainbow. We also know that light consists of waves, and that the different colors of light are produced by waves of different lengths, red light by long waves and blue light by short

waves. The mixture of waves which constitutes sunlight has to struggle past the columns of the pier. And these obstacles treat the light waves much as the columns of the pier treat the sea-waves. The long waves which constitute red light are hardly affected but the short waves which constitute blue light are scattered in all directions.

4   Thus the different constituents of sunlight are treated in different ways as they struggle through the earth's atmosphere. A wave of blue light may be scattered by a dust particle, and turned out of its course. After a time a second dust particle again turns it out of its course, and so on, until finally it enters our eyes by a path as zigzag as that of a flash of lightning. Consequently the blue waves of the sunlight enter our eyes from all directions. And that is why the sky looks blue.

Questions for Discussion

1. Writers frequently use analogy to explain something unfamiliar by describing something familiar. *What is the unfamiliar concept that Jeans describes here? What familiar thing does he use for describing it?*

2. Analogy, as a type of comparison, uses some of the writing devices of comparison: simile and metaphor, most notably. As an example, in paragraph 3 Jeans says that sunlight "has to struggle past the columns of the pier." Well, it doesn't really. Sunlight struggles past other things: dust particles, droplets of water, and molecules of air. But Jeans uses this close phrasing—a *metaphor*—to heighten his comparison. (You probably already know metaphor as an implied comparison between two unlike things; for example, "clouds sailing across the sky" implies that clouds are like ships, and "his anger flared" implies that anger is like a flame.) The sentence that follows the metaphor explains what it means by using *simile*—another comparison. Here the key word *as* tells us that Jeans is comparing obstacles in the atmosphere with columns of a pier. *Find other examples of simile—a comparison introduced by* like *or* as.

3. *In a sentence, summarize what Jeans says in this essay: "The sky is blue because. . . ." Notice that you came to this understanding of light waves by considering the action of waves of water.*

4. *From what you know about science, would you say that Jeans's analogy is valid? That is, do waves of light and waves of water react in the same way when encountering obstacles? Can light waves be described by the action of waves of water?* He's probably right as far as he goes with this analogy. We need to remember that two things chosen for analogy don't have to be alike in every respect. Light waves differ from sea waves in many ways, one of the most obvious being that sea waves are wet—that is, we can touch them. The writer chooses in what way he will compare two things, and that way must be valid: what matters here is whether light waves do act like sea waves when they encounter obstacles.

5. Jeans's purpose for writing this essay is rather clear-cut: to explain why the sky looks blue. To achieve this purpose, however, he must convince the reader that he knows what he is writing about; that is, the reader must accept his authority. He accomplishes this acceptance by his choice of words and selection of details. For example, in line 11 he refers to *scattered* as a "technical" term for the action just described. Since only an expert in the subject would know this technical use of a familiar word, we are willing to grant him a certain credibility: we're willing to believe him. *Find a number of other instances in this essay that represent Jeans's authority to write on the subject.*

6. *Notice how Jeans has organized his essay. What is the subject of the first paragraph?* Waves of water. And no thesis is yet expressed. The second paragraph acts as a transition, indicating the reason for noticing the water's action and making the analogy clear. The next paragraph describes light waves in terms of the analogy with sea waves; for example, sunlight "has to struggle past the columns of the pier." Finally, the last paragraph describes only light waves, thus balancing paragraph 1,

which described sea waves. A simple outline might appear as follows:

    I. Sea waves
    II. Transition introducing sunlight
    III. Action of sunlight like action of sea waves
    IV. Sunlight

7. We've noted that the thesis sentence doesn't appear in the first paragraph. In Question 3 you expressed the thesis as you saw it, probably something like "The sky is blue because the short, blue waves of sunlight, when they meet obstacles, are dispersed in all directions like short sea waves when they encounter columns of a pier." Now, Jeans nowhere makes a statement similar to this. But he builds it. The first sentence in paragraph 2 is close to being a thesis: "We have been watching a sort of working model of the way in which sunlight struggles through the earth's atmosphere." Then he adds to it the first sentence of the third paragraph: "The waves of the sea represent the sunlight." *Which sentence of the* last *paragraph, then, would you say completes Jeans's statement?*

    You may say the last sentence, but you'd probably need to include the sentence before it too, in order to complete the idea.

Sentence Patterning

As a student writer you've no doubt written sentences with *who* or *which* clauses and may have wondered how to punctuate them. As indicated in the Sentence Patterning under "Mr. McElroy" (p. 60), there are two ways: set off with commas or not set off with commas. If the *which* (or *who*) clause does not end the sentence, it is enclosed with *two* commas or takes *none;* at the end of a sentence it is either preceded by a comma or not. These statements tell you nothing unless you know *when* to use the commas and when not to. The rule, as stated on p. 61, is easy: if the clause *identifies* the thing it follows (tells *which one*), it is *not* enclosed with commas. If it interrupts the main idea to add further information (useful, interesting, helpful, but not essential), it takes commas. (*That* clauses, incidentally, are always essential, hence are never set off by commas.)

In this exercise we're looking only at essential *which* clauses, those *not* enclosed in commas. The Jeans essay has two that we'll use for sentence patterning. The first is from paragraph 3:

SENTENCE

> The mixture of waves <u>which constitutes sunlight</u> has to struggle past the columns of the pier.

In this sentence, *which* stands for *mixture,* and the clause is necessary for identifying which "mixture of waves" constitutes sunlight. Copy the sentence exactly, study the pattern, and then write your own imitation of it. Use no commas.

PATTERN

> _____ which _____ _____
> _____.

EXAMPLE

> The initial excitement <u>which accompanies the soaring of an airplane</u> is like catching the wind when sailing.

The second sentence for patterning adds a little complication: the *which* clause is introduced by a preposition, in this case *in.*

SENTENCE

> We have been watching a sort of working model of the way <u>in which sunlight struggles through the earth's atmosphere</u>.

This sentence has the *which* clause at the end. In it *which* stands for *way,* and the clause is essential for identifying what is meant by *way.* Copy the sentence, study the pattern, and write a sentence of your own. Use no commas. You can substitute a different preposition for *in* if your sentence calls for a different one. You might use *by, of, to, about, through,* or another that fits your meaning. (There's a list of prepositions in the Appendix and on p. 80.)

PATTERN

_____ in which
_____.

EXAMPLE

The movement of an airplane through air is similar to the way <u>in which a boat moves through water.</u>

Now write a few more sentences using *which* or *who,* and decide whether the clauses should be set off with commas or not.

WRITING ASSIGNMENT

An analogy differs from a comparison in that the aim of an analogy is to describe *one* thing—accomplished by describing a more familiar thing. A comparison, on the other hand, looks at both subjects somewhat equally, with the aim of describing *both.* For this writing assignment, choose something (*one* thing) you can describe by comparing it with something else.

As an example, one student, a pre-architecture major who wanted to help other architecture students understand essay writing, chose to describe essay writing in terms of constructing a building. After an introduction that set up the analogy, the rest of the essay described the building process: determining a theme, sketching out ideas, considering the needs of an "audience," directing the flow of movement, and finally completing the structure. Obviously the writer was describing the process of writing by using building terms and activities familiar to other architecture students.

To get an idea of the range of subjects you can choose from, scan the list below:

skiing	studying
flying	growing up
cooking	reading
selling	writing
sewing	quarreling
doing dishes	listening to music
sailing	taking a test
walking	registering for classes
playing baseball	growing old
swimming	working a crossword puzzle
watching television	recovering from illness
babysitting	catching a cold
shampooing hair	washing the dog

Choose two items from the list, one to be described in terms of a second. For example, "skiing is like growing up," or "sailing is like flying," or "registering for classes is like shampooing hair." Try out a few combinations. Choose your subject from this list if you like, but you may think of other subjects that you can write on competently.

Remember that, like Jeans, you should be somewhat of an authority on the subject. The subject that you choose to describe must be one that you know well but may be unfamiliar to your reader. You are to describe that subject in terms of something else that *is* familiar to your reader. That is, you are an expert on both subjects but your reader knows only the second one. As an example, the student who compared writing essays to building knew something about designing and constructing a building; he also knew how to write an essay. The readers, other architecture students, presumably knew about building, so building terminology was used. The student who compared sailing to flying was an expert sailor and also had done some flying; the reader is assumed to know what flying is like and is asked to think of sailing as she thinks of flying.

Organize your essay as Jeans did. Devote the first paragraph to the familiar subject, the one you are using to describe the more difficult subject. Make your second paragraph a transition in which you make clear what you are describing, and in what terms. Your third paragraph will refer to both subjects in order to describe your primary subject, and your final paragraph will describe only your main subject. For example, if your aim were to describe sailing in terms of flying, you'd have an outline something like this:

I. Flying
II. Transition: introducing sailing
III. Sailing is like flying
IV. Sailing

Experiment with using similes and metaphors, but don't overdo it; Jeans didn't. And write one sentence that fits one of the patterns you practiced in Sentence Patterning.

The difficult part of this assignment is to remember that you are describing one subject in terms of another: light waves in terms of sea waves, sailing in terms of flying. When you have finished writing your rough draft, reread what you have written and check for focus. Is it clear which of your subjects you have intended to describe, and which one is being used to carry out that description? Have you written as one with authority? Make adjustments as necessary. You may have to add details that a casual reader needs in order to get your point. You may need to explain terms. You may have to revise sentences.

After thorough revision, write a clean final copy.

12

Lift Your Feet

ANDREW WARD

Andrew Ward was born in Chicago in 1946 and grew up there and in India. His father was an educator and his mother a social worker. Ward himself is the author of numerous books, writes for magazines and newspapers, and has been a contributing editor of *Atlantic Monthly*. The essay below is excerpted from one of his books, *Fits and Starts: The Premature Memoirs of Andrew Ward*. This piece is from a chapter that describes the effect on the family of one of his mother's personal characteristics.

Vocabulary Preview

line
4	paramount	of highest importance; supreme
5	hygienic	sanitary; germ-free; promoting health
22	disorienting	confusing as to time and place
29	tatting	a fine lace made by looping and knotting thread carried on a hand shuttle (a spool-like instrument)
33	psychosomatic	a physical illness caused or aggravated by mental or emotional processes
35	Teutonic	of an ancient Germanic people

Essay Preview: Questions to Answer as You Read

1. What is the mother's behavioral characteristic that brings about the effects described here?
2. What effect does this "ambition" have on the author's wife?

3. What effects does it have on other members of the family?

Lift Your Feet

All her life, my mother wanted busy children. Nothing infuriated her more than the sight of one of her offspring lying around, staring into space. But she had a conflicting ambition which proved paramount: that her house remain at all times tidy and hygienic, that it exhibit, in effect, as little evidence of human activity as possible.

You could turn your back for a moment in my mother's house, leave a half-written letter on the dining room table, a magazine open on the chair, and turn around to find it had been "put back," as my mother phrased it, "where it belonged."

My wife, on one of her first visits to my mother's house, placed on an end table a napkined packet of cheese and crackers she had made for herself and went to the kitchen to fetch a drink. When she returned, she found the packet had been removed. Puzzled, she set down her drink and went back to the kitchen for more cheese and crackers, only to return to find that now her drink had disappeared. Up to then she had guessed that everyone in my family held onto their drinks, sometimes with both hands, so as not to make water rings on the end tables. Now she knows better. . . .

These disappearances had a disorienting effect on our family. We were all inclined to forgetfulness, and it was common for one of us, upon returning from the bathroom and finding that every evidence of his work-in-progress had vanished, to forget what he'd been up to. "Do you remember what I was doing?" was a question frequently asked, but rarely answered, for whoever turned to address himself to it ran the risk of having his own pen, paper, book, tatting, suddenly disappear into the order of my mother's universe. . . .

My mother's cleaning seems to have come to a head while I was in college. She started to get terrible headaches and psychosomatic digestive problems. Pretty soon, she hired some cleaning women to come in every week. They were

Teutonic, like her grandmother, and did a good job, and she was delighted to find that she didn't have to clean up after them half so much as she had cleaned up after her family. My sister has developed a second-hand passion for clean windows, and my brother does the vacuuming in his house, perhaps to avoid having to be the one to lift his feet. I try not to think about it too much, but I have latterly taken to cleaning the baseboards once a week. I figure if you don't keep after them they'll just get filthy, and then where will we be?

Questions for Discussion

1. The thesis statement in this essay tells the cause of the problems described here. *What is that cause?*
2. The mother's ambition for a neat and tidy house presents several problems for the family. *In this story, what problem does it create for the author's wife?*
3. It seems that it doesn't take long for outsiders to learn about the mother's passion for tidiness. *How does the family adapt to that passion?*
4. Paragraph 5 concludes with some long-term effects on various members of the family. *Starting with the mother herself, name these effects.*
5. This essay has a rather simple format: one cause and several effects. In brief outline form it looks something like this:

    I. Cause (thesis)
    II. Clarification of cause
    III. First effect: on author's wife
    IV. Second effect: on the family
    V. Third effect: in the long term

    Paragraph 2 intervenes between cause and effects. *What does it accomplish for you the reader?*
6. *What is Ward's attitude toward his subject? Is he criticizing his mother? praising her? Does he consider neatness a virtue? Study the last paragraph and the effects brought out there: the mother has health problems (caused, apparently, by the same psychological drives which generated*

the passion for a tidy house); the sister cleans windows obsessively; the brother vacuums his house; and the author pragmatically cleans baseboards. Are these effects good or bad?

We might conclude that the mother is the only one who suffers. But Ward treats the entire situation rather lightly, ending with a parody of something he probably heard his mother say; he even jokes about his mother's relationship with the cleaning women. We have the impression he's letting us in on a standing family joke.

7. *Why might Ward devote a chapter of his book to his mother's passion for neatness? What reaction might he hope to achieve in his audience?*

What is your reaction to this description of Ward's mother? Do you remember someone you know who has a similar obsession? This may be what Ward was anticipating. His goal of course is to entertain (certainly not to *inform* you—it's immaterial to you what his mother was like), but he may have been banking on this empathy, this I-know-exactly-what-you-mean reaction in the reader, in order to bring about this entertainment. It's important for writers to anticipate—and make use of—the reactions of their readers.

Sentence Patterning

One aspect of revising what we've written is to look for places where we can economize on words. In making our writing more concise—without omitting any of our meaning—we can get our points across more directly, more surely. One way to get conciseness is to use participles instead of clauses, as you may remember from "Blubber on Ice." Participles are adjectives formed from verbs; like other adjectives, they modify nouns: the *puzzled* woman, the *frightened* child, the well-*trained* dog.

In the sentence that begins on line 16, Ward begins with a participle. Here's the sentence as we'll use it for patterning:

SENTENCE

> Puzzled, she set down her drink and went back to the kitchen for more cheese and crackers.

A wordier way to convey this idea is to begin: "She was puzzled. She set down her drink. . . . " This in fact is what Ward is saying with his reduced form. In this exercise you will begin your imitative sentence with a participle that describes your subject. (In this position, the participle must describe the subject of your sentence, not another noun; otherwise you'll have a participle that doesn't clearly describe anything.)

Another feature of this sentence is the compound verb—two verbs (*set* and *went*) that follow the same subject (*she*). This is another way to make our writing more concise. A wordier way to say the same thing is "She set down her drink, and she went back to the kitchen. . . ." When the same subject is used twice, it can be omitted the second time, thus compounding the verbs by joining them with a conjunction.

Copy the sentence above, and then study the pattern and example below; write a sentence that imitates the pattern.

PATTERN

_____d, _____[verb]_____ and
_____[verb]_____.

EXAMPLE

> Tempted, the kitten pounced on the receding piece of string and watched it slip away between her paws.

WRITING ASSIGNMENT

Does someone in your family have an idiosyncrasy—a little personal peculiarity that makes life a little difficult (or fun, or exciting) for the rest of the family? If so, perhaps you could write an essay similar to Andrew Ward's. Or maybe the apparently simple action of adopting a pet made some tremendous changes for you and others. You might remember getting your driver's license and the changes it made in your life. This writing assignment is about one cause and several effects of that one cause. Here are a few topics, although you can probably think of something else that suits you better:

An idiosyncrasy of a family member
Adopting a pet
Getting a driver's license
Getting a job
Having a roommate for the first time

Don't make this a serious, informative essay. Have as your goal the entertainment of your reader, keeping in mind that the way your dad drives is not terribly important to your reader but that reading about it could be fun if you write about it as fun. So choose details that the reader might enjoy—not necessarily *big* things; a little thing like getting a cracker snack all together in one place can make a good story. This incident as told by Ward is something the audience can relate to; it's told simply, in everyday terms, but also clearly. Most important, it's firmly connected to the point of the essay.

Another cause-and-effect essay in this book, "The Bounty of the Sea" by Jacques Cousteau, has a very different purpose—and a very different cause-and-effect structure as well. In that essay the causes and effects form a chain, an effect becoming the cause of another effect, and so on. The structure of "Lift Your Feet" is simpler: several effects of a single cause. This is the structure you are to use in writing this assignment.

Try following the outline presented in Question 5. Begin by stating the cause and your thesis; then in another paragraph clarify your cause with an explanation of the cause-and-effect relationship. Be specific. In the next two paragraphs give some longer examples of the effects brought on by this cause, and in your last paragraph summarize—either the long-term or the more immediate effects.

After you've finished your first draft, reread what you've written. Are your effects actually that—effects—or just something related to the cause by time or place? Have you made clear how your effects derive from your cause? Have you been specific enough in explaining your cause and effects? Have you succeeded in being mildly humorous?

Check your essay for errors in grammar, punctuation, and spelling. Remember that this writing should be in *edited* American English—the best work you're capable of, like something you might read in published articles. When you're satisfied with your revisions, write a clean copy, and give it a final proofreading.

13

Letter of Complaint

Most people at some time have reason to write a letter of complaint: a product they have purchased is not operating properly, or one they've ordered is defective, has been substituted with something unacceptable, or has been damaged in shipment. There are many reasons. The letter below represents an actual case of complaint; its writer is turning to the general manager of the company as a last resort. (This version is edited from the original and names have been changed.)

Essay Preview: Questions to Answer as You Read

1. What is the writer complaining about?
2. What does she expect the recipient of the letter to do?
3. What is the tone of the letter?

Letter of Complaint

3642 W. 148th Street
Middleton, IL 60945
October 7, 19—

Charles F. Mitchell, General Manager
Greco Motor Division
National Motors Corporation
1023 E. Wells Avenue
Ashton, MI 49560

Dear Mr. Mitchell:

On March 1, 19—, my husband and I picked up our new Greco sedan at Hauer Greco Dealers in Darby, Illinois (copy of bill of sale attached). It was a beautiful car and we were proud to own it. However, since that time we have had repeated trouble with it.

In the seven months we've had the car, it has been in the repair garage five times, and it's still not working properly.

1. The first time it was in we had hose clamps replaced after notification from National Motors that the clamps might be defective.
2. The second time was to have transmission noise corrected. Parts had to be ordered, so we took the car home again while we waited.
3. When the transmission parts arrived, we took the car in for a third time. In order to do so, however, we had to first jump the battery because it was dead.
4. After getting the car back we left for a vacation in Minnesota. We stopped for gas about 60 miles from Eau Claire, Wisconsin, and when we were ready to drive on we found the battery dead again. The station attendant jumped it and advised us to stop at the Greco garage in Eau Claire. After six hours in the repair shop, the car—again—seemed to be fixed.
5. On September 13, back home again, the battery died while I was out buying groceries. I had it towed to the Greco garage, the third time it was in with the same problem. The service people at the garage checked the electrical system and found no malfunction, then recharged the battery. They also repaired the rear defogger, which had not operated since we got the car.

As you can see, I have not fared well with my Greco sedan. I say "I" because during this time my husband died of a heart attack. Now as a widow I'm left with the insecurity of owning a practically new car that may at any time unpredictably turn up with a dead battery. I'm sure you will agree that I should not expect this performance from a Greco. I think you'll agree also that I should have reason to expect your licensed mechanics to discover the source of the problem.

I want the assurance, Mr. Mitchell, that my seven-month-old car is in good operating condition. I don't want to worry every time I go out about whether the battery is dead. While this may be a small matter to you, it is an important one to me. I'll be waiting to hear what action you've taken.

                              Sincerely,

                              Mrs. Ray Schultz

Attachment

Questions for Discussion

1. *What tasks do the details and tone of the first paragraph accomplish?*

   The letter begins positively, acquainting the recipient with the facts and conveying a cooperative tone.

2. *How does the letter end? How has the tone changed? What does the writer expect the general manager of the company to do?*

   The letter ends as positively as it began, but here it states firmly—yet politely—what outcome the writer expects. Mrs. Schultz is in control of the anger and frustration she justly feels, yet at the same time she is not willing to tolerate inaction concerning the defective car.

3. *Trace the details of the problem. What was the first problem, the second, and so on? What is the effect of enumerating the details?*

4. *Notice the format of the letter. Where does the writer put her address? her name? the date? How much space is there between the recipient's address and the salutation ("Dear Mr. Mitchell")? Where is the complimentary close ("Sincerely") situated in relation to the return address? Why is the word "Attachment" included?*

Sentence Patterning

One frequent cause of vagueness in student writing is the use of *this* without a clear antecedent. As a consequence, the reader often must guess what it means. The

Letter of Complaint

problem, of course, may stem from the fact that the writer herself may not have a clear idea of its meaning. The cure for such fuzzy writing is to use *this* as an adjective, not a pronoun: not simply *this,* but *this something;* not "I should not expect this from a Greco," but, as written in the letter,

SENTENCE

> I'm sure you will agree that I should not expect this performance from a Greco.

Writing the sentence this way of course makes it necessary for the *writer* to know what he or she is referring to, and this clarification may improve the rest of the writing as well. Copy the sentence as it is.

Here's the pattern:

PATTERN

> this [something] ——————————.

Note the example below, and then write a sentence of your own that imitates that pattern.

EXAMPLE

> I think you'd remember if you'd felt this symptom before.

Now try writing other sentences that use *this* as an adjective (*this something*) instead of as a pronoun.

WRITING ASSIGNMENT

Your assignment is to think of a situation that has upset you recently and to write a letter of complaint to someone who has the authority to correct that situation. You may have bought defective merchandise or been treated rudely by a salesperson or been billed incorrectly for services rendered or had any number of other things happen. If possible, choose a very real situation that may be cleared up if you actually send your letter. (In response to her letter to the head of the auto company, Mrs. Schultz received a polite letter from someone in Mr. Mitchell's office. More important, the Hauer Greco service department replaced the alternator on her car and she has had no further trouble with the battery.)

Collect specific details on your subject: dates, names, model numbers if applicable, invoice numbers, etc. Find out the name and address of the person you need to write to. You may be able to get the information in your telephone directory, or you may even call the company for a name. Another source is *Standard and Poor's Register of Corporations, Directors, and Executives,* which you can find in your library reference room. Ask your librarian if you need help finding it. Once you have these details in hand, ask yourself specifically what happened. Work out the details in some notes.

Next write a rough draft, observing the following conventions for business letters:

1. Begin with a positive paragraph that presents the problem and your willingness to cooperate.
2. In a paragraph or two, with or without an enumeration as in the model, write in detail what the problem is. Be specific. Use chronological order. Be as objective as you can. Control your anger and frustration, and don't be sarcastic. Make sure that the recipient of the letter knows exactly what your complaint is.
3. End on a positive but firm note, and state clearly what you expect.

Revise your letter carefully. Delete unnecessary words or details. Use specific words in place of general ones. Check spelling and punctuation carefully, because the letter you send out represents *you* and indicates how much you care about details. When you're fully satisfied that this letter will make a favorable impression on your reader, rewrite it according to the format shown on the following page. Type the letter if possible. Aim for a neat, well-balanced appearance; the margins here are approximate and should be adjusted depending on the size of your letter. Finally, proofread carefully, so that you have ABSOLUTELY NO COPYING ERRORS.

Letter of Complaint

```
                        Return address
                        City, State, ZIP Code
                        Date

Name of recipient
Address of recipient
City, State, ZIP Code

Dear _____:

_____
_____
_____.

_____
_____
_____
_____
_____
_____.

_____
_____
_____.

                        Sincerely,
                        (your signature)


                        Your name


Attachment (if applicable)
```

14

The Arctic Storm

FRANKLIN RUSSELL

Franklin Russell, born in 1926 in New Zealand, began newspaper work in New Zealand and Australia. At the time of writing *Watchers at the Pond* he was a freelance writer living in Canada. The book which resulted from his meticulous observation of pond life presents a scientifically objective and poetically sensitive account. The story as originally published involves four "watchers": a red-tailed hawk, a snowshoe hare, an old muskrat, and a man. Two of these—the hawk and the hare—are participants in the short excerpt below, and a third, the man, narrates this frigid drama.

Vocabulary Preview

line		
2	cumulative	increasing by successive additions
13	peninsula	a land area projecting out into the water
18	pellet(s)	a little ball, or rounded mass
22	ricochet(ed)	to bounce off a surface at an angle
26	maelstrom	a large or violent whirlpool
26	eddying	moving with a circular motion against the main current
30	rime	a white mass of tiny ice crystals
39	impel(led)	to urge to action
40	foraging	searching for food
43	quest(ed)	to seek; to hunt
49	conifer	an evergreen, cone-bearing tree
50	junco(s)	a small, gray, sparrow-like bird
54	dubious	doubtful

| 55 | sanctuary | a place of refuge or protection |
| 56 | intrusive | entering as an unwanted element |

Essay Preview: Questions to Answer as You Read

1. In what month might this winter storm be taking place?
2. From what point might the narrator be observing this storm?
3. How long does the storm last?
4. What evidence of Russell's ability to observe and report natural happenings can you find in this narrative?

The Arctic Storm

1   The winter moved to its final degree. The enduring cold was having a cumulative effect on the life of the pond so that here and there the resistance to death was weakening. The snowshoe hare paused near the pond, his face plastered with caked snow. He was shivering. He was having difficulty sustaining body heat with a diminishing supply of bark and buds. The red-tailed hawk ranged farther across country. He woke chilled in the night and saw an owl drift across the moon....

2   Soon the overcast moved in, and the uneasy sound of rising wind was an audible dimension of new and bitter cold.... By midafternoon, it was so cold that the snowshoe hare was driven to shelter in deep snow among the dry chattering undergrowth near the sand and rock peninsula. The sky was now milky white, shot with streaks of black, and the wind groaned into the bare rattling forest. The first snowflakes fell as the overcast closed down tightly; the great arctic storm had begun.

3   As the snow, consisting of small, hard pellets, began streaming across the pond, all the overground creatures sought shelter. The birds headed for evergreens and dense thickets. The red-tailed hawk huddled in the racing gloom behind an oak trunk, and stray pellets ricocheted off his plumage. The wind whipped the fresh-dropped snow along the ground and piled it in long drifts. The pond, partially sheltered from the north by a tree-covered plateau and ridge,

was a maelstrom of eddying snow. Above, the storm tore on to the marsh.

4   Shortly before dusk the snow changed in character. The pellets became mixed with large, damp snowflakes that stuck where they hit and turned to rime, forming on tree trunks, branches, stones, banks, and brush. The snow built massively into the force of the wind, crystal on crystal, and by dusk most of the trees were misshapen with rime-ridden branches and trunks and their limbs crackled against the strength of the wind. . . .

5   The wind was forming long drifts wherever the ground caught its headlong snow-laden passage for the briefest moment. At the beginning of the storm, a star-nosed mole had been impelled by hunger to leave his underground tunnel system near the swamp to go foraging along the edge of the pond. But on returning to the entrance of his tunnel into the earth, he found the territory made strange by drifts of snow. He quested back and forth, then plunged his starred snout into the snowdrift in an effort to break into the hidden tunnel. He dug into the drift, but the fine snow clogged his efforts. The pond darkened. The mole's search grew more urgent as he felt the increasing cold.

6   The storm reached into the evergreens for refugee birds, and they withstood it till a conifer branch, heavy with rime, swung down into some clinging juncos, which scattered into the hissing darkness. Once aflight, they had to keep flying, blundering through the fleeting bare outlines of trees and thickets. Some clutched and held to twigs, but the force of the storm pushed the rest of them south in a dubious quest for sanctuary.

7   The intrusive wind, in all its hostility, was shaped by the same cycle of birth and death that regulated the pond. At midnight it slackened, and almost immediately the thaw began. The rime fell and exploded in silent showers of white. The shivering gray squirrel, his leaf home ruined, had found temporary refuge in a hollow elm. The arctic owl had pushed through the rime and had flown off rapidly. The snow concealed the storm's victims. When the dawn came at last, the rime was still falling into puffs of white smoke and odd branches cracked and fell. The pond had endured a long night.

Questions for Discussion

1. We learn in the biographical sketch that Russell has no specialized scientific training for writing an essay of this nature. However, the essay itself gives ample evidence of his concern for detail and of the library and laboratory research he must have done in preparation for his "watching" project. In paragraph 1, for example, Russell notices that "resistance to death was weakening." Further in the same paragraph, he writes not about a "rabbit" and a "hawk" but about a "snowshoe hare" and a "red-tailed hawk." This man is not the everyday observer of a storm. *Find other evidence throughout the essay of Russell's understanding of his subject.*

2. Because of his acquired knowledge of nature, Russell is able to describe his observations in more specific terms than a casual observer would. This gives him an advantage, to be sure, but we all have libraries available to us too. He also observes closely, and this too is an ability that can be acquired by any person with normal abilities. Most of us don't bother to look closely. How often, for example, do you watch the sun set or a summer storm come and go without really *seeing*—beyond noting the brilliant colors or the darkening clouds or how wet you get? But see how Russell observes. He notices things—even a little starving mole or a shivering gray squirrel or the texture of the snow. *Find several other examples of how closely Russell observes the storm and its effects.*

3. *What is the narrator's vantage point for observing this storm? Does he ever mention himself in the narrative?* The story of the storm has many participants—the snowshoe hare, the red-tailed hawk, the star-nosed mole (and other creatures, like the old muskrat, that had to be deleted when the essay was shortened). But nowhere is the narrator present. In fiction, he would be called a "self-effacing narrator," one who deliberately steps out of the story in order to relate the events objec-

tively. So where is the narrator? Somewhere outside the story, either reporting events as he has seen them happen or relating them as he knows they would happen.

4. *What is the controlling idea of this essay?* Russell provides direction when he says in line 16, "the great arctic storm had begun," and he completes this thought with his last sentence, "The pond had endured a long night." So he's writing about the progress of a storm and its effect on the pond and the nearby inhabitants. *But what about the storm and the pond? What happens? Why does Russell want to tell you about this storm? Just to inform you of what a bitter storm is like on a forest pond at the end of winter? Well, that, yes, but what else? What is it like?* The first sentence of the last paragraph is a clue, and the word *endure* in the very last sentence is another clue. And the second sentence at the beginning of the essay is another.

So, without stating the idea as a thesis sentence, Russell tells us that a bitter storm at the end of winter is expectedly severe on the creatures that must endure it.

5. *Look at the verbs in this narrative. Are they present time or past? Do they convey a consistent time throughout the essay?* In another nature narrative in this book, "Blubber on Ice," male sea elephants are described as they battle for possession of females. That essay recounts a *habitual* process and uses *present*-time verbs. "The Arctic Storm," on the other hand, describes not how winter storms happen but how a *particular* storm began and ended at a particular time in the past. And so *past*-time verbs are used consistently. *Read "Blubber on Ice" and compare the differing effects of the two ways of relating actions.*

Sentence Patterning

Sometimes a participial phrase (see "Blubber on Ice," p. 83) modifies not the subject or another noun in the sentence but *its own noun,* one that is not part of the main sentence but is connected to the participial phrase. Constructions of this kind have a name—*nominative ab-*

solutes (because they have their own noun—a nominative—and no grammatical function in the sentence). They can be useful in writing.

Russell uses two of them in "The Arctic Storm." One occurs in the first paragraph and one in the last. Here's the first:

> The snowshoe hare paused near the pond, <u>his face plastered with caked snow.</u>

In the underlined absolute, the participle, *plastered*, does not modify *hare* in the main clause but *his face* instead. The entire construction adds more information to the main clause and might in fact be thought of as another shortened clause. Expanded, it would read:

> His face was plastered with caked snow.

We'll use Russell's second absolute construction for imitation. The sentence reads:

SENTENCE

> The shivering gray squirrel, <u>his leaf home ruined,</u> had found temporary refuge in a hollow elm.

The absolute, underlined, might be thought of as a shortened form of another clause:

> His leaf home was ruined.

Note the punctuation of absolutes: they are enclosed with commas. When they occur as an interruption of the sentence, as in the "squirrel" sentence above, they take two commas, one before and one after.

Copy the sentence above and study the pattern and example below. Then write a sentence of your own in imitation of the pattern.

PATTERN

_____, _____ [nominative absolute],
_____.

Franklin Russell

EXAMPLE

The fast-moving summer storm<u>, its dark clouds churning menacingly,</u> struck the little farm without warning.

WRITING ASSIGNMENT

Franklin Russell narrates the progress of a winter storm, starting at its beginning and ending when it's over. In between he gives lots of details and specific images and makes clear what effects the storm has on the plant and animal life in its path. He writes objectively, without ever intruding on the story himself.

You are asked in this assignment to write a similar essay. Choose an act of nature that you've observed or might observe. You may select one of these or something else:

A winter storm	An earthquake or tremor
A summer storm	The coming of a
An incoming tide	particular spring
A flood	A particular sunrise
A fire	A particular sunset

Unlike the writing assignment in "Blubber on Ice," here you are writing about a *particular* occurrence of an event—one that happened at some point in the past. Your verbs, therefore, will be in past time, not present.

Organize your essay by starting out with the beginning of the event. Relate its progress, indicating effects it has on the surroundings. As an example, if you were recounting the progress of a sunrise, you might, in addition to observing the changing colors of the sky, note that birds began to chirp or take to flight or forage for food. If you can, write from a fresh observation rather than relying on memory. Be a close observer; note fine details. Your narrative will end when the event you're narrating ends. In your final paragraph, write a thesis statement that summarizes your controlling idea, stating the point of your essay. This idea, your point, has been *in your mind* from the very beginning, determining what you have written and how you have written it. But you don't express it until the end. Then everything you've said should fall into place.

Again, remember to keep yourself out of the narrative. Report objectively: *you* didn't see, *you* didn't hear; instead, things happened and creatures did something. Use specific words and details as you report the progress of the event. Try to fit in a nominative absolute, and make all your verbs past tense.

Once you've finished writing your draft, let it rest for awhile if you can. Then go back to it and reread. Are you thoroughly objective, staying out of the narrative yourself? Have you been specific enough in your descriptions? Have you used past-time verbs throughout? Have you noted effects of your event on surrounding nature? Have you made your point? Have you corrected errors? You'll need to go over your essay several times. When you're finally satisfied with your revisions, write a clean draft and proofread it.

15

What Color Is an Orange?

JOHN McPHEE

John McPhee studied at Princeton and Cambridge and has been a published writer since the mid-1950s. In addition to being a playwright for television, an associate editor of *Time* magazine, and a staff writer for *New Yorker,* he has writen a number of books and has contributed articles to several popular magazines. He is highly respected for his prose style, which is characterized by precision of phrasing and attention to descriptive detail. It has been said of him that, with the oddity of some of his subjects, he almost seems to seek out unpromising subjects just for the challenge of conquering them. Such a subject may be *Oranges,* a fascinating book-length exposition devoted entirely to the orange. In this excerpt, he contrasts the two colors that oranges may be when they are ripe.

Vocabulary Preview

line
1	correlation	mutual relationship; connection
4	emerald	a bright-green precious stone
14	unespied	unseen
27	cadmium orange	a yellowish orange color
28	complement(s)	to complete; to bring to perfection
29	ellipsoid	circular or not quite fully circular
33	Valencia	a popular orange, harvested in Florida from March to June; juicy, tart, and almost seedless

Essay Preview: Questions to Answer as You Read

1. What does McPhee say makes oranges orange?
2. Where do oranges that are green when they're ripe grow? those that are orange?
3. How do green oranges compare with orange oranges in flavor?

What Color Is an Orange?

The color of an orange has no absolute correlation with the maturity of the flesh and juice inside. An orange can be as sweet and ripe as it will ever be and still glisten like an emerald in the tree. Cold—coolness, rather, is what makes an orange orange. In some parts of the world, the weather never gets cold enough to change the color; in Thailand, for example, an orange is a green fruit, and traveling Thais often blink with wonder at the sight of oranges the color of flame. The ideal nighttime temperature in an orange grove is forty degrees. Some of the most beautiful oranges in the world are grown in Bermuda, where the temperature, night after night, falls consistently to that level. Andrew Marvell's poem wherein the "remote Bermudas ride in the ocean's bosom unespied" was written in the sixteen-fifties, and contains a description, from hearsay, of Bermuda's remarkable oranges, set against their dark foliage like "golden lamps in a green night." Cool air comes down every night into the San Joaquin Valley in California, which is formed by the Coast Range to the west and the Sierra Nevadas to the east. The tops of the Sierras are usually covered with snow, and before dawn the temperature in the valley edges down to the frost point. In such cosmetic surroundings, it is no wonder that growers have heavily implanted the San Joaquin Valley with the Washington Navel Orange, which is the most beautiful orange grown in any quantity in the United States, and is certainly as attractive to the eye as any orange grown in the world. Its color will go to a deep, flaring cadmium orange, and its surface has a suggestion of coarseness, which complements its perfect ellipsoid shape. . . .

2   Some oranges that become orange while they are still unripe may turn green again as they ripen. When cool nights finally come to Florida, around the first of the year, the Valencia crop is fully developed in size and shape, but it is still three months away from ripeness. Sliced through the middle at that time, a Valencia looks something like a partitioned cupful of rice, and its taste is overpoweringly acid. But in the winter coolness, the exterior surface turns to bright orange, and the Valencia appears to be perfect for picking. Warm nights return, however, during the time of the Valencia harvest. On the trees in late spring, the Valencias turn green again, growing sweeter each day and greener each night.

Questions for Discussion

1. *According to McPhee, what gives oranges their orange color? Why are Florida oranges sometimes green when they're ripe? Which Florida orange in particular is green when ready for harvesting?*

    In another part of his book *Oranges,* McPhee tells how orange growers change the color of their green, ripe oranges. The fruit is either gassed, he says, or dyed. The gassing, or "de-greening," is a natural process using ethylene gas (given off naturally by some fruits, like bananas and apples), which is circulated among the oranges to help destroy the green pigment, chlorophyll, in their skins. Since both the orange color and the green are contained in the skin of a ripe orange, breaking down the green allows the orange pigment to emerge. The second method of changing the color, dyeing, is less common and is restricted by law. California law forbids it, and Florida law requires that dyed oranges be so labeled and contain ten percent more juice than the established minimum for undyed oranges.

2. While this essay on oranges is made up of only two paragraphs and is in fact an excerpt from a larger work,

it is still a complete piece in itself, presenting a statement on the color of oranges. *In your own words, state McPhee's message about oranges.*

This is his thesis, which he expresses in his first and second sentences and repeats in the last phrase of his final sentence: the color of an orange has no correlation with its taste, or an orange can be as sweet and ripe when it is green as it will ever be. The second statement is repeated at the end: "growing sweeter each day and greener each night."

3. After making his statement that oranges take on their characteristic color only in the presence of cool weather, McPhee gives an example of a locale where the oranges are green when ripe and then two places where they are orange. He thus is setting up a comparison/contrast to illustrate his point. Structurally the essay looks like this:

    I. Thesis   lines _____
   II. Green oranges—Thailand   lines _____
  III. Orange oranges   lines _____
       A. Bermuda
       B. California
  IV. Green and orange—Florida   lines _____
   V. Final reference to thesis   lines _____

Compare the essay with this outline and indicate in the spaces at the right what lines correspond to each part of the outline.

4. One characteristic of McPhee's writing style is that it is *clear;* as a consequence, a reader has no trouble following the train of thought. One reason for this clarity is that McPhee uses very few long, Latinate words—words that frequently end in *-tion* or *-sion* and represent some abstract idea. *Compare, for example, his second sentence, as it appears below, with the rewriting of it in a wordy, pompous (unreadable!) style:*

    McPhee: An orange can be as sweet and ripe as it will ever be and still glisten like an emerald in the tree.

> Rewrite: An orange has the potential to have as much succulence and maturation that it can at any time ever have and at the same time gives forth an illumination like a precious emerald in its arboreal setting.

Suddenly McPhee's clean style becomes heavy, and the reader's mind almost refuses to deal with it. Observe how the transformation took place: "can be" became "has the potential to have," and "sweet and ripe" became "succulence and maturation." *What are some other ways that these two sentences differ?*

Choose another of McPhee's sentences and try to rewrite it in this style. When you've finished, read it over. See how heavy it is, how it obscures meaning. Some writers actually try to write in this style, thinking it gives the impression of learning and sophistication, but readers hate it because it requires so much effort to read.

5. Another characteristic of McPhee's style is *coherence*. All of his sentences are interconnected—their relationships are clear and his ideas flow from one to another. *How does he achieve his coherence? To get started on an answer to this question, observe how often he repeats his key word* orange. *Can you find any sentence in which he doesn't use it at least once?*

Repetition of key words is an effective device for linking ideas, and in this piece it is McPhee's major method for achieving coherence. (There are two sentences that do not repeat *orange,* and they seem, coincidentally, to lack the smooth connections of the other sentences.)

Sentence Patterning

One method of achieving coherence and smoothness of style in writing is by subordinating some ideas to others. While there are many ways of doing this, one common method is using the adverbial clause. This is a clause that begins with an adverbial conjunction (as the first clause of the preceding sentence does: "While there are . . . "). Here are some of those conjunctions, arranged by function—the relationship they show to the rest of the sentence:

Time	Contrast	Cause
after	although	as
as	even though	because
as long as	though	since
as soon as	whereas	
before		*Condition*
during	*Manner*	if
since	as	unless
until	as if	
when		*Degree*
whenever	*Purpose*	as far as
while	so as	so far as
	so that	

Clauses that begin with these words are subordinate; they cannot be written as sentences. Therefore, when a sentence begins with a subordinate clause, it must end with an independent clause. The sentence below, adapted from lines 31–33 of McPhee's essay, begins this way.

SENTENCE

<u>When cool nights finally come to Florida,</u> the Valencia crop is fully developed in size and shape.

The subordinate clause, here introduced by *when,* is underlined. The pattern of the sentence is diagramed below.

PATTERN

[adverbial conjunction]   [subordinate clause],
           [independent clause].

Copy McPhee's sentence exactly as it is written above, noting the comma between the clauses, and then write a sentence of your own that follows the pattern. Below is an example of a sentence written after the pattern.

John McPhee

EXAMPLE

Because its full, rich flavor and color are unsurpassed, cheddar cheese made in Wisconsin is worth looking for in the store.

WRITING ASSIGNMENT

John McPhee writes about two kinds of the same thing. Fully ripe oranges can be either green or orange in color, the only difference being the environmental conditions during ripening. So he contrasts green oranges with orange ones in respect to where they are grown and how they are ripened. Referring again to the outline in Question 3, we see that after presenting his subject he writes first about green oranges, then orange, and then, in paragraph 2, oranges of both colors, ending with a final reference to his thesis.

In this writing assignment, you too are asked to contrast two things that differ mainly in one way, perhaps in where or how they were made. Here are a few subjects for you to choose from or use to suggest others:

Subject	*Two Aspects*
cheese	Wisconsin cheddar and Vermont cheddar
	natural and processed
sweaters	knit and crocheted
	handknit and machine knit
books	hardcover and softcover
cheese sandwiches	grilled and toasted
writing	typing and handwriting
	typing and word processing
	pencil and pen

Once you have decided on a subject, ask yourself questions about it. McPhee, for example, once establishing that a cool temperature is what makes oranges orange, might have asked:

Where are oranges green when ripe?
Where are they orange when ripe?
Who has written something about oranges?
What variety of orange grows in California?
Where are they grown in California?
What do these oranges look like?
What variety of orange grows in Florida?
When do oranges ripen in Florida?
What do Florida oranges look like when ripe? when unripe?
How does an unripe orange taste? a ripe one?

And so on. To explore a new subject and find out what you already know about it, probe your mind with questions.

Next begin to organize your ideas into groups. Try doing as McPhee did, discussing one side of the subject first (like green oranges) and then the other side (like orange oranges). Then finally discuss both. While you're exploring and arranging ideas, begin thinking of a point—what your essay is all about—and write this down in a single sentence. This sentence will be your thesis.

When you have enough ideas for a start, begin writing. Introduce your subject first—both aspects of it—and write your thesis. Then discuss your subject as you outlined it, first one aspect, then the other. Begin a new paragraph when you discuss both together and finally come to a conclusion that restates your point.

When you've finished writing, check your coherence. Do your ideas flow smoothly from one sentence to another? Specifically, have you repeated key words? (If you're not sure what your key words are, look at your thesis—they *ought* to be there. Note McPhee's use of *orange* in his thesis.) Sometimes also we lose coherence when we omit ideas. We skip from one thought to another without an important intermediary thought.

Check for errors too—in grammar, punctuation, and spelling. Then rewrite, proofreading your final copy.

16

Three Disciplines for Children

JOHN HOLT

John Holt is author of *Freedom and Beyond,* a book about reform in education from which the following excerpt is taken. Holt has taught school at all levels—elementary, secondary, and university—and, writing from his own experience and knowledge, brings fresh insights into the task of bringing up and educating children. He has expressed his philosophy in numerous books and articles written for an audience of educators and anyone else interested in making school a more pleasurable and learning-inducive environment. His discussion below goes beyond the common idea that discipline must be based on fear of punishment.

Vocabulary Preview

line
2	discipline(s)	training to produce a change in behavior; self-control as a result of that training; punishment
24	impartial	fair; not favoring one over another; without bias or prejudice
25	wheedle(d)	to coax; to influence by flattery
40	ritual	a set form or order for conducting religious and other solemn ceremonies; a set of procedures followed regularly
87	impotent	lacking physical strength; powerless; ineffectual

129

89 vengeful   desiring to punish another for an injury or wrongful act

Essay Preview: Questions to Answer as You Read

1. According to Holt, what three kinds of discipline do children learn from?
2. What is one example that Holt gives to illustrate the first kind? the second? the third?
3. What is one danger in applying the third kind of discipline?

Three Disciplines for Children

A child, in growing up, may meet and learn from three different kinds of disciplines. The first and most important is what we might call the Discipline of Nature or of Reality. When he is trying to do something real, if he does the wrong thing or doesn't do the right one, he doesn't get the result he wants. If he doesn't pile one block right on top of another, or tries to build on a slanting surface, his tower falls down. If he hits the wrong key, he hears the wrong note. If he doesn't hit the nail squarely on the head, it bends, and he has to pull it out and start with another. If he doesn't measure properly what he is trying to build, it won't open, close, fit, stand up, fly, float, whistle, or do whatever he wants it to do. If he closes his eyes when he swings, he doesn't hit the ball. A child meets this kind of discipline every time he tries to *do* something, which is why it is so important in school to give children more chances to do things, instead of just reading or listening to someone talk (or pretending to). This discipline is a great teacher. The learner never has to wait long for his answer; it usually comes quickly, often instantly. Also it is clear, and very often points toward the needed correction; from what happened he can not only see that what he did was wrong, but also why, and what he needs to do instead. Finally, and most important, the giver of the answer, call it Nature, is impersonal, impartial, and indifferent. She does not give opinions, or make judgments; she cannot be wheedled, bullied, or fooled; she does not get angry or disappointed; she does not praise or blame; she does not remember past failures or hold grudges; with her one always gets a fresh start, this time is the one that counts.

2   The next discipline we might call the Discipline of Culture, of Society, of What People Really Do. Man is a social, a cultural animal. Children sense around them this culture, this network of agreements, customs, habits, and rules binding the adults together. They want to understand it and be a part of it. They watch very carefully what people around them are doing and want to do the same. They want to do right, unless they become convinced they can't do right. Thus children rarely misbehave seriously in church, but sit as quietly as they can. The example of all those grownups is contagious. Some mysterious ritual is going on, and children, who like rituals, want to be part of it. In the same way, the little children that I see at concerts or operas, though they may fidget a little, or perhaps take a nap now and then, rarely make any disturbance. With all those grownups sitting there, neither moving nor talking, it is the most natural thing in the world to imitate them. Children who live among adults who are habitually courteous to each other, and to them, will soon learn to be courteous. Children who live surrounded by people who speak a certain way will speak that way, however much we may try to tell them that speaking that way is bad or wrong.

3   The third discipline is the one most people mean when they speak of discipline—the Discipline of Superior Force, of sergeant to private, of "you do what I tell you or I'll make you wish you had." There is bound to be some of this in a child's life. Living as we do surrounded by things that can hurt children, or that children can hurt, we cannot avoid it. We can't afford to let a small child find out from experience the danger of playing in a busy street, or of fooling with the pots on the top of a stove, or of eating up the pills in the medicine cabinet. So, along with other precautions, we say to him, "Don't play in the street, or touch things on the stove, or go into the medicine cabinet, or I'll punish you." Between him and the danger too great for him to imagine we put a lesser danger, but one he can imagine and maybe therefore

want to avoid. He can have no idea of what it would be like to be hit by a car, but he can imagine being shouted at, or spanked, or sent to his room. He avoids these substitutes for the greater danger until he can understand it and avoid it for its own sake. But we ought to use this discipline only when it is necessary to protect the life, health, safety, or well-being of people or other living creatures, or to prevent destruction of things that people care about. We ought not to assume too long, as we usually do, that a child cannot understand the real nature of the danger from which we want to protect him. The sooner he avoids the danger, not to escape our punishment, but as a matter of good sense, the better. He can learn that faster than we think. In Mexico, for example, where people drive their cars with a good deal of spirit, I saw many children no older than five or four walking unattended on the streets. They understood about cars, they knew what to do. A child whose life is full of the threat and fear of punishment is locked into babyhood. There is no way for him to grow up, to learn to take responsibility for his life and acts. Most important of all, we should not assume that having to yield to the threat of our superior force is good for the child's character. It is never good for *anyone's* character. To bow to superior force makes us feel impotent and cowardly for not having had the strength or courage to resist. Worse, it makes us resentful and vengeful. We can hardly wait to make someone pay for our humiliation, yield to us as we were once made to yield. No, if we cannot always avoid using the Discipline of Superior Force, we should at least use it as seldom as we can.

Questions for Discussion

1. Holt's essay has a very simple structure. *Complete the following outline by naming the topic of each paragraph:*

    I. Discipline 1: ⎯⎯⎯⎯⎯⎯⎯⎯⎯⎯
    II. Discipline 2: ⎯⎯⎯⎯⎯⎯⎯⎯⎯⎯
    III. Discipline 3: ⎯⎯⎯⎯⎯⎯⎯⎯⎯⎯

2. *Holt's thesis is obviously and clearly stated in the first sentence. Which part of this sentence tells the subject of the essay?*

Besides stating the subject, the first sentence makes an assertion about the subject. That is, it makes the point—tells what's important—about the three kinds of disciplines. *What* is *Holt's point?*

What is important about discipline in this essay, and hence the author's reason for writing about it, is that growing children learn from these three kinds. A thesis statement that makes an assertion, or point, is preferable in essay writing to a simple statement of subject, like "The purpose of this essay is to describe three kinds of disciplines."

3. Holt's essay consists of three long paragraphs, each a model of what a paragraph should be. Each focuses on a single aspect of the subject, deals completely with that aspect of the subject, and is clearly related to the essay as a whole. We thus say that it is (a) unified, (b) complete, and (c) coherent.

Notice that paragraph 1, after the thesis, begins:

> The first and most important is what we might call the Discipline of Nature or of Reality.

This is Holt's *topic sentence,* so-called because it names the topic of the paragraph, for throughout the paragraph Holt discusses only this kind of discipline. Thus the paragraph is *unified*. We might say the discussion is *complete* too, because Holt adequately explains that aspect of his subject and doesn't come back to it in another paragraph. And finally, through a second function of the topic sentence, the paragraph also is clearly linked to the thesis sentence; it is *coherent*. The words "The first and most important" and the repetition of the key word *discipline* relate this paragraph to the thesis.

Find the topic sentences of the next two paragraphs and identify the topics plus the words that relate these paragraphs to the thesis.

4. *For what audience is Holt writing this classification of kinds of discipline? Consider lines 15–17, 57–62, and others that you think apply.*

While paragraph 1 mentions school and advises what should be happening in the classroom, paragraph 3 is

134 Three Disciplines for Children

very clearly directed to parents, as paragraph 2 also seems to be. While the book, *Freedom and Beyond,* as a whole is written for people who have some authority to make changes in how children are educated, in these paragraphs Holt seems to be writing either to parents alone—who sometimes have a voice in school matters—or to parents and teachers alike.

5. Holt explains his three ways of looking at discipline by using numerous examples. Notice how in lines 10–12 he moves from a general, non-specific statement about "what he [a child] is trying to build" to some very specific action verbs that define what it is that the child is trying to build. *Find other examples of specific details that made Holt's discussion vivid to you as you read.*

6. Computer-assisted instruction (CAI) has become so common that most students have used it at some time for learning math, practicing a foreign language, doing grammar drills, or something else. One of the advantages of CAI is that the computer doesn't scold or blame, can't be talked into something, doesn't get angry or embarrass the user, and always allows a fresh start. The learning gained from the discipline of the computer thus has many similarities with that gained from what Holt calls the Discipline of Nature or Reality.

   Find similarities between the second Discipline, that of What People Really Do, and the practice of writing through imitating model essays.

7. In paragraph 3, Holt brings up the subject of spanking. Psychologists through the years have taken one side or the other, saying at one extreme that spanking should be avoided at all costs and at the other that at times it is absolutely necessary. *Summarize what Holt has to say on the subject.*

Sentence Patterning

One common way of structuring sentences is to begin with a subordinate (dependent) clause and then state the main (or independent) clause. It's an efficient method of writing, because the relationship between the two clauses is made clear by the subordinating conjunction that introduces the dependent clause. *Because,* for instance, shows a causal relationship; *before* shows a time relationship; and *if* indicates condition. (Refer again to the list of subordinating conjunctions on p. 126.) The pattern of the preceding chapter is an example: When cool nights finally come to Florida, the Valencia crop is fully developed in size and shape.

Holt uses this pattern frequently in his essay; notice the many *if* clauses in paragraph 1. He also turns the pattern around, beginning with the main clause and ending with the subordinate clause, as in the sentence below:

SENTENCE

> He avoids these substitutes for the greater danger <u>until he can understand it and avoid it for its own sake.</u>

The subordinate clause is underlined. For imitation we'll use the sentence as Holt wrote it, with this pattern:

PATTERN

> [independent clause]   [conjunction]
>   [subordinate clause]   .

First copy the sentence, noting that there is no comma between the clauses. As you write your own sentence, begin the second part with a subordinating conjunction from the list on p. 126. Here's an example:

EXAMPLE

> Two-year-old Louisa sat down on the floor and began removing her shoes and socks <u>as the congregation stood up and sang the first hymn.</u>

After you've written your sentence, try rewriting it with the clauses reversed, inserting a comma between the clauses because your sentence is now beginning with the subordinate clause.

WRITING ASSIGNMENT

In this excerpt from *Freedom and Beyond,* John Holt approaches a broad subject, discipline of children, and breaks it down into three parts. He divides the large subject into small chunks and then describes each one. The subject is thus simpler, more manageable. Another way of looking at the subject is by *classification;* that is, the kinds of discipline that teach children can be classified, or grouped, into three categories. Again, the subject is more manageable—something like grouping items on a shopping list according to the stores where they can be purchased. Division and classification are two sides of the same coin, two ways of managing information.

The organization of an essay that discusses parts of a subject is simple: start with an introduction that presents your subject and your thesis, discuss each of your parts, and conclude. Holt's essay, being an excerpt from a larger work, does not have a separate introductory paragraph, nor does it have a concluding paragraph. His first sentence serves as his statement of thesis and introduction of subject, and his manner of concluding is to make a point at the end of each paragraph. When you write this assignment, either observe Holt's pattern or, if you or your teacher prefers, have separate opening and closing paragraphs.

The topics below will lead to classification or division essays. Choose one of these topics or something similar.

Kids' behavior in church
Kinds of "Superior Force" discipline
Reasons for spanking children
Games children play
Kinds of silence

Kinds of video games
Kinds of communication
Kinds of nicknames

After deciding on a topic, make a list of all the kinds of that thing that occur to you. Then group the items on your list into three categories, according to common features; discard those that don't fit one of your categories. You now have a manageable body of information for which you can write a thesis, similar to Holt's first sentence. If you want to admit that you're not covering the entire field, *qualify* your statement by inserting words like "at least" or "the most important." For example:

> A child, in growing up, may meet and learn from at least three different kinds of discipline.

or

> A child, in growing up, may meet and learn from several different kinds of discipline, the most important of which are the Discipline of Nature, the Discipline of Culture, and the Discipline of Superior Force.

To organize your paper, all you need to decide is how to order your three points. You might put the most important one either last or first.

As you write your paper, use specific examples for each part of your topic. Holt, for instance, in his first category uses building with blocks and playing the piano. Explain each of your points clearly, showing how each fits into its category. Make a concluding point at the end of each paragraph, or make an overall point at the end.

After writing, check your essay for clarity of your divisions. Is each clearly different from the others? Have you explained each so that your reader will understand it as you do? Have you used specific examples? Does your thesis indicate precisely that this is a division or classification of a subject? Is your arrangement of categories the most logical, or would it be better if you moved parts around? How are your spelling and punctuation? your verbs? your pronouns? Are there any other errors you can correct? After you've revised as completely as you can, copy your essay into a clear final draft.

17

Preface to *Reversals*

EILEEN SIMPSON

Eileen Simpson, a practicing psychologist, is a victim of dyslexia (a reading disability in which words are inaccurately perceived). In the Preface to her autobiography, *Reversals,* she explains why she decided to write about her affliction. She has also written a novel, *The Maze,* and several short stories.

Vocabulary Preview

line
7	abyss	a bottomless gulf; anything too deep to be measured
13	milieu	environment; surroundings
14	dyslexic	a person who has dyslexia; having the condition
29	dyslexia	impairment of the ability to read because words and letters are seen inaccurately, sometimes reversed
31	obscure	not clear; vague; not understood
35	literate	able to read and write
43	handicap	something that restricts normal activity
44	repress(ed)	to force into the unconscious; to control severely
44	traumatic	painful emotionally (or physically)
49	autobiographical	written about one's own life
50	anonymous	having an unknown or unacknowledged name

50	pseudonymous	written under a fictitious name
52	candidly	honestly; frankly; openly
53	inhibition	anything that holds one back from doing something
63	limbo	a place or condition of oblivion or neglect
65	patronize(d)	to treat in a condescending manner
65	relapse	a return to illness or some other unpleasant condition

Essay Preview: Questions to Answer as You Read

1. How common is dyslexia?
2. Why is dyslexia often not diagnosed?
3. According to Eileen Simpson, why are there very few autobiographical accounts of dyslexia?
4. What feelings did Simpson have to overcome in order to write her book?

Preface to *Reversals*

1   There was something wrong with my brain. What had previously been a shadowy suspicion that hovered on the edge of consciousness became certain knowledge the year I was nine and entered fourth grade. I seemed to be like other children, but I was not like them: I could not learn to read or spell. Had my present friends, acquaintances, colleagues, and I grown up together, there would have been an abyss between them and me. The books they were then reading, I did not read. Their compositions merited gold stars, won prizes; mine were unacceptable. They were at the top of their classes; I was at the bottom. Throughout my childhood and youth the nature of my disorder remained mysterious to me and those in my milieu. When I was twenty-two it was diagnosed—not by a psychologist but by a poet: I was dyslexic.

2   Much later, when I had become sufficiently detached from the past to want to understand it, I discovered that what I had thought was a unique affliction occurs in all countries of the

world, in all classes of society, and seems to have little to do with cultural, emotional, or family circumstances. Roughly one tenth of the population is dyslexic. There are those who believe that in the United States alone as many as 23 million are affected to some degree, as compared, say, with two million American stutterers.

3   Statesman, public servants, generals, surgeons, writers—Woodrow Wilson, Nelson Rockefeller, General George Patton, Dr. Harvey Cushing, Gustave Flaubert, Hans Christian Andersen, and W. B. Yeats—are counted among their number.

4   Although the word *dyslexia* (often used loosely and inaccurately) has become fashionable today, a good deal about it remains obscure, and many of its victims continue to go unrecognized and untreated. Experts in the field have been hampered in their research because they have not been able to find out what it is like, from the inside, to live in a literate society and be unable to read and write. What has been wanting is the dyslexic's own story. As Dr. Lloyd J. Thompson has said in his book, *Reading Disabilities: Developmental Dyslexia:*

> Very few anonymous reports . . . of dyslexia can be found in the literature. . . . The writer has attempted many times to persuade dyslexics to write their personal experiences, but without success. It is possible that these people are still sensitive about their handicap, or that they have glossed over, forgotten or repressed the details of the traumatic experiences. Or that they still have difficulty putting their experiences into correctly spelled words. For this reason they may be reluctant to reveal any vulnerable spot to a secretary available to do the writing for them.

5   The autobiographical accounts one does find are brief, and, for all the reasons suggested, anonymous or pseudonymous. Even nowadays, when the confessional mode is in style, and people talk candidly about what used to be called their private lives, the inhibition against revealing intellectual failures and limitations is strong. The old shame and fear of ridicule remain forever lively. Andersen was world famous and much decorated when he wrote:

Isn't it strange that at the age of 66 I can still suffer and feel those torments of my youth . . . ? In my dreams I am still a schoolboy and Meisling [his teacher] is rude. . . .

6   For years now I have "passed." Were it not for the periodic threats of exposure—anyone who passes learns to live with them—I would almost have forgotten what it was like to live in the limbo of illiteracy. But in order to write this book under my own name, I had to fight the old shame and the fear of being patronized: I suffered a relapse. My symptoms returned fullblown, providing me with a sharp reminder of what life had been like before I was "cured." There are undoubtedly details of the early years that I have forgotten. Others that remain repressed. Everything that I remember I have set down, as I remember it.

Questions for Discussion

1. This essay is an *exposition*—an explanation of why Simpson wrote her book on dyslexia. So it ends up showing causes and effects—causes, or reasons, for her writing, and effects of the writing. Her first reason for writing was the fact that she is a dyslexic. A second is that the disorder is common to many people. *A third, more pointed, cause is explained in paragraph 4. Put it in your own words.*

    In addition to stating that research is hampered by lack of autobiographical accounts, Simpson presents another causal explanation—this one for why people have hesitated to write such reports. *What reasons does she give in paragraph 4 and paragraph 5?*

    Finally, in paragraph 6, she tells the *effect* on herself of this writing. *In your own words, what was this effect?*

2. *Keeping in mind that this essay is an explanation of why Simpson wrote her book, express her thesis in your own words and as you see it.*

    You may have written something like this: "I wrote this account of my experiences with dyslexia because such a record is needed to increase understanding and knowledge of the disorder." This is Simpson's main idea, even though she doesn't express it in so many words. The closest she comes to these words is her sentence that begins on line 35: "What has been wanting is the dyslexic's own story." This she says after indicating why that story is needed.

3. *What is the basis of Simpson's authority to write a book on dyslexia? In addition to being a dyslexic herself, what else qualifies her?* (See the introductory biographical sketch on p. 139.) *Are these credentials enough to satisfy you about her authority on the subject?*

4. Simpson says that one of her reasons for writing her book was to provide information for research on dyslexia. *Do you think her audience is limited to professionals, or might she have intended a broader audience? What evidence in her Preface supports your answer?*

5. *What is the effect of the narrative in the first paragraph? What do you know after reading it that you didn't know before?*

6. Simpson quotes twice from other authors. *Notice how she leads into the quotations, informing the reader of (a) who is writing, (b) where the original words are found, and (c) how the quoted passage relates to what she has just written herself. Find these three points for the first quotation, which begins on line 39.*

The first two are obvious; the third is indicated by the transitional *as*, showing that what follows illustrates what was said in the previous sentence.

In the second quotation, who is "Andersen"? Conventionally, quoted writers are referred to by their last names once their full names have been given. *Where was Andersen named earlier? In the lead-in to this quotation, Simpson doesn't name the title of the source. Would you like to know where she found it? Or is it enough to know something of Andersen's circumstances at the time he wrote the words?*

Sentence Patterning

Eileen Simpson seems to favor *what* clauses, for she has used them several times in this short passage. Our sentence patterning will imitate one of them, but you might want to locate others. The one we're using, slightly shortened, occurs in paragraph 1.

SENTENCE

> What had previously been a shadowy suspicion became certain knowledge the year I was nine and entered fourth grade.

This sentence has a *what* clause that serves as the subject of the sentence. The structure is worth practicing because actually it is rather common. Copy the original sentence, study the pattern and the example sentence, and then imitate the pattern with a sentence of your own. Don't be tempted to put a comma at the end of your complete *what* clause—that is, before the verb; it's not needed and would break up the flow of your sentence.

PATTERN

What _____ [verb] _____
_____.

EXAMPLE

> What I didn't know about smoking was the difficulty of stopping and the expense of continuing.

WRITING ASSIGNMENT

Write a cause-and-effect essay similar to Simpson's. Choose a situation (for Simpson: why I'm writing this book) and present some reasons for that situation (for

Simpson: I'm dyslexic, many people are dyslexic, and more information is needed on the dyslexic experience). Here are some subjects you might like to choose from:

Why I'm attending college
Why I like (don't like) to read
Why I like (don't like) to write
Why I'm living at home (away from home)
Why I smoke (don't smoke)
Why I like (don't like) to watch (play) baseball (football, basketball)

If you should choose one of these subjects, your essay will be highly personal, since each one refers to the *I*. The use of the pronoun *I* is entirely appropriate, but you'll need to be careful not to forget your audience. While Simpson began on the personal level, she very quickly broadened her topic to include all dyslexics—23 million, she estimates—plus all people interested in treating or understanding dyslexia. You can do something similar with your subject, whatever you choose.

After choosing a subject, try to get some ideas going by asking yourself some questions:

When did this situation begin?
How did it begin?
Who was there?
What did other people say?
What did I think?
How did I feel?
What else has influenced this situation?
Has any other person been a factor?
How do I feel about this situation?
How might I change it?
Do I want to change it?

Continue asking questions as long as necessary until you understand how you relate to your subject and what you think about it. Keep in mind that your key word is *why*. You're looking for reasons—causes.

So begin, as Simpson did, with a narrative paragraph—one that goes back to the beginning of the situation or points up your awareness of it. Then proceed to give causes, reasons, being careful to broaden the significance by including other affected persons. You may have two or three paragraphs on causes or reasons (Simpson has four). Finally, if your subject lends itself to a paragraph on effects, you may end that way, as Simpson does. Otherwise, end with a summary of causes and a restatement of your thesis. (While Simpson's thesis comes in paragraph 4, you may want to express yours earlier, perhaps at the end of your narrative paragraph.) Outlined, your essay may look like this:

   I. Narrative and thesis
  II. First reason
 III. Second reason
  IV. Third reason
   V. Effect and conclusion

If you've recently read something relevant to your subject, you may want to quote part of it. If so, observe the conventions of leading into the quotation by (1) naming the author, (2) indicating the source, and (3) relating it to what you've just said. Also, be sure to quote exactly. You may want to *block quote,* as Simpson did in her preface. If so, every line is indented at the left margin, and quotation marks are omitted.

As usual, revise your work thoroughly before submitting it for evaluation. Have you broadened the significance of your subject outside your own personal scope? Is the point of your essay obvious (a clearly stated thesis)? Are the reasons you've presented actual *reasons*—or are they just related ideas? Do you need to include additional details or explanations for the reader's benefit? Do your sentences need revision? What are the strengths of your essay? See if you can make them even stronger. How is your essay weak? If you can correct that weakness, do so.

Rewrite your revised draft, carefully proofreading (not just *reading!*) the final draft to make sure you don't have any copying errors.

18

The New Ambidexters

ELLEN GOODMAN

Ellen Goodman has been writing for the *Boston Globe* newspaper since 1967 and has had her column syndicated throughout the country since 1976 with the Washington Post Writers Group. She won the Pulitzer Prize in 1980. Her columns are timely, thoughtful, and sometimes challenging to comfortable beliefs and customs. The following essay—written in 1977 and taken from *Close to Home,* a collection of some of her articles—responds to the language of politics, in particular to the Right and the Left.

Vocabulary Preview

line
3	right	conservative, sometimes reactionary (another word for extremely conservative) in politics, tending to favor capitalism (or even fascism), returning to a former position, and little government interference; the term derives from the position of the seats in some European legislatures
3	left	liberal or radical (extreme) in politics, tending towards socialism or even communism, favoring reform or progress; derives from the position of the seats in some European legislatures
6	chronicling	telling the history of

6	evolution	change; process of development
18	ambidextrous	able to use both hands equally well
24	dialectician(s)	expert in logical argumentation, weighing contradictory statements with the intention of resolving them
37	dole	welfare or relief payments from the government
46	rue	to regret

Essay Preview: Questions to Answer as You Read

1. In what new way is Goodman using the term *ambidextrous*?
2. Does Goodman think of herself as one of The New Ambidexters?
3. What do you think is Goodman's purpose for writing this essay (other than the obvious one of meeting a newspaper deadline)?

The New Ambidexters

1   The political expert explained it carefully over dinner. The country, he said, is turning to the right, but the New Right is farther to the left that it used to be. At the same time, the Left is farther to the right than it was in the Old Days when it was called the New Left.

2   By the time he was through chronicling the evolution of politics in America, I was totally unable to remember which hand I was supposed to cut my food with. Was it the right or the left, and was it important?

3   Now, I had read the Gallup poll, which said that 47 percent of the American people consider themselves to be right of center, and I had heard the accounts of the new conservative bash at the St. Regis hotel in New York last week. But, to be perfectly frank about it, I don't think that we can understand what's going on in politics in the classical terms of political anatomy. I don't think we are turning to

the right, or the left, for that matter. I think most of us are turning ambidextrous.

4 To sound more trendy about the whole thing, we seem to have become The New Ambidexters.

5 There is much more widespread uncertainty, often a frustrating sense of the complexity of social issues. Every time someone offers a solution someone else offers a criticism. Most of us have become walking dialecticians, carrying our own debates in our arms. We are constantly arguing with ourselves—"on the one hand . . . on the other hand. . . ." We are, in short, card-carrying members of the New Ambidextrous Party.

6 The New Ambidexters believe, for example, that on the one hand, government should provide services and, on the other hand, government should keep out of our lives. The New Ambidexters believe that the corporations have murderously gunked up the environment and put ruinous chemicals in our food, but that government regulations interfere too much with business.

7 The New Ambidexters believe that welfare mothers should get off the dole and go to work, and that mothers of small children should stay home with them. They believe that we've all become far too selfish, too "me-first," but that individuals have the right to lead their lives as they choose.

8 The Ambidexters simply hold onto a wide range of opinions simultaneously, without always seeing them as contradictory. They want government to provide more and cost less. They want security and independence. They believe in responsibility and freedom.

9 The same people who rue the disruption of the family don't believe that people should be forced to stay in rotten marriages. The same people who believe in roots and community believe—on the other hand—in mobility and adventure.

10 Most of them, of course, weren't born ambidextrous. They have lived long enough to see the cost accounting of change.

11 They have seen that change, even the solutions, comes with a full attachment of new problems. When the government sets up a program to help those who can't work, they end up also helping those who won't work. When the government helps the aged who don't have families to depend on,

they end up with more aged depending on the government instead of families. As divorce becomes more acceptable in society, there are more divorces for society to accept.

12   The Ambidexters don't want to go back to the thirties or the fifties. Few people want to remove the Social Security system or take away compensation for unemployment. They have no interest in returning to desperation. But when they look ahead to the future they weigh the issues in both hands.

13   The Ambidexters are aware that there are still serious social problems. They believe that government should Do Something. National health care. Day care. Welfare reform. But there are the other problems. Big government. Family responsibility. Taxes.

14   So, in view of the complexity of the situation, the one solution the Ambidexters seem to have agreed upon for the moment is to sit on their hands. The right hand, and the left.

December 1977

Questions for Discussion

1. *Is Ellen Goodman's intent serious in this analysis of American politics, or is she simply entertaining the reader? Be sure to consider paragraphs 2 and 14 in making your answer; on the other hand, look at paragraph 5 too. Use these and other references to the text as support for your answer.*

2. Goodman's purpose in writing this essay may have been to entertain or to inform. Yet she also had a very practical purpose: to meet a deadline. In this way newspaper columnists are like student writers. Both have deadlines, but they don't write simply for the purpose of turning something in. *What purposes might students have for writing papers other than meeting the teacher's deadline?*

3. *What is Goodman's thesis? What is the point of her essay? Can you rephrase the thesis in your own words in order to express the point?*

   You have probably considered one of the sentences in paragraphs 3 and 4 to express Goodman's idea that the terms *right* and *left* no longer adequately describe our political leanings.

4. Goodman uses transitions in a special way. They not only show how parts of the essay are related but sometimes also *make the point*. She prepares you, the reader, for this use in paragraph 5: "We are constantly arguing with ourselves—'on the one hand . . . on the other hand. . . . ' "

   Find examples in the remainder of the essay of Goodman's use of "on the other hand" to make her point that politically we can't seem to make up our minds.

5. Thesis sentences frequently appear at the end of the first paragraph, especially in academic writing. Goodman's thesis, however, does not appear in this position. In fact, you have to read three paragraphs of introductory matter before you know what stand she is taking on her subject. *Do you think the thesis should have come earlier? What purpose does the early part of the essay serve? Think in terms of audience, writer's credentials, subject, and purpose. Support your claims with specific references to the text.*

6. By the end of the third paragraph you know what the subject is, the writer's attitude toward the subject, something about her credentials on the subject, and, most important, her *stand* on the subject. This is important: that the introduction present not only the *subject* but also the writer's *position* on the subject—the point.

   Find sentences in the first three paragraphs that present the subject—that tell what the essay is about. *Then contrast these statements with the thesis, in which Goodman takes a stand on the subject of right and left in politics.*

   Remember that a thesis statement does two things: names the subject and takes a stand. To see how this happens in another example, look at the thesis in "The Bounty of the Sea" (p. 188):

   > If the oceans should die, this would signal the end not only for marine life but for all other animals and plants of this earth, including man.

In this sentence, Jacques Cousteau names his subject—the death of the oceans—and then makes his point—that everything else will die as well.

Now look at your thesis sentence in the last essay you wrote for this class. Do you state both your subject and your point (your stand on the subject)? If not, rewrite the sentence so that it accurately reflects the point you intended to make in that essay.

7. Goodman makes her point by defining *ambidextrous* in a new way. *What method of development does she use in order to accomplish this definition? In other words, how is the essay organized?*

Like the transitional phrase "on the other hand," the organization of "The New Ambidexters" is integral to its point. In order to show that most Americans are neither right nor left politically, Goodman balances the two—contrasts them. She says, for example, that Ambidexters believe "government should provide services" but "government should keep out of our lives."

The essay thus is similar to a listing of political subjects with two sides. On a piece of paper, draw a line down the center and head the first column *right* and the second *left*. Then fill in the columns with items from Goodman's contrasting statements. Your two lists, when you have completed them, may very well conform to the kind of balanced lists that Goodman herself might have needed before writing her essay.

8. While the basis of Goodman's essay is two contrasting lists, the essay doesn't have the appearance of a list. *What devices does she use to convert her lists into an essay? In paragraph 11, for example, what is the function of the first sentence? What does Goodman do to show how the next three sentences are connected to the first?*

As another example, the paired details in paragraph 7 are explained in paragraph 8 by means of balanced—paired—characteristics of the Ambidexters. Notice that paragraph 8 has the same pattern of development as paragraph 11: topic sentence followed by three explanatory sentences of structure.

9. Goodman has fourteen paragraphs in an essay of roughly 500 words. Most of her paragraphs are short—some with only one or two sentences. This pattern is not usual for college essays and most other essay writing, though it *is* conventional in newspaper writing. The column format of newspapers, in which only a few words appear on a line, would make a paragraph of the usual essay length go on for many lines. Since readers like to see a little "white space" now and then, shorter paragraphs are called for.

Chapter 16, "Three Disciplines for Children," describes an essay paragraph as a group of related sentences that make up a unified, complete, and coherent unit that relates to the essay as a whole. *Apply this description to Goodman's paragraphs. Do they fit? Are they unified? complete? coherent? related to the essay as a whole? The point to look at most closely, since her paragraphs are so short, is completeness. Look, for example, at the very short paragraph 10 and the one that follows it. Are both paragraphs centered on the same idea? Could they be combined to make up a single unified paragraph?*

Could paragraphs 7 and 8 be combined? In Question 7 we saw that paragraph 8 explains the details in paragraph 7. Would a combined paragraph be unified—based, that is, on one central idea?

Paragraph 4 is made up of only a single sentence. Can you think of some reasons why it should remain as it is? As we've indicated elsewhere in this book, short sentences are sometimes effective because they are different from the other sentences around them. This can be true also of paragraphs. As a matter of fact, as writers we need to know that occasionally we might compose a single-sentence paragraph in order to draw attention to and emphasize its point.

Sentence Patterning

You've probably heard that sentence fragments are serious errors in writing and should be avoided at all times. But did you notice Ellen Goodman's fragments? There are six in paragraph 13. And do you remember Maya Angelou's fragments in her description of Mr. McElroy? How do these writers get away with them? They manage it because they know how and when to use them. And in this sentence-patterning assignment you are officially given permission to use fragments too—if you follow the pattern.

We've talked before about how Goodman balances contrasting items, and here she is doing it again: three fragments about what the government should do and three about why it shouldn't do them. She could have avoided the fragments, of course, by using colons and commas, as follows:

> They believe that government should do something: national health care, day care, welfare reform. But there are the other problems: big government, family responsibility, taxes.

These sentences are acceptable both grammatically and stylistically. But Goodman chose to use fragments. Why? Probably for the same reason writers use short sentences—to draw attention to and thus emphasize the point.

Knowing how to use fragments effectively is a useful skill, and that is one reason why you're being asked to practice them here. The other reason is so that you can avoid writing them unintentionally. Below is Goodman's paragraph 13, then the pattern, and finally an example of how the pattern might be imitated. After studying the pattern, copy Goodman's sentences and fragments as they appear; then write your own in imitation, using a current national or local issue as your subject.

SENTENCE

> The Ambidexters believe that government should do something. National health care. Day care. Welfare reform. But there are other problems. Big government. Family responsibility. Taxes.

Ellen Goodman

PATTERN

_____.
_____. _____. _____. _____.
_____. _____. _____. _____.

EXAMPLE

There are many reasons for not polluting the environment. Clean air. Pure water. Species preservation. But carrying out conservation presents problems. Taxes. Restrictions. Species over-population.

WRITING ASSIGNMENT

Suppose that you are a columnist for your local newspaper. You can write on any subject you want as long as you make it interesting for the readers. First choose from the following list the kind of columnist you want to be:

sports	food and nutrition
business	fashion
politics	gardening
real estate	news commentary

Now you have established who you are: a sports commentator for the *Milwaukee Sentinel,* for example.

Next you need to decide on something to write about: a current subject of local or national interest. Remember that you are not a reporter but a commentator; you don't report news, you voice an opinion about it. As you try to decide on your subject, you may want to keep in mind your audience. Who might be reading this column in your newspaper? What would those readers be interested in? What can you say that will keep them reading till the end? What can you say that your editor would accept?

Oops! Here we have another person entering the scene—an intermediary, someone coming between us and our readers—our editor. Writing for an editor shouldn't be such an unusual practice for you, however, because in a way you do it frequently. An English teacher is somewhat like an editor: judging the quality of your writing, suggesting how it might be revised, sometimes telling you what to write in the first place.

So now you know, for the purpose of this writing assignment, who you are, what your subject is, who your readers might be (and their preferences), and who will have to pass your column before it gets into print. Next you need to consider format. You can use Goodman's article as your pattern. Remember the short paragraphs. Write one single-sentence paragraph (where it will do the most good, through emphasis), but write some longer ones too, as Goodman did. Make sure that, because of your short paragraphs, your ideas are not weakly developed. You still need adequate support for all your ideas, even though you might divide up your statements (as, for example, Goodman did in paragraphs 7 and 8, 10 and 11, and 12 and 13).

Make sure you have a thesis sentence, and put it somewhere near the beginning, though not necessarily in the first paragraph. Does your thesis express not only your subject but also your point? Compare your thesis with Goodman's and Cousteau's to see if it has these two parts.

After you've written your column, read your thesis over again, checking to see that it accurately and precisely expresses the subject and point of your essay as actually carried out. If it doesn't, rephrase the thesis so that it *is* accurate, or revise the essay if it seems to be off the subject. Sometimes our ideas grow and develop as we write, and that's good. But sometimes we slide off the subject, and then we need to cut out sentences and paragraphs. While cutting hurts, we're better off without those sentences and paragraphs that aren't contributing anything to the subject. Finally, correct all errors. You want your work to be that of a literate columnist.

When your newspaper column is written, revised, and passed by your "editor," you may want to submit it to a real newspaper and see what comes of it. Some newspapers welcome free-lance writing that is competently and interestingly written.

19

Ticaspleeze and Trees

MICHAEL D. McCARTHY

Michael D. McCarthy wrote this essay as a sophomore in college. The assignment was to write a descriptive essay that employed figures of speech in order to make the description vivid. In carrying out this assignment, Mike came up with the following essay. Not only are the figures numerous, but language and detail are tightly compressed with a high density of meaning. On occasion the meaning is perhaps too dense. For example, in paragraph 3 one might wonder why the children laughed when told that their mother was sick. But, as Mike explained to his teacher, it was common knowledge in the family that Mom didn't want to go to the opera any more than the kids did—hence Dad's "paper" (that is, meaningless) words. The compression of meaning happened as a result of Mike's work with his rough drafts. He cut and pruned and revised, as his rough drafts show in the next chapter, until finally he turned in the finished draft. Polished a little more, it appears below.

Vocabulary Preview

line
10	taken aback	surprised; startled and confused
20	agendum	singular of *agenda,* a list of things to be done; *agendum* sometimes refers to a single item on the list, sometimes to the entire list
25	reek(ed)	to give off a strong smell
39	stoic	indifferent to pain; calmly enduring bad fortune or suffering

41	benevolent	kindly; performing charitable acts
48	tarp(s)	short for *tarpaulin,* a sheet of waterproof material, spread over something for protection
65	dogmatically	without allowing for discussion or dispute; obstinately, determinedly

Essay Preview: Questions to Answer as You Read

1. What would you guess is the age of the narrator at the time this incident takes place?
2. Why does he have to go to the opera?
3. How does "Dad" feel about going to the opera?
4. What is happening to the lobby of the opera house?

Ticaspleeze and Trees

1   Mother's favorite walnut clock tick-tocked towards noon while, underneath, three of its children waited for the family "discussion" to begin. Hardly discussions at all, these gatherings were an excuse for Dad to discipline, delegate jobs, and dictate morality. Six small round fishbowls each containing a single blue fish inspected Dad as he eased himself into the family sofa. Six eardrums beat simultaneously as he spoke, "I want one of you to go to the opera with me tonight."

2   Not taken aback by this peculiar request, my older brother, a stickler for logic and reason, retorted, "What's the matter with Mom?"

3   Dad's paper words were not so quick in reply, "She's not feeling well this evening," he said to his shoes. Laughter boomed forth from our ever silent throats and echoed without a sound from the walls. "Well?" Dad said, itching for a reply.

4   I had half-turned to my brother when my silver-tongued sister, wise in the ways of dealing with Dad, melted the silence. Her gentle words explained that her agendum was jam-packed with wholesome, wholly false, activities. Without

waiting for a non-existent reply she glided out of our company, secure that she would not be called back.

"I don't want this ticket to go to waste." Dad's words reeked of anticipation. If it's true that he who hesitates is lost, I wandered through yet uncharted ground. My brother then "reasoned": "Since Michael is younger and therefore more impressionable than I, it would therefore be more beneficial for him to go." Older brother's handpicked words and twisted logic covered Dad like a warm wool blanket. Nothing I could say would unwrap the comforter from him. Words were not spoken. My friend silence had betrayed me. I was doomed to be cultured. Dad simply grinned his parental approval.

"How many of you sheep really want to wait in the bleeding rain to see this anyway?" I screamed mutely to Dad's imaginary embarrassment. I shielded my eyes from the pointed autumn droplets long enough to see his patiently stoic expression. It contrasted sharply with my expression of helpless despair.

Finally saved from the rain by a benevolent green canopy (benevolent? it was her job), I was frozen stiff by a low voice.

"Ticaspleeze," came the voice from inside a bright blue braided uniform. Dad produced two tickets, which the uniform ripped and gave back halved.

White paint-stained ladders, paint buckets covered by dried drippings, grey-white tarps, unfinished work and the wet-dry smell of new plaster rushed to greet Dad and me as we stepped into the lobby of Orchestra Hall. Plaster chips crackled under our weight as we quickly made our way through the remodeling rubble. Paint splotches were everywhere. The room resembled the remains of a five-minute indoor snowstorm without one melted snowflake. From the glass countertop under which slept the outrageously expensive candy to the velvet ropes which politely told patrons where not to walk, all were spotted by some sterile white paint that insulted the walls.

Breezing past red double doors and taking exaggerated steps down the gentle sloping of the aisle, we arrived at our twenty-third-row end seats. We removed our saturated overcoats and dumped them on a third seat next to me. The red velvet, well-cushioned seats embraced and welcomed us to the hall.

11 I enjoyed watching the other patrons file slowly but dogmatically into their seats. I saw the same couples, thirty times over, bicker as to who would sit on the aisle. Another regular was the pair who, after negotiating past twenty-one knees, decided they were in the wrong row. But unique to this theatre were the bird ladies perched on the edge of their too-small seats dying to be recognized. Once prey is spotted, a bird will swoop down amidst a flurry of the hi-how-are-yous and glad-to-see-yous. I thought it hurt them when the lights went down—dashing further hope of being seen.

12 The lights did go down and the music rose from the orchestra pit. Had I been younger, I would have been amazed at the sight of an old man shaking a pointed stick at a fat lady who did nothing but shout back at him. The music died and the lights came to life once more.

13 One thought persisted during the entire silent ride home and followed me into bed. It was not that Dad and I slept through the entire intermissionless program—that was quickly forgotten and remained secret ever after. I was, however, wondering why nature strips her trees before winter and dresses them in the spring.

Questions for Discussion

1. In paragraph 5 the narrator says, "I was doomed to be cultured." *Considering the outcome of the tale, how might this "culture" be defined? What does the narrator have at the end that he didn't have at the beginning?*

2. No particular sentence in this essay can be designated as the thesis. However, certain sentences are keys to making the meaning clear. One is the statement, "I was doomed to be cultured." Here the choice of words, "doomed" and "to be cultured," indicates the narrator's reluctance to go to the opera and his doubt as to

the success of the venture. At the end, after he and his dad have slept through the performance, the narrator knows that the culture they received was not the appreciation of good music well performed, but rather an adornment to be worn for creating a favorable impression on others. The words and music already gone from his head, he wonders if nature's adornment makes any more sense than culture's. The thesis, then, might be something like, "A person doesn't get 'cultured' simply by attending an opera." Or, "If this is culture, who needs it?"

Find examples of the lack *of culture at the opera. Find examples of the family's reluctance to participate in this culture.* Even though the thesis is not directly expressed in this essay, it is clear that Mike had one in mind. His selection of details and choice of words all focus on one central idea.

3. *Thinking in terms of the thesis as expressed in Question 2, explain the meaning of the title. What does* ticaspleeze *mean? Why is* trees *included in the title?*

4. The real force in Mike's paper is the figurative language he uses. "Six small round fishbowls each containing a single blue fish" is much livelier phrasing than "six blue eyes" or "three blue-eyed children." While most academic writing does not rely nearly as heavily on figures of speech as this essay does, the figures add an extra dimension to description and frequently can be useful in other kinds of writing as well.

Here are the figures of speech that Mike uses, some of them known by their Greek names, along with examples (with line numbers in parentheses) from Mike's essay. *See if you can find other examples, either in "Ticaspleeze" or in some other writing.*

Figures Involving Sentence Patterns
Antithesis: two contrasting ideas placed side by side.

Laughter boomed forth from our *ever silent* throats. (15)

Appositive: a noun placed beside another noun to refer to the same person or thing and to explain the first noun.

   . . . my older brother, a *stickler* for logic and reason, retorted . . . (11)

Parallelism: similarity of structure in a pair or a series.

   . . . these gatherings were an excuse for Dad to *discipline, delegate jobs,* and *dictate morality.* (4)

Figures Involving Unusual Word Use
Hyperbole: exaggeration.

   Six eardrums beat simultaneously. (7)

Irony: the use of words to convey the opposite of the literal meaning, or pretended ignorance.

   She's not feeling well this evening. (13) (Mother was feeling fine, as the children and father knew; she just didn't want to attend the opera.)

Litotes: understatement, usually with a negation.

   Dad's paper words were not so quick in reply. (13)

Metaphor: an implied comparison of two unlike things.

   Six small round fishbowls each containing a single blue fish inspected Dad as he eased himself into the family sofa. (5)

Oxymoron: two contradictory terms side by side.

   I *screamed mutely* to Dad's imaginary embarrassment. (36)

Personification: the attribution of human qualities to inanimate objects or abstractions.

   My friend silence had betrayed me. (32)

Puns: plays on words.

Her gentle words explained that her agendum was jam-packed with *wholesome, wholly* false activities. (20)

Simile: an explicit comparison of two unlike things; similar to metaphor but uses a word indicating the comparison—*like, as.*

Older brother's handpicked words and twisted logic covered *Dad like a warm wool blanket.* (29)

Synecdoche: a figure of speech in which a part is used to indicate the whole, or vice versa.

Dad produced two tickets, which *the uniform* ripped and gave back halved. (45)

5. *What is the effect of the synecdoche in paragraph 8, in which "the uniform" is used to indicate the doorman? Is this figure of speech more effective than the more literal term* doorman?

   What is the effect of the metaphor in paragraph 1, "Six small round fishbowls each containing a single blue fish"? Is it more effective than the more literal "six blue eyes"?

   What is the effect of the simile in paragraph 5: "Older brother's handpicked words and twisted logic covered Dad like a warm wool blanket"? What impression do you get of Dad? of older brother's words?

6. *Mike doesn't say how old he was when the incident described in his essay took place, but can you make a guess? What evidence from the essay supports your assumption of that age?*

7. We have already seen how Mike uses figurative language to make his description vivid. We can also see how he uses direct quotations to effectively present the words of the people taking part in the story (as George Gaylord Simpson does in "Shearing Sheep in Patagonia"). Another descriptive technique Mike uses is specific details. Notice, for example, how in paragraph 9 he describes the unusual appearance of Orchestra Hall. He begins with "white

Michael D. McCarthy

paint-stained ladders" and "paint buckets covered by dried drippings" and goes on throughout the paragraph to describe the lobby under renovation. *Find other specific details in this paragraph.*

Then look at paragraph 11 to see how he describes the other people waiting for the opera to begin. What are three types of opera-goers he describes?

Sentence Patterning

In order to achieve a tightly compressed style, Mike often uses phrases to indicate ideas that might otherwise have been expressed in clauses. In paragraph 10, for instance, he has a double participial phrase that expresses two ideas before he ever gets to the main clause:

> *Breezing* past red double doors and *taking* exaggerated steps down the gentle sloping of the aisle, we . . .

The two implied clauses are

> We breezed past red double doors.
> We took exaggerated steps down the . . . aisle.

Notice in these clauses that the subjects of the verbs—the *do*ers of the actions—are the subject of the main clause: *we*. But they're omitted from the phrases, giving a shorter form. (The *-ing* participles are similar to the *-ed* participles practiced in "Blubber on Ice," p. 83, and "Lift Your Feet," p. 99.)

Practice this kind of sentence by first copying the sentence below and studying the pattern; then write a sentence of your own which uses participial phrases for describing action.

SENTENCE

> <u>Breezing past red double doors</u> and <u>taking exaggerated steps down the gentle sloping of the aisle</u>, we arrived at our twenty-third-row end seats.

Ticaspleeze and Trees

PATTERN

```
____ing _____ and ____ing _____
_____,       [independent clause]
_____.
```

EXAMPLE

Speeding down the street and turning sharply at the corner, the Camaro narrowly missed the van parked on the side street.

("The Camaro" is agent, or doer, of three actions: it *missed* the van, but also it was *speeding* and was *turning*. Since the agents of the participles are the same as the agent of the main verb, *missed*, the participial phrases are clear.)

WRITING ASSIGNMENT

In "Ticaspleeze and Trees" Mike has taken a rather simple event, going to the opera, and given it meaning by describing it with vividness and perception. Several factors are important in making this description work:

1. His experiences and reactions are those of a child, yet
2. He looks back at the incident from his adult perspective, and
3. He uses his adult skills to bring the incident back to life, and
4. In particular, his figurative language conveys images and reactions that were only impressions on his mind at the time the trip occurred.

Your writing assignment is to choose an incident from your life that you remember vividly. You are to write *descriptively,* using specific words and details to allow your reader to picture the people and surroundings that make up this incident. To get started, try free writing. Don't use an outline or thesis sentence; just begin writing. Try to write fast to keep up with your ideas; don't worry if they're out of order. And don't stop to correct spelling or grammar. Just try to write without stopping.

Now you have a start. Without having to struggle through making a neat and tidy introduction, you got your ideas down. Some people prefer to begin most of their writing this way, because it frees their ideas. But now the hard part starts. You need to take this mess of ideas and make some sense of them: organize them, move parts around, add to them, delete irrelevant details, determine a thesis, make corrections. As you work with the result of your free writing, try to use specific words and details to describe people and their actions. Use some figurative language—not necessarily as much as Mike used, but some, in order to make the incident, the people, and your personal reactions more vivid. Try also to use at least one sentence that has a participial phrase similar to the one you practiced in Sentence Patterning. Make sure that the agent (the *do*er) of the action of your participle is the same as the agent (the subject, or *do*er) of your main verb.

Make a clean copy of the essay you developed from your free writing. The next chapter discusses the revisions that Mike McCarthy practiced when writing his essay. Refer to it after your teacher has read your first draft and you're ready to revise your descriptive essay.

20

Ticaspleeze and Trees
(Revision)

MICHAEL D. McCARTHY

Next to the extensive use of figurative language, the characteristic of "Ticaspleeze" most noticeable to Mike's teacher was the amount of revision he gave the paper. The essay as it appears in the preceding chapter is much like the final version Mike submitted to his teacher; editorial changes were few and minor. This published version, however, is very different from Mike's *first* draft of the paper, and even from his second draft. Mike took this essay through three drafts, all of which are reproduced on the following pages as he wrote them. The third draft is the one he turned in and shows the teacher's comments.

Essay Preview: Questions to Answer as You Read

1. At what levels did Mike make revisions: (a) word? (b) sentence? (c) paragraph?
2. In Draft No. 1, which kind of revision did Mike do more of, adding or deleting? in Draft No. 2?

First Draft

ticaspleze, and trees. ↗ discipline / delegate / dictate

~~In the fall of my 12 year,~~

1   My mother's favorite clock tick-tocked its way towards noon ~~on a~~ while underneath 3 ~~of~~ of ~~the~~ owner's *its* children waited for the family discussion to begin / Hardy dicussions at all, these gathering were an excuse for my dad to delegate jobs, dictate morality or merely to discipline. ~~This morning was different. As my dad eased himself into Electricity in the form of nervous glances hushed remarks and~~ 6 *small* fishbowls each containing a ~~blue~~ single blue fish inspected my dad as he eased himself onto the family sofa & eardrums beat simoltaneously as he spoke. "I want one of you to go to ~~the opera~~ *THE OPERA* with me tonite ~~the words he used smelled of exp~~ *downtown* the tone he used ~~had an~~ *carried the* odor of expectation. ~~My sister, seemingly insulted at this pseudo question.~~ *home from college older* My brother, a stickler for logic and reason retorted. What's the matter with mom? My ~~dad's~~ *paper* words were not so quick in reply, She's not feeling well this evening, he said ~~sheepishly~~ *TO HIS SHOES*. Laughter boomed ~~out of~~ from our silent mouths. Well? he (~~said~~, itched) for a reply. ~~The three of us turned to each other as if to~~

169

First Draft—continued

A+ good   TICKASPLEEZ

~~discuss~~ I turned to my brother ~~as if to discuss this matter when~~ my silver-tounged older sister, wise in the ways of dealing with dad, spoke ~~gently explained~~ words ~~that her~~ addenda was jam-packed with wholesome activities. Without waiting for reply she glided out of the den secure she would not be called back ~~in~~. I dont want this ticket to go to waste. This time my dads words reeked of anticipation. If its true that he who hesitates is lost, I was standing on yet uncharted ground. My brothers words cut through the silence as he reasoned. Since michael is younger and therefore more impressionable than I, it would THERE FOR ~~therefore~~ be more beneficial for him to go. ~~For the first time that morning, my dad grinned.~~ My brother's hand-picked words covered my dad like a warm wool blanket.

{ TEMPO TOO FAST

2   Nothing I could think of could pull the comforter off my dad which, in the silence had wrapped itself around him 3 times! ~~My silence had betrayed me~~ I was doomed to be cultured. Words ~~did not have to be~~ were not spoken. ~~My~~ Dad simply grinned his paternal approval.

3   How many of you really <u>want</u> to wait in the bleeding rain to see this anyway!!! I screamed mutely to Dad's imaginay embar-

170

First Draft—continued

rasment. I shielded my eyes ~~(from the knife-like droplets)~~ just long enough to see his patiently stoic expression. ~~I tried to mimic this look but produced only a look of grim frustration. After several minutes of trying to modify my expression to match his,~~ by controlling minute facial muscles, I gave up ~~I felt the rain suddenly come. I immediately looked skyward, but instead of seeing the~~ clearing ~~sky, I saw the protective rain canopy.~~ This contrasted sharply with my expression of helpless depair.

4   Finally sheltered from rain by a canopy, ~~my progress was~~ a low voice stopped me dead in my tracks. Tickaspleze came the voice from a bright blue uniform. Dad produced ~~handed~~ the tickets which the uniform deftly and mechanically ripped and gave back half.

5   White paint-stained ladders, paint buckets, ~~with drippings down the side,~~ grey tarps, unfinished work, and the smell of new plaster rushed to greet Dad and me as we stepped into the lobby of Orchestra hall. Plaster chips crackled under our weight as we made our way through the remodling rubble. Paint splotches were everywhere. The room looked like a ~~an~~ 3 min indoor snowstorm with not one of the snowflakes melting. From the glass countertop under which slept the outrageously ex-

171

First Draft—continued

pensive candy to the velvet ropes which politely told patrons where not to walk, all was spotted by the same sterile white paint that insulted the walls.

6 ~~Walking~~ Breezing past red double doors and taking eggaducted steps down the gen-~~tile~~ tle sloping of the aisle, We arrived at our seats. (halfway down the center section of the side.)

7 We removed our saturated overcoats and dumped them on a third seat next to me. ~~The seat must have belonged to a more intelligent patron because it was vacant all evening.~~ The ~~red velvet~~ well cusioned red velvet chairs embraced us as we ~~prepared for the culture to unfold before us.~~ watched the other patrons file slowly but with much determination into their seats.

8 ~~I am somehow amused viewing people as they got themselves settled before a show.~~ There is always the couple who after climbing past 20 knee~~caps~~s, decide they are in the wrong row. There is a couple who bicker as to ~~whom~~ will shall sit on the aisle seat. There are the ladies who ~~look like~~ resemble giant mounds of soap bubbles~~,~~. ~~the These laidies~~ they wait to be recognized by other soap bubbles. I would think it hurts them when the lights go down--~~thus it~~ dash~~es~~ing their hopes of being recognized to the ground.

First Draft—continued

9   The lights did go down and the music rose from the orchestra pit. Had I bean younger, I would have been amazed at an old man shaking a pointed stick at a fat girl. who did nothing but shout back at him. The music died and the lights came up once more. *and followed me into bed*

10 One thought ~~I~~ persisted the entire silent ride home. It was not the fact that dad & I slept through the entire show that was quickly forgottern and remained a secret everafter. I was, however, ~~wondering why nature~~ in asking a question unanswered from my childhood--Why does nature make the trees take off their clothes before winter and then put there clothes on again in the Spring?

Second Draft

SIMULTANEOUSLY

(his tone carried the faint but distinct odor of expectation

1   Mother's favorite ^walnut clock tick-tocked   PICSI IMAGINARY I'm AGANARY
    its way towards noon while underneath, 3
    of its owner's children waited for the
    family "discussion" to begin. Hardly dis-
    cussions at all, these gatherings were an
    excuse for Dad to discipline, delegate
    jobs and dictate morality. Six small
    round fishbowls each containing a single
    blue fish inspected dad as he eased him-
    self into the family sofa. Six eardrums
            LOOK UP
    beat simoltanously as he spoke. "I want
    one of you to go to the opera with me ~~to-~~
    ~~nite~~ tonight."

wandered

2   Not taken back by this peculiar request,
    my older brother, a stickler for logic and
shot back v. reason, ~~retorted~~, What's the matter with
    mom? Dad's paper words were not so quick
    in reply, "She's not feeling well this
    evening," he said to his shoes. Laugh-
    ter boomed forth from our ever-silent ~~mo-~~
    throats and echoed without a sound from
    the walls. ⊥ "Well?" Dad said itching
    for a reply. I half-turned to my brother
    when my silver-tonuged sister, wise in the
            melted
    ways of dealing with dad, ~~cracked~~ the
    silence. Her gentle words explained that
    her addenda was jam-packed with wholesome,

Second Draft—continued

wholely false, activities. Without waiting for a non-existant reply, she glided out of our company secure she would not be called back. ~~in~~

3   "I dont want this ticket to go to waste." This time dad's words reeked of *expectation*. ~~anticipation.~~ If it is true that he who hesitates is lost, I stood on ^yet uncharted ground. My brother's words sliced the silence as he reasoned. Since Michael is younger and therefore more impressionable than I, it would therefore be more beneficial for him to go. My brother's hand picked words and twisted logic covered my dad like a warm woolen blanket. Nothing I could say could unrap the comforter from my dad. ~~Silence ha~~ Words were not spoken. Silence had betrayed me. I was doomed to be cultured. ~~My~~ Dad simply grinned his paternal approval.

4   How many of you really want to wait in the bleeding rain to see this any way? I screamed mutely to ~~my~~ dad's imaginary embarrasment. I shielded my eyes from the pointed droplets long enough to see his patiently stoic expression. This contrasted sharply ~~was~~ with my expression of helpless despair.

5   Finally saved from the rain ~~from~~ *by* a benevolent green canopy, (Benevolent?, It

175

Second Draft—continued

was her job~~)~~, a low voice ~~stopped me dead in my tracks.~~ froze me.

6   "Ticaspleez." came the voice from a bright blue uniform. Dad produced the tickets which the uniform ripped and gave back half.

7   White paint stained ladders, paint buckets covered by dried drippings, grey-white tarps unfinished work and the smell of new plaster rushed to greet ~~to greet~~ Dad and me as we stepped into the lobby of Orchestra Hall. Plaster chips crackled as we → under our weight made our way through the remodleing rubble. Paint splotches were everywhere. The room resembled the remains of a 5 minute indoor snowstorm without one melted snowflake*s*. From the glass countertop under which slept the outrageously expensive candy to the velvet ropes which politely told patrons where not to walk, all were spotted by the same sterile white paint that insulted the walls.

8   Breezing past red double doors and taking eggadurated steps down the gentle sloping of the aisle, we arrived at our 23 row ~~aisle~~ *end* seats. We removed our satarated overcoats and dumped them on a third seat next to me. The well cushioned red velvet seats embraced and welcomed us to the hall.

Second Draft—continued

DOGMATICALLY

9 ~~I am somehow amused viewing people as they get themselves settled before a show.~~ I enjoyed watching the other patrons file slowly but ~~with much determination~~ *dogmatically* into their seats. I ~~see~~ *saw* the same couples I've seen 30 times before bicker as to who will sit on the aisle. Another "regular" ~~is~~ *was* the couple after negotiating their way past 24 knees decided they were in the wrong row. But, unique to this theatre were *the* ladies resembleing giant mounds of soap bubbles. These wait to be recognized by other soap bubbles. I would think it hurts them when the lights go down dashing any hopes of being recognized to the ground.

10 The lights did go down and the music rose from the orchestra pit. Had I been younger, I would have been amazed at the sight of an old man shaking a pointed stick at a fat lady who did nothing but shout back at him. The music died and the lights came to life once more.

11 One thought persisted the entire silent ride home and followed me into bed. It was not the fact that dad and I slept the entire program—that was quickly forgotten and remained everafter. *secret* I was, however, wondering why nature strips her trees before winter and ~~clothes~~ dresses them in the Spring.

were an excuse for dad to dictate morality
were an excuse for *No* Dad to dictate morality...

Third Draft

Michael D. McCarthy

Ticaspleeze and Trees

1   Mother's favorite walnut clock ticktocked towards noon while, underneath, three of its children waited for the family "discussion" to begin. Hardly discussions at all, these gatherings were an excuse for Dad to discipline, delegate [*fascinating metaphor*] jobs and dictate morality. Six small round fishbowls each containing a single blue fish inspected dad as he eased himself into the family sofa. Six eardrums beat simultaneously as he spoke, "I want one of you to go to the opera with me tonight."

2   Not taken aback by this peculiar request, my older brother, a stickler for logic and reason, retorted, "What's the matter with Mom?"

3   Dad's paper words were not so quick in reply, "She's not feeling well this evening," he said to his shoes. Laughter [*Why laughter?*] boomed forth from our ever silent throats and echoed without a sound from the walls. "Well?" Dad said, itching for a reply.

4   I had half-turned to my brother when my [*sp*] silver (toung)ed sister, wise in the ways of dealing with Dad, melted the silence. Her

178

Third Draft—continued

gentle words explained that her agendum was jam-packed with wholesome, wholly false, activities. Without waiting for a non-existant reply she glided out of our company, secure ^*that* she would not be called back.

5   "I don't want this ticket to go to waste." Dad's words reeked of anticipation. If it's true that he who hesitates is lost, I wandered through yet uncharted ground. My brother then 'reasoned', "Since Michael is younger and therefore more impressionable than I, it would therefore be more beneficial for him to go." Older brother's handpicked words and *interesting* twisted logic covered dad like a warm wool *analogy* blanket. Nothing I could say would (unrap) *sp* the comforter from him. Words were not spoken. My friend silence had betrayed *nice.* me. I was doomed to be cultured. Dad *phrasing* simply grinned his paternal approval.

6   "How many of you sheep really want to wait in the bleeding rain to see this anyway?" I screamed mutely to *D*ad's imaginary embarrasment. I shielded my eyes from the pointed ^*autumn* droplets long enough to *It* see his patiently stoic expression. ~~This~~ contrasted sharply with my expression of helpless despair

Third Draft—continued

7   Finally saved from the rain by a benevolent green canopy (Benevolent? It was her job.), I was frozen stiff by a low voice.

8   "Ticaspleeze," came the voice from inside a bright blue braided uniform. Dad produced two tickets which the uniform ripped and gave back half. *halved*

9   White paint stained ladders, paint buckets covered by dried drippings, grey-white tarps, unfinished work and the wet-dry smell of new plaster rushed to greet dad and me as we stepped into the lobby of Orchestra Hall. Plaster chips crackled under our weight as we quickly made our way through the remodeling rubble. Paint splotches were everywhere. The room resembled the remains of a five minute indoor snowstorm without one melted snowflake. From the glass countertop under which slept the outrageously expensive candy to the velvet ropes which politely told the patrons where not to walk, all were spotted by same sterile white paint that insulted the walls.

10 Breezing past red double doors and taking exaggerated steps down the gentle sloping of the aisle, we arrived at our twenty-third-row end seats. We removed our saturated overcoats and dumped them on a third seat next to me. The red velvet, well-cushioned seats embraced and welcomed us to the hall.

Third Draft —continued

11   I enjoyed watching the other patrons file slowly but dogmatically into their seats. I saw the same couples, thirty times ~~before~~ *over*, bicker as to who would sit on the aisle. Another regular was the pair *neat number* who, after negotiating past twenty-one knees, decided they were in the wrong row. But, unique to this theatre were the bird ladies perched on the edge of their too-small seats dying to be recognized. Once prey is spotted, a bird will swoop down amidst a flurry of hi-how-are-yous and glad-to-see-yous. I thought it hurt them when the lights went down--dashing further hope of being seen. ~~to the ground.~~

Mike, this essay is very good. You have so tightly compressed the action and your metaphors describing it that it is fascinating reading.

12   The lights did go down and the music rose from the orchestra pit. Had I been younger, I would have been amazed at the sight of an old man shaking a pointed stick at a fat lady who did nothing but shout back at him. The music died and the lights came to life once more.

13   One thought persisted *during* the entire silent ride home and followed me into bed. It was not ~~the fact~~ that dad and I slept through the entire intermissionless program--that was quickly forgotten and remained secret ever after. I was, however, wondering why nature strips her trees before winter and dresses them in the spring.

The child's perspective is well controlled, the reduction of excessive words admirable.

A—

181

Questions for Discussion

1. Mike's first draft illustrates the value of revision. It has incompletely framed ideas, inaccurate punctuation, and numerous spelling errors. It also lacks the refinement of expression found in the final draft. Studying each successive draft reveals Mike's mind at work: crossing out a sentence, substituting a synonym, changing phrases, trying out spelling. *If he had turned in his first draft as a completed assignment, what grade do you think it would have received?*

2. The difference between A papers and D or F papers is frequently nothing more than the difference that revision makes. Yet students so often deny themselves the chance to improve the products of their writing by hastily turning in what is no more than a freshly copied version of their rough draft. But the kind of work Mike put into his paper takes time—days and hours, time to puzzle over words and phrases, time to let the paper set until the writer can approach it again with a fresh mind. It also takes a strong desire for a superior finished product and a little knowledge of how to achieve that superiority.

   The assignment, you remember, was to write a descriptive essay that used figures of speech to make the writing more vivid. (Some of the more common figures are explained on pp. 162–164.) So one of Mike's aims was to add figures, as well as to sharpen those he had already used. In paragraph 4 of the third draft, for example, he refers to "wholesome, wholly false activities." This pun, or play on words, involving the use of two similar words side by side in two different ways, was a late addition. *Trace its growth through the three drafts. How did the phrase appear in Draft No. 1? What is the difference between the way the phrase is written in the second and third drafts?*

   In tracing this phrase, we see Mike employing two kinds of revision: first, *addition,* by adding the pun; and second, *correction,* by changing the spelling of "wholely" to "wholly."

3. He also made effective use of substitution. *Notice, for example, the clever change in paragraph 11 of the third draft.* "After negotiating past twenty-one knees" evokes a much lighter, more sympathetic reaction from the audience than the "twenty knees" of the first draft. *Note how the substitution occurs in Draft No. 2, paragraph 9.*

4. The second draft shows the evolution of another substitution in paragraph 9. In the third draft (corresponding paragraph 11), the first sentence reads:

   > I enjoyed watching the other patrons file slowly but dogmatically into their seats.

   In Draft No. 2 it reads:

   > We watched the other patrons file slowly but with much determination into their seats.

   How Mike came to change "with much determination" to "dogmatically" is shown on page 4 of the second draft. First we see "dogmatically" tried in the top margin. Looking at paragraph 9, we see that the first sentence, about the writer's amusement at viewing people getting settled, has been struck out. (If you compare Drafts No. 1 and No. 2 you'll see that Mike is trying this sentence—also struck out in Draft No. 1—in a new position, where he again apparently decides it doesn't work.) Then in the next sentence we see "with much determination" struck out and "dogmatically" written below it. The change is complete, for this is the way the sentence reads in Draft No. 3.

   Analyze the effect of this minor change. Why do you think Mike bothered to make it? Do you think it has anything to do with the use of "slowly"? Read the two versions aloud to feel the rhythm. Which sounds best? Which has better balance?

5. Another revision for the purpose of gaining rhythm and balance happened in paragraph 1. Here Draft No. 1 tells the story, where the second sentence reads:

184 Ticaspleeze and Trees (Revision)

> Hardy dicussions at all, these gathering were an excuse for my dad to delegate jobs, dictate morality or merely to discipline.

But *note the arrow running to the top margin,* where we see the words *discipline, delegate,* and *dictate.* Mike had evidently decided to rearrange their order, because in Draft No. 2 we read:

> Hardly discussions at all, these gatherings were an excuse for Dad to discipline, delegate jobs and dictate morality.

Again, read the words aloud:

> discipline, delegate jobs and dictate morality

Compare with the original:

> delegate jobs, dictate morality or merely to discipline

Consider again the rhythm and balance. Which version seems to give equal weight to all three d-words? Which one gets the most effect from the alliterative d's?

6. In the revision analyzed in Question 5 above, Mike also improved the spelling: *hardly* from *hardy, discussions* for *dicussions,* and *gatherings* for *gathering.* This is another way that Mike revised his earlier drafts. His final draft has very few errors, whereas the first draft has many. Writers frequently misspell words as they're writing a rough draft. Totally wrapped up in their idea and how to transmit it on paper, they give very little thought to the appearance of their words. Only later, after their thoughts are down on paper, do they go back to look at the forms their words have taken and then make corrections. Some misspellings are readily recognized and easily corrected. Others can be overlooked in the first rereading, and still other words must be looked up in a dictionary.

Mike had a further problem with spelling. He was inventing a word and so had to decide for himself how to spell it. *Trace his use of* ticaspleeze *in all three drafts, both as a title and as it appears in paragraph 4 of Draft*

No. 1, paragraph 6 of Draft No. 2, and paragraph 8 of Draft No. 3. Which of his spellings do you prefer? For what reason? What does the word mean? Why do you think Mike wanted to write it as a single word?

7. For the same reason that many writers have numerous spelling and punctuation errors in their rough drafts, many also have faulty paragraphing. They may write an entire essay as one paragraph. The essay may have logical organization and follow a well-structured outline, but its form on paper doesn't show how it's organized. Then the writer must go back to look for the logical divisions and mark them as new paragraphs. The symbol for paragraphs (¶) is handy for this marking.

The first page and a half of Mike's first draft are written without paragraphing. In Draft No. 2, however, he divides this section of writing into three paragraphs, and in Draft No. 3 he breaks it down still further.

Try to analyze Mike's reasons for making these paragraph divisions. Consider paragraph unity, noting content and dialogue. Can you say that each paragraph has a single focus? What is the focus of each? Would you divide the paragraphs differently? Why?

Sentence Patterning

We've already looked at some of the process by which Mike's second sentence evolved, how he decided on the balanced phrases "discipline, delegate jobs, and dictate morality." In this patterning assignment you're asked to imitate these phrases; you'll need to keep in mind rhythm and alliteration (repetition of consonant sounds).

Another feature of this sentence is the introductory phrase, "Hardly discussions at all," an appositive which defines "these gatherings." In imitating this portion of the sentence, you'll need two words that refer to the same thing, just as *discussions* and *gatherings* both refer to the family meetings. (Another example of an appositive is found in line 11 of Mike's essay on p. 159: "... my older *brother*, a *stickler* for logic and reason. . . . " Here the appositive, *stickler,* follows the other word, *brother.*)

To imitate the pattern sentence, first think of your subject, like *gatherings* in the pattern sentence or *winter* in the example sentence. Then think of another word that can serve as the appositive by renaming that subject. Finally, fill out the phrase and the sentence. (Avoid beginning your first phrase with an *-ly* word, because most of them won't work.)

SENTENCE

Hardly discussions at all, these gatherings were an excuse for Dad to discipline, delegate jobs, and dictate morality.

PATTERN

_____[synonym]_____, _____[subject]_____
_____[alliterative word]_____, _____[alliterative word]_____, and
_____[alliterative word]_____.

EXAMPLE

More an occupation than a season, winter in Wisconsin costs money, consumes energy, and confines folks indoors.

WRITING ASSIGNMENT

Revise your last writing assignment, or some other piece of your writing. Plan to go over it several times, making some of the kinds of changes Mike made and others that occur to you or have been suggested by your teacher. Ask yourself the following questions:

1. Can I take out any words or sentences without removing or changing meaning?
2. Should I add words or details to make my meaning clearer?

3. Where can I change words to express my idea more clearly, more directly, or more concisely?
4. Should any of my words or sentences be rearranged in order to read more rhythmically or more logically?
5. Have I used strong, active verbs as often as I can?
6. Is the grammatical subject of each sentence the same as the idea subject?
7. Have I corrected all my errors?
8. Does my essay say what I want it to, making the points I want to make, placing emphasis on the points I consider most important, not leaving the reader asking "So what?"?
9. If I were grading my final draft, what grade would I give it?

Many student essays fail to communicate with readers because the writers leave out ideas and details that are essential for explaining what the writers have in mind. Remember that your readers can't read your mind. They have only what you put on paper. If this was a problem with your last essay, your teacher or other readers probably indicated so. In that case, go back to probing your mind again to pull out details that will help your readers understand what you're saying.

After you've gone over your essay several times, looking for ways to improve it and reading it aloud at times to see how it sounds, write a clean final draft, one that has a title and that you consider good enough to represent you to anyone who reads it.

21

The Bounty of the Sea

JACQUES COUSTEAU

Jacques Cousteau, French oceanographer and researcher, has conducted numerous oceanic expeditions that, through his books and television documentaries, have greatly increased our knowledge of the ocean and its inhabitants. For many years he has been intensely concerned about the protection and conservation of the marine environment. "The Bounty of the Sea," written in the mid-1960s, vividly presents this concern in a plea for support of environmental conservation.

Vocabulary Preview

line		
[title]	bounty	something freely given; a reward
3	teemed	swarmed; was full
5	trawler(s)	a fishing boat that drags a large baglike net along the sea bottom
7	effluents	the outflow of sewers
11	profound	deep; far-reaching; complete
12	fundamental	basic; major; elemental
18	insupportable	unbearable; unendurable
18	stench	an offensive smell; a strong and foul odor
25	remorseless	having no pity
47	plankton algae	microscopic plant life floating on bodies of water
53	scavenger	a creature that eats refuse and decaying matter

Essay Preview: Questions to Answer as You Read
1. How can you rely on the truth of what Cousteau says?
2. What is his thesis?
3. How does he support his thesis?
4. Is he convincing?

The Bounty of the Sea

1   During the past thirty years, I have observed and studied the oceans closely, and with my own two eyes I have seen them sicken. Certain reefs that teemed with fish only ten years ago are now almost lifeless. The ocean bottom has been raped by trawlers. Priceless wetlands have been destroyed by landfill. And everywhere are sticky globs of oil, plastic refuse, and unseen clouds of poisonous effluents. Often, when I describe the symptoms of the oceans' sickness, I hear remarks like "they're only fish" or "they're only whales" or "they're only birds." But I assure you that our destinies are linked with theirs in the most profound and fundamental manner. For if the oceans should die—by which I mean that all life in the sea would finally cease—this would signal the end not only for marine life but for all other animals and plants of this earth, including man.

2   With life departed, the ocean would become, in effect, one enormous cesspool. Billions of decaying bodies, large and small, would create such an insupportable stench that man would be forced to leave all the coastal regions. But far worse would follow.

3   The ocean acts as the earth's buffer. It maintains a fine balance between the many salts and gases which make life possible. But dead seas would have no buffering effect. The carbon dioxide content of the atmosphere would start on a steady and remorseless climb, and when it reached a certain level a "greenhouse effect" would be created. The heat that normally radiates outward from the earth to space would be blocked by the CO_2, and sea level temperatures would dramatically increase.

4   One catastrophic effect of this heat would be melting of the icecaps at both the North and the South Poles. As a result, the ocean would rise by 100 feet or more, enough to flood almost all the world's major cities. These rising waters would drive one-third of the earth's billions inland, creating famine, fighting, chaos, and disease on a scale almost impossible to imagine.

5   Meanwhile, the surface of the ocean would have scummed over with a thick film of decayed matter, and would no longer be able to give water freely to the skies through evaporation. Rain would become a rarity, creating global drought and even more famine.

6   But the final act is yet to come. The wretched remnant of the human race would now be packed cheek by jowl on the remaining highlands, bewildered, starving, struggling to survive from hour to hour. Then would be visited upon them the final plague, anoxia (lack of oxygen). This would be caused by the extinction of plankton algae and the reduction of land vegetation, the two sources that supply the oxygen you are now breathing.

7   And so man would finally die, slowly gasping out his life on some barren hill. He would have survived the oceans by perhaps thirty years. And his heirs would be bacteria and a few scavenger insects.

Questions for Discussion

1. This essay is an excerpt from a letter from Jacques Cousteau and the Cousteau Society requesting financial support for the Cousteau Society and its work of conserving the waters of the world. *Given this information, what reaction do you think Cousteau hoped to evoke in his audience? Did he achieve that effect with you?*

2. The oceans are generally thought to be "bountiful" in their liberal gifts of fish and other sea life for the benefit of humankind. But in this disturbing essay the ocean bestows no benefits. *What is the "bounty of the sea" that is described here? Who is responsible for bringing it about?*

3. *What does Cousteau say are his credentials for writing about this subject? Is this enough authority for you to accept what he says?*

4. *What single sentence expresses the main idea of this essay?*

   This is Cousteau's thesis; it directs your thinking as you read the remainder of the essay. Whenever you're reading an essay and trying to discover what it's all about and what position the writer is taking on his subject, look for the thesis sentence. In essays it usually comes near the end of the introduction. In Cousteau's essay, it is the final sentence of the introductory paragraph.

5. *How does Cousteau support his main idea?*

   In your own writing, try to aim for details as vivid as Cousteau's. In order to write with specific details, you must first of all write on a subject you know something about; secondly, you usually need to prod your memory to call forth these details. You thus explore a subject, bouncing it around in your mind, picking up details before you begin to write about it.

6. *How is "The Bounty of the Sea" organized? How does the third paragraph relate to the second? How does the fourth relate to the third?*

   Cousteau develops this essay in a cause-and-effect chain—two chains, in fact, that join at the end. He presents an original cause—the end of life in the oceans—and goes from there to an effect—decaying bodies—which itself becomes a cause, and so on. Each effect is not only an *effect* but also a *cause* of another effect. Thus a chain is established, with each link helping to keep the whole together, as the following diagram illustrates.

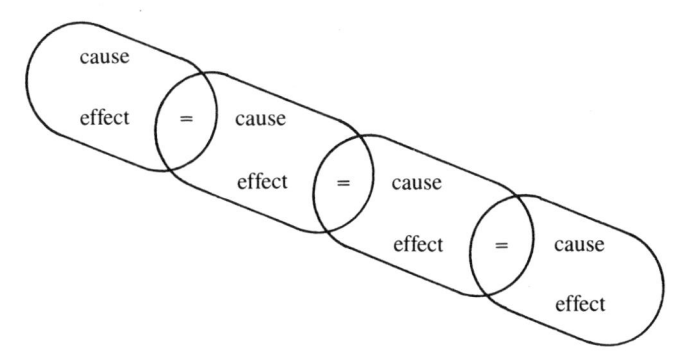

```
  cause
  effect  =  cause
             effect  =  cause
                        effect  =  cause
                                   effect
```

It's important that we don't omit any links, or the chain will be disconnected. *Study the following outline and observe how carefully Cousteau sets up his causal chain.*

- I. Introduction
  - A. Credentials of writer
  - B. Statement of problem
  - C. Statement of thesis: original cause and eventual effect
- II. First chain: heat
  - A. Decaying bodies
  - B. Increased CO_2
  - C. Higher temperatures
  - D. Melting of polar icecaps
  - E. Flooding of coastal plains
  - F. People moving inland
  - G. Insufficient food and space
- III. Second chain: drought, famine, anoxia
  - A. Scum on ocean
  - B. No evaporation
  - C. No rain
  - D. Drought
  - E. Reduced vegetation (two effects)
  - F. Famine ──────▶ G. Anoxia
- IV. Chains joined: death of man

7. When you were reading "The Bounty of the Sea," you didn't think in terms of an outline. You didn't need to, because Cousteau, as a good writer, provided cues that led you from one part to another. *Notice, for example, the cue he used to indicate he was beginning another chain. What is it?* "Meanwhile." *Now look at the beginnings of each of the paragraphs after the first.* Each beginning relates its paragraph to the preceding one. These transitions thus create *coherence*—the linking together of all parts of the essay to bring about a unified whole. *How do the following paragraph transitions relate to the paragraph before them?*

paragraph
____2____ With life departed, . . .

Jacques Cousteau

    ___3___ The ocean acts as the earth's buffer. . . . But dead seas would have no buffering effect.
    ___4___ One catastrophic effect . . .
    ___5___ Meanwhile, . . .
    ___6___ But the final act is yet to come.
    ___7___ And so man would finally die, . . .

8. Cousteau also effectively achieves coherence in another way: by means of key words. *Look again at the thesis statement at the end of the first paragraph. Underline what you consider the key words relating to this essay. Then notice how many times these words are repeated throughout the essay. Underline each repetition.* Every time a key word is repeated, the writer is referring back to his thesis and linking what he is saying with it. Key words may be referred to also by means of synonyms, related words, or pronouns. Thus, each time Cousteau mentions *ocean* (or its synonym *sea*), *die* (or its related words *death* and *dead*), or *man* (or synonyms *human race,* etc., or pronouns *them* and *his,* etc.), he is recalling his thesis and joining the parts into a whole. And Cousteau does this so smoothly that you're not even aware of it. Good writing is like that.

Sentence Patterning

Cousteau uses sentence variety in this essay. He has some very simple sentences, like "But the final act is yet to come." However, he also has some that are more complicated. Good writing uses both. Short sentences can be very effective—even emphatic—when used in combination with longer ones, but too many short sentences make writing dull. Below is one of Cousteau's more complicated sentences.

SENTENCE

    <u>If</u> the oceans should die—<u>by which</u> I mean that all life in the sea would finally cease—this would signal

194 The Bounty of the Sea

the end not only for marine life but for all other animals and plants of this earth, including man.

Practice writing this kind of sentence by imitating it, first copying the sentence exactly and then writing your own sentence following the pattern.

The sentence begins with a subordinate clause (as practiced on p. 134) followed by a *by which* clause (as practiced on p. 95), and then ends with an independent clause. The new feature of this sentence is the parallel structure of the *not only . . . but* phrases. In both Cousteau's sentence and the Example sentence below, the phrase following *but* begins the same way as the phrase following *not only*:

Cousteau:	not only	for marine life
	but	for all other animals
Example:	not only	on aquatic life
	but	on agricultural productivity

You may want to refer to the list of prepositions in the Appendix as you write your sentence.

PATTERN

If _____—by which I mean _____
_____ — _____
_____ not only _____
_____ but _____.

EXAMPLE

If acid rain should continue—by which I mean that precipitation would persist in having a high sulfuric and nitric acid content—we would probably see harmful effects not only on aquatic life but on agricultural productivity as well.

After completing your close imitation, write two or three more sentences with a freer imitation, concentrating only on the *not only . . . but* structure.

WRITING ASSIGNMENT

Write a cause-and-effect essay using a causal chain as your mode of development and "The Bounty of the Sea" as a model. Use one of the topics suggested below or one of your own.

winning	tuition increase
an act of cruelty	a tornado or hurricane
a helpful act	language
a bad choice	getting a pet
something you forgot to do	jogging or running

Once you have decided on a topic that you know something about, begin exploring what you know. What were (or would be) the consequences of the act or statement? How did (or would) those consequences lead to others? What was (would be) the final effect? Ask yourself: who? what? when? where? why? how? Keep prodding with these questions until you recall some specific details and can decide on a statement you can make about the subject. Don't write something like "Tuition will increase," because that sentence doesn't imply cause. Instead, write a sentence something like this:

If tuition increases, I'll have to leave school.

This sentence has a cause—tuition increase—and an effect—leaving school. Write your thesis like the model below, putting your cause in the *if* clause and your effect in the independent clause (after the comma).

If (or when) _____
_____ , _____
_____.

Your *if* or *when* clause is the beginning of your causal chain, and your independent clause is the end. Between them are intermediate causes and effects—the middle part of your essay.

Now write a brief outline, listing your causes in one column and your effects in another. Remember that an effect becomes a cause of the next item, all together making up a causal chain. Here's an example:

Causes	Effects
If the cost of living increases,	school administration costs will go up.
If administration costs go up,	tuition will increase.
If tuition increases,	I won't have enough money.
If I don't have enough money,	I'll have to leave school.

After working out your causes and effects, you may alter your thesis. The tuition thesis, for example, may have been revised to read:

If the cost of living continues to increase, I'll have to leave school.

In developing your ideas, you may have more than one chain, as Cousteau does; or, depending on your subject, you may have only one. If you do have only one chain, you will follow Cousteau's model essay for the first four paragraphs, skip paragraphs five and six, and then write your conclusion.

When you're satisfied with the order of your causes and effects, write your essay, following the pattern of "The Bounty of the Sea." Place your thesis at the end of your introduction, relate your paragraphs with transitional cues and key words, use specific details, and make a final point.

After you've finished writing your first draft, check the logic of your essay: are your causes really *causes,* and are your effects really *effects?* Are you omitting some important links in the causal chain? Is each paragraph clearly related to the preceding paragraph? Check for repetition of key words; you may need to add some. Do you have any errors in grammar, punctuation, or spelling? Finally, write a clean draft, making last-minute changes and proofreading to catch all copying errors.

22

Reading by Leaps and Bounds

FRANK SMITH

Frank Smith is one of today's foremost researchers on literacy. He was born in England, gained his B.A. at the University of Western Australia, and earned a Ph.D. at Harvard University. Before beginning his language research he was a reporter, magazine editor, and novelist. He teaches language education now and spends his spare time as a carpenter, dinghy sailor, and private pilot. The following essay, which defines and explains how the eye moves during reading, is adapted from his widely read *Understanding Reading,* now in its third edition. Though the intended audience is teachers of reading, the points Professor Smith makes in this essay can be of interest and value to any reader.

Vocabulary Preview

line
2	spasmodic	characterized by involuntary muscle contractions
12	periphery	outer edges; boundary
17	erratic	irregular; having no fixed course
17	fixation	a directed focus on something
40	sensory store	a brief holding of visual information while it is being identified by the brain

Essay Preview: Questions to Answer as You Read
1. What is a saccade?
2. What is the difference between a saccade and a fixation?
3. What is the average rate of fixations for good readers?
4. What readers make regressive eye movements while reading?

Reading by Leaps and Bounds

The eye movement that is really of concern in reading is, in fact, a rapid, irregular, spasmodic, but surprisingly accurate jump from one position to another. It is perhaps a little inappropriate to call such an important movement a jump, so it is dignified by the far more elegant-sounding French word *saccade* (which translated into English means "jerk").

A saccade is by no means a special characteristic of reading, but is rather the way we normally sample our visual environment for the information about the world. We are very skilled in making saccadic movements of the eye. Guided by information received in its periphery, the eye can move very rapidly and accurately from one side of the visual field to the other, from left to right, up and down, even though we may be unaware of the point or object upon which we will focus before the movement begins. Every time the eye pauses in this erratic progression, a fixation is said to occur.

In reading, fixations are generally regarded as proceeding from left to right across the page, although, of course, our eye movements must take us from the top of the page toward the bottom and from right to left as we proceed from one line to the next. Really skilled readers often do not read "from left to right" at all—they may not make more than one fixation a line and may skip lines in reading down the page. . . . All readers, good and poor, make another kind of movement that is just another saccade but that has got itself something of a bad name—a *regression*. A regression is simply a saccade that goes in the opposite direction from the line of type—from right to left along a line, or from one line to an earlier one. All readers produce regressions—and for skilled readers a regression may be just as productive an eye movement as a saccade in a forward, or progressive, direction.

4   During the saccade, while the eye is moving from one position to another, very little is seen at all. The leaping eye is functionally blind. Information is picked up in between saccades when the eye is relatively still—during fixations. . . . It seems possible to pick up information only once during a fixation—for the few hundredths of a second at the beginning when information is being loaded into the sensory store. After that time, the backroom parts of the visual system are busy, perhaps for the next quarter of second, processing the information.

5   Saccades are fast as well as precise. The larger saccades are faster than the small ones, but it still takes more time to move the eye a long distance than a short one. . . . The limit on the rate at which we can usefully move from one fixation to another is set by the time required by the brain to make sense of every new input. That is why there can be little "improvement" in the rate at which fixations are made during reading. You cannot accelerate reading by whipping the eyes along faster. . . .

6   The duration of fixations and the number of regressions are not reliable guides for distinguishing between good and poor readers. What does distinguish the fluent from the less-skilled reader is the number of letters or words—or the amount of meaning—that can be identified in a single fixation. As a result, a more meaningful way to evaluate the eye movements of a poor reader and a skilled one is to count the number of fixations required to read a hundred words. Skilled readers need far fewer than beginners because they are able to pick up more information on every fixation. A skilled reader at the "college graduate" level might pick up enough information to identify words at an average rate of over one a fixation (including regressions) or about 90 fixations per 100 words. The beginner might have to look twice for every word, or 200 fixations per 100 words. . . .

7 The brain tells the eyes when it has got all the visual information it requires from a fixation and directs the eyes very precisely where to move next. The saccade will be either a progressive or regressive movement, depending on whether the next information that the brain requires is further ahead or further back in the page. The brain always "knows" where to direct the eye, in reading as in other aspects of vision, provided the brain itself knows what it needs to find out.

Questions for Discussion

1. *According to Smith, what does the eye do when a person reads? What is the difference between a saccade and a fixation?*

   The eye does not move smoothly across the page; rather it proceeds in jumps—called saccades—and each time it stops—a fixation—it picks up information. To observe how this process works, try a little experiment. Get another person and a book; then have that person hold the book up in front of him or her, just a little below eye level, and read. As the "subject" of your experiment reads, watch her eye movements. Are they smooth, or do they jump and stop as they move across the line? Now try counting the number of fixations (stops) and then estimate the number of words read per fixation. Next reverse the procedure: you be the subject and let your companion observe *your* eye movements.

2. *What is a regression? Is it profitable for reading?*

   You have perhaps been told that good readers don't go back to preceding lines of print—a regression—but always move forward at a steady pace. However, Smith says, "Not so." The eyes of good readers move anywhere on the page that they need to in order to pick up the required bits of information. They *ordinarily* move forward, and they regress perhaps less than the eyes of poor readers, but regressions for good readers *are* productive.

3. *According to Smith, how might a reader increase reading speed?*

The way to increase speed is not by forcing the eyes to move faster across the page but by picking up more information at a time—several words per fixation instead of one. Some extremely fast readers will gather enough information with one fixation per line, but most good readers will make two or three or even four stops per line, depending on line length. Smith's average of more than one word per fixation may sound a little low, but it is an *average,* meaning that regressions are averaged in, as well as the times when one reads only one word per fixation or fixates more than once on a long or unfamiliar word.

4. *What aspects of Smith's essay indicate to you that he was writing for an audience of reading teachers?*

 Except sometimes in academic compositions when students forget that *someone* (if only the teacher) will be reading what they write, writers have a particular audience in mind as they write. This audience may be rather specific, like reading teachers or the recipient of a letter, or more general, like the subscribers to *Time* magazine or the readers of the evening newspaper. Such concentration on a given audience affects our writing in certain ways: our choice of words, the amount of assumed knowledge compared to explanations, the words we choose to define, the length of our sentences, the tone (or attitude) we project. *Consider each of these points in relation to Smith's essay and his presumed audience:*

> What does his choice of words tell you about his audience?
> How much knowledge does he assume on the part of his audience?
> What words does he define?
> Are you comfortable with the length of his sentences?
> What is his tone, or attitude toward his subject?

5. *Smith in this essay defines by explanation. Do you know now what a saccade is? Could you explain to someone else how the eye moves when a person reads? What part of Smith's essay was especially helpful to you in understanding these eye movements?*

In looking at the development of Smith's definition, we don't find specific *examples,* but instead specific explanations. Note, for instance, in paragraphs 2 and 3 that he *explains* how the eye moves, or again in paragraphs 4 and 5 that he explains what happens during fixations.

6. *Make an outline of Smith's definition by summarizing the main idea of each outline point.*

   I. Introduction (paragraph 1): _____
   II. Process (paragraph 2): _____
   III. Contrast (paragraph 3): _____
   IV. Effects (paragraphs 4, 5, 6): _____
   V. Conclusion (paragraph 7): _____

What we find as we outline Smith's essay is that he defines his subject in several ways. In paragraph 2 he tells how the eye moves while reading—a *process* orientation. In paragraph 3 he *contrasts* the forward-moving saccade with another kind of eye movement. In paragraphs 4, 5, and 6 he shows the *effects* of saccadic movements and in paragraph 7 how the brain uses eye movements. As writers ourselves, it's useful to remember that definitions are frequently made in many ways, discussing the subject from several perspectives.

7. *Now that you've read the essay, which sentence in the introduction would you say best expresses Smith's thesis? Remember that a thesis states both the subject and the point.*

Probably the best choice is the very first sentence; it presents the subject, "the eye movement," which we learn is called a *saccade;* and it states the point, which is the fact that this eye movement "is really of concern in reading."

Sentence Patterning

A relative clause—usually beginning with *who, which,* or *that* (or understood *that*)—functions as an adjective, thus modifying a noun. And just as a noun may be modified by more than one adjective, it may also have more than one relative clause. The sentence for this patterning exercise has two relative clauses modifying the same noun:

SENTENCE

> All readers, good and poor, make another kind of movement <u>that is just another saccade</u> but <u>that has got itself something of a bad name.</u>

Both *that* clauses modify *kind of movement,* describing it in two ways. The clauses are coordinated with *but.* (Other coordinating conjunctions might also serve this function: *and, or, nor, yet.*) Notice also that there is no comma before the *but,* since it is joining two *subordinate,* not independent, clauses. And as you remember from p. 95, commas do not precede *that,* so there is no comma before either *that;* in this sentence they each introduce a restrictive (essential) modifier. Copy the sentence exactly.

Here's the pattern and an example of another sentence written on the pattern:

PATTERN

_____ that _____
_____ but [or other coordinating conjunction] that _____.

EXAMPLE

> An individual's vocabulary is a stock of words <u>that is acquired beginning at birth</u> and that <u>continues to increase throughout life.</u>

Write a sentence of your own following this pattern. Begin with an independent clause followed by two *that* clauses joined with a coordinating conjunction.

WRITING ASSIGNMENT

Definitions are not confined to dictionaries, and they're not always as brief as those found in dictionaries. It's frequently necessary when writing to define our terms in perhaps a few sentences or a paragraph. Sometimes, too, there is occasion for writing a longer piece whose main purpose is to define a word. Frank Smith in the third chapter of his book *Understanding Reading* found it necessary to devote several paragraphs to explaining what a saccade is. So writing a definition essay is not an unrealistic assignment. Here are some words that might generate definition essays something like Smith's:

> coughing   leaf
> hiccoughs   magnetic field
> shortstop   applause
> quasar   handwriting
> vocabulary   signature
> handshake   cartoon

Your essay will answer the question "What's (a) _____?" It will not only explain what that thing is but might also tell how that thing works, what effects it has, how it differs from similar things, how it might be treated, or anything else that could be useful to a reader trying to see your subject as you do.

Notice again how Smith defines the saccade in several different ways (refer to Question 6). Then explore your subject by asking these questions:

> What does it look like?
> How does it work?
> How is it similar to other items in the same class?
> How does it differ from other items that have some common characteristics?
> What effects does it have on other things?
> Can it be controlled? How?
> What can we do about it or with it?
> What more do we need to know about it?
> What are some examples of it in operation?

It may be necessary for you to do a little reading, perhaps referring to an encyclopedia, before defining your subject. Don't plan to do any quoting (or copying), but you may need to gather some facts. If you do consult a reference book, give credit to your source of information by citing it at the end of your essay, as follows:

Source: *The New Columbia Encyclopedia,* 1975 ed.
             (title)   (edition)

When using books other than encyclopedias, report the following information, punctuating as indicated:

Source: Author, *Title* (City of publication: Publisher, date of publication), pages.

After you've collected some ideas, sort through them for the ones you want to use. Then organize them in some logical way, as Smith did. Construct a thesis statement that expresses the point you've decided you can make about the thing you're defining. Begin your essay with a paragraph that presents the word you're defining and a brief definition of it. Also state your thesis. Do not quote from a dictionary. (While there is nothing inherently wrong with such a beginning, it's been done too many times and is now rather trite.) Begin the body of your essay by acquainting your reader in several ways with the idea that your word represents: show how that thing works, compare it with something similar, show the effects it has on something else, and/or describe that thing. Finally, come to a conclusion that summarizes your sub-points and/or makes a final statement about the significance of your subject.

After you've finished writing your first draft, reread it and revise. Try to be an objective reader and read what's actually on the page, *not* what's in your mind. Have you made yourself clear? Have you omitted important ideas? Have you used specific words? What are the strengths of your essay? Can you make them even stronger? What can you do to overcome the weaknesses? Check for errors in spelling, punctuation, and grammar.

Then rewrite your essay, giving it a final proofreading to catch copying errors. Remember that *proofreading* is not *reading*. We read for ideas, but we proofread for errors. So we must make our eyes stop—fixate—at each word and punctuation mark to check their accuracy. Correct any errors that you discover.

23

The Hidden Teacher

LOREN EISELEY

Loren Eiseley, until his death in 1977, was an educator, anthropologist, poet, and author who had a knack for combining a poetic style with scholarly subjects. For this reason some readers find his writings difficult to understand, while others are enthusiastic about his forceful style and the strength of his ideas. In his many books and articles, the overriding idea is that people must be ruled not by reason alone but by envisioning and imagining as well. It is this fusion of reason and imagination that is the theme of the following passage, excerpted from his highly acclaimed book, *The Star Thrower*.

Vocabulary Preview

line
5	supernova(s)	an extremely bright exploding star, occurring rarely
6	void	not occupied, vacant
6	triangulate	to survey by dividing the area into triangles and measuring lines and angles
9	estranged	alienated; separated in affections and/or distance
9	interim	meantime; the time between
19	impelled	urged to action
23	repulsion	the act of being driven back; a strong dislike
24	intuitively	perceiving without conscious reasoning

28	wan	unnaturally pale, suggesting weariness or illness
46	transfiguration	a change in outward appearance
65	transcending	going beyond the limits
66	ultimate	farthest; most distant; final

Essay Preview: Questions to Answer as You Read

1. Who (or what) is the "Hidden Teacher"?
2. Where do the events of the dream take place?
3. Where is the dreamer sleeping when the dream occurs?
4. What is the role of the narrator in telling this story? What is his relationship to the dreamer?

The Hidden Teacher

1. We of this modern time know . . . that [dreams] can be interior teachers and healers. . . . It has been said that great art is the night thought of man. It may emerge without warning from the soundless depths of the unconscious, just as supernovas may blaze up suddenly in the farther reaches of void space. The critics, like astronomers, can afterward triangulate such worlds but not account for them.

2. A writer friend of mine with bitter memories of his youth, and estranged from his family, who, in the interim, had died, gave me this account of the matter in his middle years. He had been working, with an unusual degree of reluctance, upon a novel that contained certain autobiographical episodes. One night he dreamed; it was a very vivid and stunning dream in its detailed reality.

3. He found himself hurrying over creaking snow through the blackness of a winter night. He was ascending a familiar path through a long-vanished orchard. The path led to his childhood home. The house, as he drew near, appeared dark and uninhabited, but, impelled by the power of the dream, he stepped upon the porch and tried to peer through a dark window into his own old room.

4. "Suddenly," he told me, "I was drawn by a strange mixture

of repulsion and desire to press my face against the glass. I knew intuitively they were all there waiting for me within, if I could but see them. My mother and my father. Those I had loved and those I hated. But the window was black to my gaze. I hesitated a moment and struck a match. For an instant in that freezing silence I saw my father's gaze glimmer wan and remote behind the glass. My mother's face was there, with the hard, distorted lines that marked her later years.

5 "A surge of fury overcame my cowardice. I cupped the match before me and stepped closer, closer toward that dreadful confrontation. As the match guttered down, my face was pressed almost to the glass. In some quick transformation, such as only a dream can effect, I saw that it was my own face into which I stared, just as it was reflected in the black glass. My father's haunted face was but my own. The hard lines upon my mother's aging countenance were slowly reshaping themselves upon my living face. The light burned out. I awoke sweating from the terrible psychological tension of that nightmare. I was in a far port in a distant land. It was dawn. I could hear the waves breaking on the reef."

6 "And how do you interpret the dream?" I asked, concealing a sympathetic shudder and sinking deeper into my chair.

7 "It taught me something," he said slowly, and with equal slowness a kind of beautiful transfiguration passed over his features. All the tired lines I had known so well seemed faintly to be subsiding.

8 "Did you ever dream it again?" I asked out of a comparable experience of my own.

9 "No, never," he said, and hesitated. "You see, I had learned it was just I; but more, much more, I had learned that I was they. It makes a difference. And at the last, late— much too late—it was all right. I understood. My line was dying, but I understood. I hope they understood, too." His voice trailed into silence.

10 "It is a thing to learn," I said. "You were seeking something and it came." He nodded, wordless. "Out of a tomb," he added after a silent moment, "my kind of tomb—the mind."

11 On the dark street, walking homeward, I considered my friend's experience. Man, I concluded, may have come to the

end of that wild being who had mastered the fire and the lightning. He can create the web but not hold it together, not save himself except by transcending his own image. For at last, before the ultimate mystery, it is himself he shapes. Perhaps it is for this that the listening web lies open: that by knowledge we may grow beyond our past, our follies, and ever closer to what the Dreamer in the dark intended before the dust arose and walked. In the pages of an old book it has been written that we are in the hands of a Teacher, nor does it yet appear what man shall be.

Questions for Discussion

1. *Establish the locale of the dream and the dreamer. Where is the dreamer when the dream occurs? We don't have the name of a place, but we have the setting; what is it? What is the setting of the dream? Note the contrasts of location, season, and time of day for the two settings. See especially lines 15–16 and 41–42.*

2. *According to the narrator, what factors in the dreamer's life might have brought on the nightmare?*

3. *In the dream, what transformation takes place as the dreamer peers through the window?*

4. *How does the dreamer interpret his dream? (It in line 52 means the reflection in the glass.)*

   The insight that came to the dreamer is one that comes to many people at some point in their lives: that they are a part of their parents and ancestors and that their children and other descendants are a part of them. Expanded to historical dimensions, we are a part of all that went before us and all that will follow us. The past exists in the present. Therefore, we cannot close the past out of our lives.

5. *Did this realization alter the condition described by the narrator in paragraph 2? Find specific lines to support your answer.*

6. *In the final paragraph, the narrator takes the dreamer's conclusion one step further. In your own words, summarize this final conclusion.*

Loren Eiseley

In paragraph 11 the narrator, Eiseley, concludes that, while we are made up of all that went before us, we also are able to transcend—go beyond—the past, shaping ourselves, becoming new creatures, accomplishing all this through knowledge.

7. Who, or what, is the "Hidden Teacher"? *In answering, see especially the first and last paragraphs.*

8. Loren Eiseley's essay has two interwoven frameworks: the dream, as told by the dreamer, and the larger scene, as told by the narrator. *How does the dream illustrate the point the narrator is making? What sentence would you say is Eiseley's thesis? How does the dream support his thesis?*

9. While this narration has a somewhat complex meaning, its organizational structure is rather simple. Reduced to a skeletal outline, it looks like this:

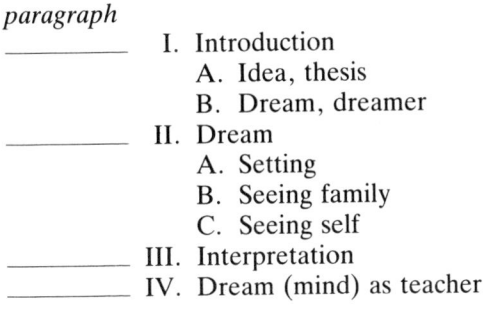

paragraph

_____ I. Introduction
                   A. Idea, thesis
                   B. Dream, dreamer
_____ II. Dream
                   A. Setting
                   B. Seeing family
                   C. Seeing self
_____ III. Interpretation
_____ IV. Dream (mind) as teacher

Determine what paragraphs coincide with each part of the outline.

10. The dream is told in a conversation between the narrator and the dreamer. *Note how the dialogue is handled. What does Eiseley do to make clear who is speaking?* In paragraph 6 he adds related information: how he is reacting to the tale. And in paragraph 7 he describes the dreamer: how he speaks, how he looks. *Find other instances of personal reactions of the narrator or observations he makes about the dreamer.* Note the consistent perspective: he doesn't inform us about the feelings or thoughts of the dreamer except as quotations—words from the dreamer himself.

Sentence Patterning

To keep their writing from being flat and lifeless, writers use various devices to emphasize certain points. One of these devices is repetition, which Eiseley uses selectively in several sentences of this essay. One occurrence is in line 54, where he sets off "much too late," a repetition and amplification of *late,* with two dashes. In another sentence, beginning on line 31, he sets off the repetition with a comma. It is this second sentence that we'll use for patterning. Copy it as it appears below.

SENTENCE

> I cupped the match before me and stepped <u>closer</u>, <u>closer</u> toward that dreadful confrontation.

Notice how the repetition of *closer* draws attention to the word and thus provides emphasis. (Incidentally, it is because of this emphasis gained from repetition that we avoid repeating unimportant words; the repetition works in the same way for them.)

Here's the pattern of our sentence and an example of another sentence written after that pattern.

PATTERN

```
                                    [same word]
_____↙      ↘_____
                                       ,
_____.
```

EXAMPLE

> In my dream I pulled myself to the edge of the open bridge and peered <u>down</u>, <u>down</u> into the abyss of churning water.

Study the pattern and then write your own sentence in imitation of the original.

WRITING ASSIGNMENT

Have you ever had a dream that you still remember vividly? Write about that dream. You may not know why you dreamed it or what it means, but it's essay material all the same. As a matter of fact, by writing about it you may come to understand it better. Your essay will differ from Eiseley's in that you are recounting your own dream, not someone else's. If you can't write about a dream, choose an unusual incident that once happened to you—perhaps something from childhood that had an influence on your life.

Details of the dream or the half-forgotten incident will probably come back to you as you write, so start by free or *pre*-writing—just writing down ideas as they come to you. Keep writing for as long as the ideas come. When they stop, don't give up; take a break. Go for a walk, stare out the window, move to another room, get a snack—something to relieve your mind of the intensity of focusing on the subject, yet keeping the lines of thought open for additional recall. If you think of more ideas, write them down.

After you've completed your preliminary writing, you have in front of you a mess of ideas—a good start for an essay but much in need of shaping. Again you may need to break in order to decide what it all means. In coming to this decision, you may want to ask yourself why you chose to write about this subject, why you still remember it, how you felt about it when it happened, what its significance is (or was) for you. Once you've established a meaning, write it down in a sentence that indicates both your subject and its meaning to you, as Eiseley's opening sentence does.

With your thesis written, you can start to organize your thoughts. Your basic outline will probably be like this:

  I. Introduction
 II. Dream or Incident
III. Conclusion

Your introduction will present your subject to the reader, setting it in time and place, and will express your thesis. In the next paragraphs you will recount your dream or experience as you remember it. Use direct quotations, if appropriate, to indicate what was said. Finally, in your conclusion, make some final statement about the significance of the dream or experience.

Plan to rewrite; you may remember further details as you write your rough draft, or even afterward. As you write and revise, try to add as many specific details as you can in order to make your experience as vivid to the reader as it is to you. Use names, places, descriptions. Make sure that you have related events as they occurred. Is the significance of this experience clear? Are you satisfied with your sentences and your choices of words? Do you see any errors you can correct?

Finally, rewrite your essay to make a clean copy, and proofread for copying errors.

24

Beginning

ISAAC ASIMOV

Isaac Asimov is a scientist and historian who has written over 200 books and innumerable articles on science, history, and literature. In addition, he has written several books on the Bible. *In the Beginning,* a book published in 1981, attempts to compare and relate the Biblical account of the Creation with the scientific explanation of origins. Asimov writes with perception and understanding of both views, respecting both and showing their similarities and differences. The excerpt below, appearing near the front of the book, presents a definition that is essential to understanding his exposition that follows it. Here he explains a fundamental difference between the two accounts.

Vocabulary Preview

line		
3	illuminate(s)	to give light to, to make clear
3	subsequent	coming after; following in time or order
15	subjective	particular to an individual; related to feelings, not thinking; not objective
19	deduction(s)	logical conclusion(s)
28	revelation(s)	striking disclosure(s) of something not previously known
29	intuitive	known immediately, without conscious thought
29	insight(s)	clear understanding(s) of the real nature of something

46	heretic(s)	a person who has beliefs contrary to church teachings
48	polemics	the practice of argumentation or controversy
65	superficial	shallow, on the surface

Essay Preview: Questions to Answer as You Read

1. According to Asimov, what is the fundamental difference between the Biblical and the scientific statements of beginning?
2. What does he mean by "compelling" evidence?
3. Why isn't Biblical authority accepted universally?
4. Why isn't the scientific statement about the beginning absolute, unchangeable?

Beginning

1. There is an enormous difference between the Biblical statement of beginning and the scientific statement of beginning, which I will explain because it illuminates all subsequent agreements between the Biblical and scientific point of view; and, for that matter, all subsequent disagreements.

2. Biblical statements rest on authority. If they are accepted as the inspired word of God, all argument ends there. There is no room for disagreement. The statement is final and absolute for all time.

3. A scientist, on the other hand, is committed to accepting nothing that is not backed by acceptable evidence. Even if the matter in question seems obviously certain on the face of it, it is all the better if it is backed by such evidence.

4. Acceptable evidence is that which can be observed and measured in such a way that subjective opinion is minimized. In other words, different people repeating the observations and measurements with different instruments at different times and in different places should come to the same conclusion. Furthermore, the deductions made from the observations and measurements must follow certain accepted rules of logic and reason.

5   Such evidence is "scientific evidence," and ideally, scientific evidence is "compelling." That is, people who study the observations and measurements, and the deductions made therefrom, feel compelled to agree with the conclusions even if, in the beginning, they felt strong doubts in the matter.

6   One may argue, of course, that scientific reasoning is not the only path to truth; that there are inner revelations, or intuitive grasps, or blinding insights, or overwhelming authority that all reach the truth more firmly and more surely than scientific evidence does.

7   That may be so, but none of these alternate paths to truth is compelling. Whatever one's internal certainty, it remains difficult to transfer that certainty simply by saying, "But I'm *sure* of it." Other people very often remain unsure and skeptical.

8   Whatever the authority of the Bible, there has never been a time in history when more than a minority of the human species has accepted that authority. And even among those who accepted the authority, differences in interpretation have been many and violent, and on every possible point no one interpretation has ever won out over all others.

9   So intense have been the differences and so unable has any one group been to impress other groups with its version of the "truth" that force has very often been resorted to. There is no need here to go into the history of Europe's wars of religion or of the burning of heretics, to give examples.

10   Science, too, has seen its share of arguments, disputes, and polemics; scientists are human, and scientific ideals (like all other ideals) are rarely approached in practice. An extraordinary number of such arguments, disputes, and polemics have been settled on one side or the other, and the general scientific opinion has then swung to that side because of *compelling* evidence.

11   And yet, no matter how compelling the evidence, it remains true, in science, that more and better evidence may turn up, that hidden errors and false assumptions may be uncovered, that an unexpected incompleteness may make itself visible, and that yesterday's "firm" conclusion may suddenly twist and change into a deeper and better conclusion.

12   It follows, then, that the Biblical statement that earth and heaven had a beginning is authoritative and absolute, but not

compelling; while the scientific statement that earth and heaven had a beginning is compelling, but not authoritative and absolute. There is a disagreement there that is deeper and more important than the superficial agreement of the words themselves.

Questions for Discussion

1. *Answer in your own words the questions preceding the essay.*
2. Asimov's thesis is the first part of the first sentence, up to the comma. In the rest of the sentence he gives his reason for writing the essay that follows. In the thesis statement, his first key word, *difference,* establishes the method of organizing this definition; contrast. Throughout the essay Asimov explains how the Biblical and scientific statements on beginnings *differ. Observe in the following outline how he shifts from one to the other.*

   I. Introduction
     A. Thesis
     B. Reason for writing
   II. Fundamental difference
     A. Biblical statements rest on authority
     B. Scientific statements are backed by evidence
   III. Evidence (science)
     A. Definition
     B. "Compelling" evidence
     C. Contradiction
     D. Refutation
   IV. Authority (Bible)
     A. Minority acceptance
     B. Differences in interpretation
   V. Disputes in science
     A. Settlement by compelling evidence
     B. Changes with new evidence
   VI. Conclusion—summary

   Finally, note how the conclusion reiterates the thesis yet states it in a fuller, more complete form. This is one of the most effective types of conclusions.

3. In addition to the organizational key word, *difference,* notice the other key words in the thesis: *beginning, Biblical,* and *scientific.* While the first key word, *difference,* indicates the organization of the essay, the others serve to provide coherence, linking each part of the essay to the thesis. *Read through the essay again and underline every occurrence of the words* beginning, Biblical *(or* Bible*), and* scientific *(or related words* science *and* scientist*).*

You have seen how the key words recur frequently throughout the essay. In paragraph 2 and paragraph 3, where Asimov gives his two contrasting definitions, he contributes additional key words. In paragraph 2 appears the fundamental word, *authority,* followed by others: *disagreement* and *absolute.* In paragraph 3, the word that is fundamental to the definition is *evidence.* Notice then how Asimov relies on the repetition of these additional key words to tie the parts of his essay together. Paragraph 4, for example, picks up the key word *evidence* and proceeds to define it. Paragraph 5 goes one step further in the definition, introducing another key word, *compelling,* showing how it describes evidence.

Repetition of key words, as we have seen, is an effective technique for tying together parts of the essay, relating them to the thesis and to one another. Unlike useless repetition of unimportant words, this kind of repetition *works* for the writer by helping the reader to follow the development of ideas.

4. *Does Asimov take a position that favors either the Biblical or the scientific statement of beginning? Is he fair in his treatment of both sides? Support your answer with evidence from the essay.*

5. In the conclusion of this essay, Asimov asserts that both the Bible and science state that earth and heaven had a beginning—an apparent agreement. But underlying this agreement is the more fundamental difference that the Biblical statement is authoritative and absolute (accepted as God's word) but not compelling, and that the scientific statement is compelling (backed by evidence)

but not authoritative and absolute. Throughout his book *In the Beginning,* Asimov then gives examples of how the Bible and science agree or disagree. Both agree, for example, that light occurred before the sun originated. Despite agreements, however, there is still controversy and taking of sides. *Can you explain the controversy between science and religion in light of their being either authoritative or compelling? Think of additional examples of agreement or disagreement.*

Sentence Patterning

While intentional repetition of key words can be a useful writing tool for achieving coherence and emphasis, needless repetition of unimportant words can produce deadly wordiness. One way to avoid such repetition is by using parallel structure. This efficient technique can compress similar ideas into similar structures and eliminate words that might otherwise be repeated. Isaac Asimov in the sentence below (from lines 54–59 in the essay) uses a series of *that* clauses to compress into a single sentence four possible occurrences in scientific research.

SENTENCE

> No matter how compelling the evidence, it remains true, in science, <u>that</u> more and better evidence may turn up, <u>that</u> hidden errors and false assumptions may be uncovered, <u>that</u> an unexpected incompleteness may make itself visible, <u>and that</u> yesterday's "firm conclusion" may suddenly twist and change into a deeper and better conclusion.

As you copy Asimov's sentence, notice the repetition of the subordinator *that* and the clause pattern that follows it each time. What is omitted in the second, third, and fourth clauses is "it remains true, in science." Write a sentence in imitation, possibly on the subject of science or religion. If you like, use a different subordinator: *because, when, after, how.*

PATTERN

[main statement]
that _____, that _____
_____, that _____
_____, and that _____
_____.

EXAMPLE

According to Mortimer J. Adler, it is worthwhile to study angels <u>because</u> many people are interested in knowing what the study may reveal, <u>because</u> great philosophers like Plato, Descartes, Nietzsche, and Kant have theorized about angels, <u>because</u> fallacies about angels need to be exposed, <u>and</u> <u>because</u> this study can help us better understand our own place in the cosmic scheme—from *The Angels and Us.* (The understood words in the second, third, and fourth occurrences of <u>because</u> are "it is worthwhile to study angels.")

WRITING ASSIGNMENT

Below are two explanations for the cause of toothaches. The first is an ancient Babylonian version of a once universally held belief. The second is a more familiar, modern account. Write an essay that contrasts the two. First decide on a fundamental difference, as Asimov showed in his brief descriptive second and third paragraphs. Then choose other differences to make up the rest of your essay. The common ground is that both stories account for toothaches. Even though you will find some similarities, like the need for a dentist to cure the pain, concentrate only on the differences. Remember that you are contrasting the two explanations.

I. *How Toothache Came into the World*
After God had created heaven,
heaven created earth;
earth created rivers;
rivers created ditches;
ditches created mud;
mud created the worm.

But the worm had nothing to eat.
So he went to the god of justice
and wept and wept;
and before Ea, the god of wisdom,
he poured forth his tears.

"What will you give me to eat?" he cried,
"and what will you give me to drink?"

"I will give you ripe figs," said the god of justice,
"and I will give you apricots."

"What good are ripe figs?" cried the worm.
"And what use are apricots?

Lift me up from the mud
and place me among men's teeth,
and set me down in their jaws,
that I may drink the blood of their teeth
and feed on the roots of their jaws!"

"Very well," said the god of justice.
"You have made your choice.
You may lie among men's teeth;
you may lie among their jaws.
But henceforth and for evermore
the mighty hand of Ea shall be against you to crush you!"

> And so it has remained. The worm preys upon the teeth and gnaws at the gums of men; but the dentist, the servant of Ea, attacks him and kills him. And that is not all. Whenever you have a toothache and you brew a drug to ease it, recite this story thrice, and you will surely be cured. (From *The Oldest Stories in the World*, ed. and trans. Theodor H. Gaster, New York: Viking Press, 1952, pp. 93–94.)

II. Cavities in the teeth are caused by tooth decay, which begins when bacteria on the teeth cause food particles to ferment. This fermentation forms an acid that destroys tooth enamel. Once the enamel has been damaged, decay attacks underlying dentin (the body of the tooth) and progresses steadily unless the decay is removed by the dentist and the tooth is filled. If the tooth is not repaired, the decay eventually reaches the nerves and the tooth begins to ache. Further inattention leads to infection, greater pain, disease, and loss of the tooth. Other diseases can attack the gums, also leading to pain and tooth loss. But regular visits to the dentist will prevent most painful problems of the teeth.

Use Asimov's essay as a model for writing yours. Establish first of all that these are two explanations for the same thing: toothache. Present a brief summary of each, and then proceed to discuss their differences. Introduce your subject and state your thesis in the first paragraph. Then write two short paragraphs which name the primary difference between the two explanations. Asimov in his essay says that Biblical statements rest on authority while scientific statements rest on evidence. You will say in one paragraph that the Babylonian account _____, and in your second paragraph that the modern account _____. What is their fundamental difference as you see it? The rest of your essay will explain this difference. You don't need to have as many paragraphs as Asimov does, but make sure that you treat both accounts somewhat equally and as fairly as you can. End your essay with a restatement of your thesis that presents in a fuller way the controlling idea of your essay.

To achieve the kind of coherence that we've seen in Asimov's essay, repeat key words frequently. The key words will appear first in your thesis and in your second and third paragraphs. For this assignment, underline your key words to help you concentrate on them.

When you've finished writing, check for transitions.

Since you're writing about two subjects and moving back and forth between them, you'll need to be especially careful to keep your reader with you. You'll do this by indicating when you're making a shift. Asimov, for example, as he shifts from the Bible to science in paragraph 3, uses the transitional phrase "on the other hand." Other contrasting terms are *however, but,* and *although,* to name a few. Asimov also indicates his shifts by naming the subject he is moving to, as in paragraph 8, where he says "Whatever the authority of the Bible," and in paragraph 10 where he says "Science, too, has seen its share of arguments. . . . " If you find as you reread your essay that you haven't made perfectly clear your shifts from one account of toothache to the other, add some kind of transition.

Then check your essay to see if it concentrates on differences between the two accounts. Do you treat both subjects fairly? Does your essay make a point? Do you have any errors? Check for those that keep recurring in your writing, and correct them. After you've read through your essay several times looking for ways to improve it, rewrite a final draft and proofread it carefully.

25

Play in Ancient Greece
EDITH HAMILTON

Edith Hamilton was born in Fort Wayne, Indiana, in 1867, and studied Greek culture at the University of Munich as the first woman student ever admitted there. In 1896 she became headmistress of the Bryn Mawr School of Baltimore, retiring twenty-six years later. It was after her retirement that she wrote *The Greek Way,* originally published in 1930. This classic in its field presents the people and culture of ancient Greece as seen by one who admired and studied them nearly all her life. The excerpt below illuminates one aspect of Greek living.

Vocabulary Preview

line
1	sparse fertility	thinly spread plant growth
1	keen	sharp
5	rampart(s)	an embankment usually topped with a wall for defense against attackers
10	sapphire	deep blue; the gem of that color
11	luminous	clear; bright, shining
12	antiquity	ancient times; the people of ancient times
21	chariot(s)	a horse-drawn, two-wheeled vehicle used in ancient times for war, races, and parades
28	strove	tried very hard (past tense of *strive*)
28	covet(ed)	to want excessively
29	Olympic	in ancient Greece, referring to the contests in athletics, poetry, and

		music that were held every four years at the plain of Olympia to honor the god Zeus
31	tragedian	a writer of tragedies—plays in ancient Greece that dealt with the problems of a noble character and ended unhappily or disastrously
41	wretched	miserable; unhappy; unfortunate
42	conceivable	able to be thought of or understood
44	mural	a picture painted directly on a wall
44	minutest	smallest
46	Solon	an ancient Greek statesman and lawgiver
50	vigor	physical energy or strength
52	enigma	a riddle; a statement that is puzzling or ambiguous (having more than one meaning)
55	Orient	Eastern, or Asian, nations (e.g., China)
57	resurrect(ed)	to revive; to bring back to life

Essay Preview: Questions to Answer as You Read

1. What three ancient Greek personages does Hamilton name?
2. How did the Greeks benefit from play?
3. In what ways do the ancient Olympic games compare with those of today?

Play in Ancient Greece

Greece is a country of sparse fertility and keen, cold winters, all hills and mountains sharp cut in stone, where strong men must work hard to get their bread. . . . Somewhere among those steep stone mountains, in little sheltered valleys where the great hills were ramparts to defend and men could have security for peace and happy living, something quite new came into the world; the joy of life found expression. Perhaps it was born there, among the shepherds pasturing their flocks where the wild flowers made a glory on the hillside; among the sailors on a sapphire sea washing enchanted islands purple in a luminous air. At any rate it has left no trace anywhere else in the world of antiquity. In Greece nothing is more in evidence. The Greeks were the first people in the world to play, and they played on a great scale.

2   All over Greece there were games, all sorts of games; athletic contests of every description: races—horse-, boat-, foot-, and torch-races; contests in music, where one side outsung the other; in dancing—on greased skins sometimes to display a nice skill of foot and balance of body; games where men leaped in and out of flying chariots; games so many one grows weary with the list of them. They are embodied in the dancing flute players.

3   The great games—there were four that came at stated seasons—were so important, when one was held, a truce of God was proclaimed so that all Greece might come in safety without fear. There "glorious-limbed youth"—the phrase is Pindar's, the athlete's poet—strove for an honor so coveted as hardly anything else in Greece. An Olympic victor—triumphing generals would give place to him. His crown of wild olives was set beside the prize of the tragedian. Splendor attended him, processions, sacrifices, banquets, songs the greatest poets were glad to write. Thucydides, the brief, the severe, the historian of that bitter time, the fall of Athens, pauses, when one of his personages has conquered in the games, to give the fact full place of honor.

4   If we had no other knowledge of what the Greeks were like, if nothing were left of Greek art and literature, the fact that they were in love with play and played magnificently would be proof enough of how they lived and how they looked at life. Wretched people, toiling people, do not play. Nothing like the Greek games is conceivable in Egypt or Mesopotamia. The life of the Egyptian lies spread out in the mural paintings down to the minutest details. If fun and sport had played any real part they would be there in some form for us to see. But the Egyptian did not play. "Solon, Solon, you Greeks are all children," said the Egyptian priest to the great Athenian.

228 Play in Ancient Greece

At any rate, children or not, they enjoyed themselves. They had physical vigor and high spirits and time, too, for fun. The witness of the games is conclusive. And when Greece died and her reading of the great enigma was buried with her statues, play, too, died out of the world. The brutal, bloody Roman games had nothing to do with the spirit of play. They were fathered by the Orient, not by Greece. Play died when Greece died and many a century passed before it was resurrected.

Questions for Discussion

1. Hamilton starts her essay considering causes for the Greek development of play. *How does she suggest the environment might have contributed to its origin?*

2. In whatever way play might have originated—whether as a tough response to a harsh environment, as a peace-loving response to a secure one, or as a creative response to a beautiful one—play was essential to the ancient Greek way of life. *In paragraph 2 Hamilton names some of the kinds of games they played. What were they?*

3. *How might the ancient Olympic games compare with the Olympic games of today? Consider events, rewards, participants, state support, etc.*

4. *What reasons does Hamilton suggest for the fact that the Egyptians did not play?*

5. *Name several benefits that came to the ancient Greeks because of their participation in games of many types.*

6. *Hamilton names three famous Greeks—Pindar, Thucydides, and Solon. What are they noted for, and what were their connections with the Greek games?*

7. *What is Hamilton's thesis? Find it in her introduction, and then locate a restatement of it in her conclusion.*

8. In developing her thesis—that the Greeks brought play into the world, developed it on a grand scale, and benefited physically, emotionally, and intellectually because of it—Hamilton uses several rhetorical modes. Her in-

troduction is clearly *causal,* an attempt to explain why the Greeks took to play. Paragraph 2 *classifies,* listing the games according to categories. Paragraph 3 gives *examples* to show how important the Olympic games were. *Paragraph 4 relies on* comparison; *look at this paragraph: what two subjects does Hamilton compare?*

Paragraph 5 functions as a conclusion, providing significance by looking at the *effects* of play on the Greeks. A skeletal outline of the essay might look like this:

I. Causes and thesis
II. Classification
III. Examples
IV. Comparison
V. Effects and significance

Sentence Patterning

Since *The Greek Way* was published in 1930, English usage and punctuation has changed a little—yet not radically. While Hamilton's punctuation might not always be as we'd use it, it doesn't give us any false signals either. And the phrasing of her sentences is still marvelous to observe and imitate. The sentence below is beautifully put together. It is long, but the coordination is so clear that nowhere do we get off the track.

Hamilton starts with two parallel *if* clauses, uses coordinated verbs (*were* and *played* joined by *and*), and then finally coordinates two *how* clauses. Copy the sentence and study the pattern, and then write a sentence of your own in imitation. You can substitute other conjunctions for *if* and *how* if you want (see list on p. 267).

SENTENCE

<u>If</u> we had no other knowledge of what the Greeks were like, <u>if</u> nothing were left of Greek art and literature, the fact that they were in love with play <u>and</u> played magnificently would be proof enough of <u>how</u> they lived <u>and how</u> they looked at life.

PATTERN

If _____, if _____
_____, _____
_____ and _____
_____ how _____ and how _____.

EXAMPLE

Though television has changed the character of professional sports, though exorbitant player salaries have distorted a sense of values, professional sports nevertheless have unified local communities and provided diversion from the anxieties of figuring out how to pay bills and how to keep jobs.

WRITING ASSIGNMENT

This writing assignment is more complex than many you've been doing. Usually you've written an essay of one type—for example, comparing two things or analyzing causes or effects of something, or using examples to make a point. In this essay, however, you will use several methods of development.

Before considering how all this will work out, let's first think about topics. With a complex development of your essay, you'll need a somewhat complex topic. Here are a few, but you might want to consider others:

Play in the United States
Professional sports in the United States
Computers for learning
Ballpoint or nylon tip pens
Compact automobiles
Microwave ovens
Motorcycles
Contact lenses
Video games
Calculators

Reading down the list, you see that the topics are broad. One of your tasks will be to determine a focus in developing your topic, and then to maintain that focus. That is, just as Hamilton didn't write everything she knew about Greek games, you won't write everything you know about professional sports in the United States, if that's your topic. What she did was to use what she needed to make her point, that games had beneficial effects on the Greeks. So it's important for you to know what point you're making *before you start*. If you're writing about ballpoint pens, your point might be, "The ballpoint has revolutionized the way Americans think about pens."

Once you've decided on a topic and the point you want to make, you can proceed to examine how you're going to support your point. The outline, again, is as follows:

    I. Causes and thesis
   II. Classification
  III. Examples
  IV. Comparison
   V. Effects and significance

Start thinking about what you can do to fill in each part. If you're writing about ballpoint pens, determine what might have led to their development. You might go about this task in two ways: by doing a little research or by guessing. Actually, you'd probably be best off if you did both. That is, Hamilton did extensive research on how the Greeks lived. But who knows why they took to games? There's no record, so *on the basis of what she knew* Hamilton guessed—inferred—about causes. Before you finish your first paragraph, state your thesis.

In your second paragraph, name different kinds—classes—of your subject. If you're writing about contact lenses, you might talk about hard, soft, and extended wear types. Then you might sub-classify according to different kinds or brands under each heading. Again, you might need to do a little research.

In the next paragraph you can get specific in another way. Choose one aspect of your subject and use examples to support your point. If you're writing about contact lenses, you might discuss their features by recounting the experiences of people who have used the various types.

Next, make a comparison. Compare ballpoints to fountain pens, for example, or microwave ovens to conventional ovens. Still keep in mind what your overall point is. And finally, in your last paragraph, deal with the effects of your subject, suggesting its significance and making a restatement of your thesis.

As you reread your essay, concentrate again on your focus and make adjustments as necessary to have all parts centering on your point. Add details where necessary and delete where your ideas don't support your thesis. If you've borrowed information from another source, document it according to the convention suggested on p. 205. Check for errors. When you're satisfied with your revisions, write a clean final copy and proofread it.

Essays for Further Reading

26

Theme Writing

DOROTHY CANFIELD FISHER

Essay Preview: Questions to Answer as You Read
1. How does Fisher suggest a person start writing?
2. What can English classes teach about writing?
3. What part of the rough draft is most likely the worst? Why?

Theme Writing

Scientists tell us it is harder to start a stone moving than to keep it going after it gets started. And every writer can bear witness that the most unyielding stone is mobile as thistledown compared to the inertia of the average human mind confronted with a blank sheet of paper.

It is hard to write. It is infinitely harder to begin to write. Don't I know it? I have been earning my living by my pen for twenty-five years. I shouldn't like to guess how many hundred words I've put on paper, and I have never in my life sat down at my desk and started off without hesitation, repugnance, and wild flounderings. Other authors confess that it is much the same with them. There are exceptions—stories, even novels, where the opening words pop right into one's mind, part of the first conception, but these inspirations are far between.

I set down all this not to discourage those of you who are wondering if perhaps it might not be possible to become an author, still less to add to the gloom of wrestling with the English compositions you all have to write. On the contrary, I hope to encourage you by letting you know that those hopeless moments of inhibition before the blank page, those chewed, balky penholders are only the common lot. There is nothing the matter if you can't start writing without effort. Nobody can.

4   But perhaps this sounds a little bit like the fortune teller who predicted, "You will have forty years of bad luck and then—then you will be used to it." It is not so bad as that. It is quite true that no one ever learns to write both well and easily. But there are tricks to every trade and some of the most useful of them all are ways of tricking your own rebellious nerves. Perhaps it would help you to know of one that works with most writers. Whenever they have a piece of writing to do, *they begin to write*—to write something, anything. They conquer the inertia of their minds by a spasm of effort, just as a man might give a great heave to a boulder that blocks his way. Grimly, doggedly, they keep on writing. Often what they are setting down is flat, stale balderdash, and they know it. No matter! If they are experienced writers they keep right on, do not stop—not to sharpen a pencil, or get a drink of water, or go to look out of the window, although they yearn to do all these things. They have learned by experience that if they sit and stare at the paper they are lost. The rosy, hazy half-thoughts which flit about the back of the mind always vanish when one tries to think them out. The only way to catch them is to put down on the paper as many of them as possible.

5   So the struggling author plods ahead, filling page after page with horrible, unwieldy sentences, haphazard, unleavened ideas, and after a time it begins to move more smoothly. Is it because of habit, or because the subconscious mind wakes up, or is it something similar to physical momentum? Nobody knows, but it almost always works. The great boulder begins to roll evenly and more and more in the desired direction. Apter phrases suggest themselves. The whole subject begins to take on shape. Even now it is not good. But there is something there, some stuff which can later be licked into shape. Then comes the moment when the writer realizes that he has said somehow all that was in his mind.

6   The work is far from being finished, but the hardest part is over. Now comes the mechanical task of breaking up un-

gainly sentences, cutting out the flat words and phrases, thinking up colorful ones to fill the gaps, shifting related ideas into paragraphs. It is a matter of skill and judgment, only a little harder than correcting grammatical errors—far different from the agony of trying to create, or rather to drag out the raw material from the fringe of consciousness.

7. It is mechanical work but very necessary. Inexperienced writers don't do enough of it. Very young writers often do not revise at all. Like a hen looking at a chalk line, they are hypnotized by what they have written. "How can it be altered?" they think. "That's the way it was written." Well, it has to be altered. You have to learn how. That is chiefly what English classes can teach you. They can't give you thoughts and material to write about. Only your inherited brain cells and the enriching experience of life as you live it can do that. But you can learn to put what material you have into form. In manual training you wouldn't hand in a lot of sticks and boards bunched together with string, and call it a table. It's no better to hand in a detached bundle of statements, starting nowhere in particular, trailing along a while and then fading out—and call it a theme.

8. All your first drafts will need revision, but the middle and end of them may not need a great deal. You had steam up when you wrote them; you were commencing to feel what you wanted to say. *But watch your beginning.* That was written when arm and brain were cold. Try as you may to put it into shape, the first page or so is generally hopeless. Then cut it out and begin where the real life begins. You may hate to sacrifice that laboriously written first page, but if it isn't right, can't be made right, it isn't worth keeping. When you wrote it you were only warming up your arm. Do that behind the grand stand, and when you start the game be ready to pitch real ball.

Questions for Discussion

1. What does Fisher say are her credentials—her authority—for writing on this subject?
2. Who do you think is her intended audience?

3. What assurance does Fisher give to inexperienced writers?
4. What should writers do when they find it hard to start writing? Have you tried this? Has it worked for you?
5. What should writers do if what they're writing is bad? Does that sound reasonable to you? How many times have you thrown away bad starts and started over?
6. What does Fisher compare inexperienced writers to? Why?
7. Name some ways to revise rough drafts. How many of them have you tried?

27

Probing for Ideas

FRANK J. D'ANGELO

Essay Preview: Questions to Answer as You Read
1. What are the "topics"?
2. What does D'Angelo say the principles of composition are?

Probing for Ideas

Although no two people would develop a general subject in exactly the same way, each of us to a certain extent must nevertheless follow certain lines of development in our thinking because the mind is organized according to certain principles. It recognizes temporal, spatial, logical, and psychological principles and relationships in the universe.

Principles of composition such as analysis, classification, comparison and contrast, and cause and effect are *ways of thinking*. For example, not a day goes by that you don't analyze, classify, compare and contrast, or discover cause-and-effect relationships in the world around you. You see a tree and note the shape of its branches, the size of its trunk, or the color of its leaves. You classify it by naming it. You compare it to other trees. You observe it changing in time, notice that termites are causing it to decay or that it has been struck by lightning. When the tree is not in the immediate range of your vision, you substitute images or words to call it to mind, and these words or images facilitate your thinking about the tree. Every time you analyze, classify, exemplify, enumerate, compare, contrast, or discern cause-and-effect relationships, you are inventing ideas.

3   Compositional categories such as an analysis, classification, and comparison and contrast, besides being principles of thought, are categories that suggest questions that can be used in exploring ideas for writing. These categories are sometimes called *topics,* a word that originally meant "places." (I have referred to them previously as *modes.*) The topics were literally conceived of as places in the mind or in books where ideas were stored, where one could go to get ideas. The term *topic* today is more frequently used to refer to the subject matter of a discussion or conversation. But I would like to use the term to refer to *categories that can be used to direct the search for ideas or the arrangement of these ideas into some orderly pattern.*

4   What I would like to propose is that in examining a subject to get ideas for writing, you use these topics or modes and the questions they suggest in a systematic way. To help you do this, I have put these categories into a scheme to enable you to use them more efficiently:

Topics of Invention
A. Static
 1. Identification
 2. Analysis
    a. Partition
    b. Enumeration
 3. Description
 4. Classification
 5. Exemplification
 6. Definition
 7. Comparison and contrast
    a. Similarity
       (1) Literal
       (2) Figurative
    b. Difference
       (1) In kind
       (2) In degree
B. Progressive
 1. Narration
 2. Process
 3. Cause and effect

This visual scheme has two advantages. It shows you how the topics are related to one another, and it will enable you to remember them better for future use.

5   The static, logical topics are for the most part abstracted from time and space. Description, of course, is an exception, but what unites all of these topics is our ability to view them apart from their existence in time.

6   Obviously, many relationships exist among these categories. Probably all of the topics work together in the composing process, but for practical purposes you can separate them out. You can't classify without comparing or divide something into parts without noticing differences. All of these topics relate to dynamic processes in the human mind.

7   In order to use the topics to explore a subject, you need merely to move from one topic on the diagram to another, applying them to the subject at hand. You can start anywhere on the diagram that you like. Thus, you might begin by describing or defining your subject, or comparing it to something else. Then you move on to the other topics, all the while obtaining a clearer idea of your subject as you apply each topic in turn. Once you have gone through the topics, you can repeat the procedure as often as you desire. The process is recursive. The result of applying these topics to a particular subject is that when you complete this procedure, you should have something to say, or at least you will be aware of the gaps in your knowledge and go on from there.

8   It may be that the topics may best be applied by putting them in the form of questions. The following are just a few of the many questions suggested by these topics:

Identification
Who or what is it?
Who or what is doing it or did it?
Who or what caused it to happen?
To whom did it happen?

Analysis
What are its pieces, parts, or sections?
How may they logically be divided?
What is the logical order?
What is the exact number?

Description
What are its constituent parts?
What are its features or physical characteristics?
How is it organized in space?

Classification
What are its common attributes?
What are its basic categories?

Exemplification
What are some representative instances, examples, or illustrations?

Definition
What are its limits or boundaries?
What are its classes?
What are its common attributes?
What is its etymology?

Comparison
What is it like?
How is it similar to other things?
How does it differ from other things?

Narration
What happened?
What is happening?
What will happen?
When did it happen?
Where did it happen?

Process
How did it happen?
How does it work?
What are its stages or phases?
How do you make it or do it?

Cause and Effect
Why did it happen?
What are its causes?
What are its effects?
What is its purpose?
How is it related causally to something else?

9   Another plan is to put the topics in the form of statements and apply these directly to the topic you are exploring. The advantage of this procedure is that you will have fewer questions, statements, or topics to remember:

> Identify the subject.
> Describe it.
> Divide it into parts.
> Define it.
> Classify it.
> Give some examples.
> Point out its similarities to or differences from something else.
> Tell what happened, when it happened, and where.
> Tell how it happened or how it is changing in time.
> State its causes or effects.

10 In probing, clearly, you cannot apply all of the topics or questions to every subject. But merely by using some of them you will be able to get enough ideas to begin your writing.

Questions for Discussion

1. How does D'Angelo explain the principles of composition as ways of thinking?
2. What new use does he suggest for these principles (topics)?
3. How are classification, description, etc., useful in probing for ideas?
4. D'Angelo sees three uses for the topics, or principles of composition:
   a. Ways of thinking
   b. Ways of exploring ideas
   c. Ways of organizing essays

   Try out these uses as you write an essay, beginning from the time you get the topic, or subject, through exploring ideas, and on to organizing and writing the essay.

Developing a Paragraph from a Topic Sentence

JIM W. CORDER

Essay Preview: Questions to Answer as You Read

1. What is a topic sentence?
2. How does Corder suggest using topic sentences when "inspiration doesn't come"?
3. What do topic sentences do for readers?

Developing a Paragraph from a Topic Sentence

Some identifiable patterns of paragraphing exist. They can sometimes be used in any kind of writing, and they can often be used in particular kinds of writing. They may be especially helpful when you are stuck—when you are blocked in your writing and can't see how to proceed, it's often possible to get started again by deliberately adopting a method or pattern other writers have worked out and frequently used.

One such method is the development of a paragraph from a *topic sentence*. When a sentence serves as a *topic sentence* for a paragraph, it sets a theme for the entire paragraph: every other sentence in the paragraph is related in some specific way to the topic sentence; it is the fixed post to which all the other sentences are tied. In a paragraph built from a topic sentence, the other sentences serve to illustrate what the topic sentence says, or to explain it, or to amplify it, or to modify it; or they are in some way extensions of the topic sentence. Look at some examples.

3   The first example below opens with a primary assertion, the generalization that serves as topic sentence. The rest of the paragraph is devoted to one specific episode that dramatizes the truth of the primary assertion, or topic sentence:

> A great thirst is a great joy when assuaged in time. On my first walk down Havasu Canyon, which is a small hidden branch of the Grand Canyon, never mind exactly where, I took with me only a one-quart canteen, thinking that would be enough water for a fourteen-mile downhill hike on a warm day in August. On the rim of the canyon the temperature was a tolerable ninety-six degrees, but it rose about one degree for each mile down and forward. Like a fool I rationed my water, drank sparingly, and could have died of sunstroke. When late in the afternoon I finally stumbled—sundazed, blear-eyed, parched as an old bacon rind—upon that blue stream which flows like a miraculous mirage across the canyon floor I was too exhausted to pause and drink soberly from the bank. Dreamily, deliriously, I slogged into the waist-deep water and fell on my face. Like a sponge I soaked up moisture through every pore, letting the current bear me along beneath a canopy of willow trees. I had no fear of drowning in the water—I intended to drink it all.—Edward Abbey, *Desert Solitaire*

4   The second example works in a different way. It is the second paragraph in an article about new architecture in Columbus, Indiana. The last part of the preceding paragraph is included so as to make the context clearer:

> ... it has become a bustling, vital community, a showcase of contemporary architecture—and the envy of urban developers everywhere.
>
> There are no fewer than 41 modern buildings, all designed by nationally and internationally famed architects. On Sundays, the citizens of Columbus worship in churches designed by Eero and Eliel Saarinen. They borrow books at a library built from the innovative plans of I. M. Pei and embellished with a bronze arch sculpted by Henry Moore. They shop in a glass-enclosed piazza designed by Cesar

246 Developing a Paragraph from a Topic Sentence

> Pelli, and send their children to schools conceived by architects Harry Weese, Eliot Noyes and John Warnecke. Along with distinctive new structures, the spirit and pride of Columbus have risen as well. All over town, old commercial buildings and residences are being fully restored. As Mayor Max Andress puts it, "A sense of quality has rubbed off all over Columbus."—*Time,* "Showplace on the Prairie"

5   The first sentence or topic sentence, makes the primary declaration: "There are no fewer than 41 modern buildings, all designed by nationally and internationally famed architects." The next three sentences are clearly an extension of this topic, listing specific architects and buildings. But at the fifth sentence something new, though related, occurs. The first part of the sentence, "Along with distinctive new structures . . . ," connects this sentence with the original topic sentence. But the remainder of the fifth sentence, ". . . the spirit and pride of Columbus have risen as well," adds a new element to the paragraph, amplifying the topic sentence. The last two sentences are, then, more clearly related to the fifth sentence than they are to the original topic sentence.

6   In the example below, the topic sentence, which is first, barely suggests a theme that is then played out in the rest of the paragraph:

> This autumnal mellowness usually lasts until the end of November. Then come days of quite another kind. The winter clouds grow, and bloom, and shed their starry crystals on every leaf and rock, and all the colors vanish like a sunset. The deer gather and hasten down their well-known trails, fearful of being snowbound. Storm succeeds storm, heaping snow on the cliffs and meadows, and bending the slender pines to the ground in wide arches, one over the other, clustering and interlacing like lodged wheat. Avalanches rush and boom from the shelving heights, piling immense heaps upon the frozen lake, and all the summer glory is buried and lost. Yet in the midst of this hearty winter the sun shines warm at times, calling the Douglas squirrel to frisk in the snowy pines and seek out his hidden

stores; and the weather is never so severe as to drive away the grouse and little nut-hatches and chickadees.—John Muir, "Shadow Lake"

The first sentence, or topic sentence, makes a suggestion of the coming of winter. The remaining sentences then show how the events around the author bring the "hearty winter." The paragraph below develops from a topic sentence in another way:

> The well's importance goes far beyond that. Its discovery indicates that a major new gas-exploration effort in the Tuscaloosa Sand geological formation of southern Louisiana is hitting pay zones. That promises new production not only for Louisiana but for an energy-hungry nation that counts natural gas as both its cleanest-burning and most critically scarce fuel. Last week the Louisiana Office of Conservation estimated that gas reserves in the Tuscaloosa Sand may reach 3 trillion cu. ft. That would be equal to 86% of last year's production in Louisiana, which leads the nation in gas output, and 18% of annual consumption in the whole country. To its discoverers that much gas would be worth $5.5 billion at existing wellhead prices on Louisiana's intrastate free market.—*Time*, "Giant Gas Gusher in Louisiana"

The topic sentence simply announces that the discovery of a new gas well has far-reaching significance. The rest of the paragraph then spells out the well's importance. Notice that the sentences form a kind of chain reaction to show quite literally how the importance of the gas well "goes far beyond that." In the second sentence, we learn that new explorations are "hitting pay zones," and that means, in the third sentence, new production for the nation, and that means, in the fourth sentence, a potential reserve of 3 trillion cubic feet, and that means, in the fifth sentence, a bountiful new supply, and that means, in the sixth sentence, a bountiful new income. Each sentence literally goes beyond the preceding sentence, just as the topic sentence predicts.

Paragraphs that are built upon topic sentences have diverse uses. In a piece of writing built upon some logical sequence, for example, topic-sentence paragraphs provide a neat, clear, and orderly method. Suppose, for example, you are explaining some process in which the stages must be made clear and in which each stage requires some additional explanation. In such an account a series of topic-sentence paragraphs may be especially useful; each paragraph might deal with a stage in the process, announced in a topic sentence at or near the first of the paragraph, with the particular stage being explained in the course of the paragraph. Certain kinds of emotional exhortation may be handled in topic-sentence paragraphs—each paragraph opens with a declaration in its topic sentence, for example, and the rest of the paragraph provides room to explore the strength and appeal of the declaration in particular circumstances.

Remember, too, that topic-sentence paragraphs are practical in a pinch. If inspiration doesn't come and all else fails, a declarative sentence and a series of quick illustrations (as in the Muir paragraph above) or a declarative sentence and one fully developed illustration (as in the Abbey paragraph above) will make a paragraph. Three or four declarative sentences (provided they are related in some way) and a double handful of vivid examples will make a short essay, such as you might write in an examination. No one can guarantee that such paragraphs or such an essay will be excellent, but sometimes when you are stuck, simple competence looks attractive.

Don't imagine, however, that topic-sentence paragraphs are just simple gimmicks. Development of a paragraph from a topic sentence is a method that may be useful to you any time you wish to be sure that a reader can follow with ease the sequence of your thinking. If, for example, the stages of your thinking on a given subject occur as topic sentences at the beginning of your paragraphs, then readers should have little difficulty tracking you. Notice how the topic sentences in the passage below do three things: they establish a theme for their paragraph, they connect with each other, and they conduct you through the author's sequence of thought:

Pulling Up Roots

Before 18, the motto is loud and clear: "I have to get away from my parents." But the words are seldom connected to action. Generally still safely part of our families, even if away at school, we feel our autonomy to be subject to erosion from moment to moment.

After 18, we begin Pulling Up Roots in earnest. College, military service, and short-term travels are all customary vehicles our society provides for the first round trips between family and a base of one's own. In the attempt to separate our view of the world from our family's view, despite vigorous protestations to the contrary—"I know exactly what I want!"—we cast about for any beliefs we can call our own. And in the process of testing those beliefs we are often drawn to fads, preferably those more mysterious and inaccessible to our parents.

Whatever tentative memberships we try out in the world, the fear haunts us that we are really kids who cannot take care of ourselves. We cover that fear with acts of defiance and mimicked confidence. For allies to replace our parents, we turn to our contemporaries. They become conspirators. So long as their perspective meshes with our own, they are able to substitute for the sanctuary of the family. But that doesn't last very long. And the instant they diverge from the shaky ideals of "our group," they are seen as betrayers. Rebounds to the family are common between the ages of 18 and 22.

The tasks of this passage are to locate ourselves in a peer group role, a sex role, an anticipated occupation, an ideology or world view. As a result, we gather the impetus to leave home physically and the identity to *begin* leaving home emotionally.

Even as one part of us seeks to be an individual, another part longs to restore the safety and comfort of merging with another. Thus one of the most popular myths of this passage is: We can piggyback our development by attaching to a Stronger One. But people who marry during this time often prolong financial and emotional ties to the family and relatives that impede them from becoming self-sufficient.

> A stormy passage through the Pulling Up Roots years will probably facilitate the normal progression of the adult life cycle. If one doesn't have an identity crisis at this point, it will erupt during a later transition, when the penalties may be harder to bear.—Gail Sheehy, *Passages*

11   Paragraphs developed from topic sentences have many uses, but notice that they don't all look alike and that not all paragraphs have clearly defined topic sentences.

12   Paragraphs with topic sentences (that is, sentences that identify the central theme of the paragraphs) come in different forms, as the examples shown a little earlier may suggest. Topic sentences themselves come in different forms. The kind of topic sentence I have been talking about (a single sentence establishing a subject or a theme for a paragraph) is a simple, more or less noticeable form.

13   Sometimes, however, it takes two sentences to establish a theme for a paragraph, and sometimes a topic or theme can only be discovered by assembling it from several sentences within a paragraph. In other words, you shouldn't expect all the paragraphs you read to have a clearly defined single topic sentence; neither should you suppose that all of your own paragraphs ought to have such a topic sentence. A recent study of paragraph form shows that somewhat fewer than half of the paragraphs examined had a single, plainly recognizable topic sentence. In the same sampling, only about 13% of the paragraphs began with the topic sentence. The same study shows, incidentally, that sometimes a topic sentence governs a series of paragraphs. Remember, however, that paragraphs developed from topic sentences are useful, and it's entirely likely and appropriate that you may be asked to write paragraphs with clear topic sentences and whole papers in which each paragraph has a clear topic sentence.

Questions for Discussion

1. According to Corder, what is a topic sentence, and how does it function in a paragraph?
2. The author gives several examples of how topic sentences function in paragraphs. Then he suggests another

way to use topic sentences: something to do when inspiration fails. Explain how this use works.
3. How do topic sentences help readers?
4. Do paragraphs always have topic sentences? If they don't, how does the reader know what the topic is?

29

Specific Details

DAVID SKWIRE AND
FRANCES CHITWOOD

Essay Preview: Questions to Answer as You Read

1. What is "abstract writing"?
2. What is wrong with abstract writing?
3. How can writers avoid abstract writing?
4. Can writers be too specific?

Specific Details

Abstract writing is writing that lacks specific details and is filled with vague, indefinite words and broad, general statements. Every piece of writing needs generalizations, of course, and vague words such as *nice* and *interesting* can be useful. But writing that is dominated by such words is abstract writing, and abstract writing is the main cause of bored readers. It is often a reflection of lazy or careless thinking. It can interfere with full communication of meaning. It prevents many students from developing their themes adequately. ("I've already said all I have to say. How am I supposed to get 300 more words on this subject?")

Abstract writing occurs when someone writes:

Too much poverty exists in this country.

INSTEAD OF

I see one-third of a nation ill-housed, ill-clad, ill-nourished.

Mr. Jones is a tough grader.

INSTEAD OF

Mr. Jones flunked 75% of his class and gave no higher than a C to the students who passed.

Don't fire until they're extremely close.
INSTEAD OF
Don't fire until you see the whites of their eyes.

The story is quite amusing in places, but basically is very serious.
INSTEAD OF
Underneath the slapstick humor, the story presents a bitter attack on materialism and snobbishness.

Religious faith is important, but practical considerations are also important.
INSTEAD OF
Trust in God, and keep your powder dry.

3 Nothing is technically wrong with the above examples of abstract writing, but we need only compare them to the rewritten concrete versions to see their basic inadequacy. They convey less information. They are less interesting. They have less impact. There is nothing wrong with them except they are no good.

4 The use of specific details is the most direct way to avoid abstract writing. We tend to get irritated with a politician—or college dean—who, when confronted by a crucial issue, releases a press statement declaring, "We will give this matter our careful consideration." We get irritated not because the matter doesn't require careful consideration, but because the abstractness of the statement makes us suspect that we have just received a strong whiff of hot air. That suspicion will probably decrease significantly if the statement goes on to tell us the names of the people who will confer on this issue next Monday under orders to present recommendations within two weeks, those recommendations to be acted on inside of forty-eight hours. In this case, the specific details have served to support the generalization, have given us a clear notion of what the generalization means, and have helped create an impression of seriousness and sincerity.

254 Specific Details

Politicians and college deans are not the only people who sometimes seem too fond of hot air. Much of the material we read every day is abstract: flabby, dull, vague, and essentially meaningless. Like hot air, it lacks real body, real substance. The sports columnist writes, "The team should do better this year," and leaves it at that, instead of adding, "It should finish in third or fourth place and even has a fighting chance for the pennant." The teacher writes an angry letter saying, "This school ignores all vital needs of the faculty," and sounds like just another crank unless the letter goes on and points to *specific* needs that have in fact been ignored.

Student writing, from essay exams to themes in composition courses, could be vastly improved if more attention were paid to eliminating excessive abstraction and adding specific details. The more specific details, the less chance of hot air. Students should not tolerate the same things in their own writing that antagonize them in someone else's. Our use of language, not to mention our level of thought, would probably improve a hundredfold if we established an informal rule *never* to make an unsupported general statement, a general statement not backed up by specific details.

This rule sounds easy enough, but it means what it says. It means a writer should never try to get by with sentences such as, "The day was too hot"; "The hero of the story was very ambitious"; "The establishment is corrupt"; "The Industrial Revolution brought about many changes." These sentences are neither ungrammatical nor necessarily incorrect, but if they are not backed up by specific details they are worthless. "The day was too hot" is uninteresting and unpersuasive. *Back it up.* The reader should know that the temperature was 93 degrees, that Bill's sweaty glasses kept slipping off his nose, that even the little kids who usually filled the street were inside trying to keep cool, that a cocker spaniel who had managed to find a spot of shade was too exhausted and miserable to bother brushing away the flies. Whatever the piece of writing—a letter of application for a job, an analysis of a short story, a final exam in history—specific details give the writing life and conviction that abstractions alone can never achieve.

One more point about specific details: within reason, *the*

more specific the better. As long as the detail is relevant—as long, that is, as it backs up the generalization and is not instantly obvious as too trivial for consideration—the writer is unlikely to go wrong by being too specific. On a history exam, a student may generalize, "In the Revolutionary War, the Americans had many difficulties." As specific support for that statement, the student may go on to write, "The number of Tories was quite large." But better in all respects would be, "Tories numbered as much as 30% of the population." The more specific the better, and one can almost always be more specific. Eventually, it is true, one can defeat one's purpose; it would be a mistake to give the reader the names and addresses of all the Tories during the Revolutionary War. The writing would then become so overwhelmed by specifics that the major point would be lost. Elementary common sense is usually the best guide in preventing that kind of mistake, and in actual practice few student writers run up against the problem of being too specific.

9   To summarize: support all your generalizations with relevant specific details. Remember that, within reason, the more specific the details, the better the writing.

Abstract (weak)

The telephone is a great scientific achievement, but it can also be a great inconvenience. Who could begin to count the number of times that phone calls have come from unwelcome people or on unwelcome occasions? Telephones make me nervous.

More Specific (better)

The telephone is a great scientific achievement, but it can also be a great pain. I get calls from bill collectors, hurt relatives, salespeople, charities and angry neighbors. The calls always seem to come at the worst times too. They've interrupted my meals, my baths, my parties, my sleep. I couldn't get along without telephones, but sometimes they make me a nervous wreck.

Still More Specific (much better)

The telephone is a great scientific achievement, but it can also be a great big headache. More often than not, that cheery ringing in my ears brings messages from the Ace Bill Collecting Agency, my mother (who is feeling snubbed for the fourth time that week), salesmen of encyclopedias and magazines, solicitors for the Policeman's Ball and Disease of the Month Foundation, and neighbors complaining about my dog. That's not to mention frequent wrong numbers—usually for someone named "Arnie." The calls always seem to come at the worst times, too. They've interrupted steak dinners, hot tubs, Friday night parties, and Saturday morning sleep-ins. There's no escape. Sometimes I wonder if there are any telephones in padded cells.

Questions for Discussion

1. Here are the preview questions again. Now you should be able to answer them:
   a. What is "abstract writing"?
   b. What is wrong with abstract writing?
   c. How can writers avoid abstract writing?
   d. Can writers be too specific?
2. Compare the three examples at the end of the essay. What specific details make the second one better than the first? What, specifically, makes the third better than the second?

30

The Maker's Eye: Revising Your Own Manuscripts

DONALD M. MURRAY

Essay Preview: Questions to Answer as You Read

1. How must writers read what they've written in order to revise it?
2. What seven things should writers look for when revising their work?
3. What does the "maker's eye" do while revising?

The Maker's Eye: Revising Your Own Manuscripts

1   When the beginning writer completes his first draft, he usually reads it through to correct typographical errors and considers the job of writing done. When the professional writer completes his first draft, he usually feels he is at the start of the writing process. Now that he has a draft he can begin writing.

2   That difference in attitude is the difference between amateur and professional, inexperience and experience, journeyman and craftsman. Peter F. Drucker, the prolific business writer, for example, calls his first draft "the zero draft"—after that he can start counting. Most productive writers share the feeling that the first draft—and most of those which follow—is an opportunity to discover what they have to say and how they can best say it.

3   To produce a progression of drafts, each of which says more and says it better, the writer has to develop a special reading skill. In school we are taught to read what is on the page. We try to comprehend what the author has said, what he meant, and what are the implications of his words.

4   The writer of such drafts must be his own best enemy. He must accept the criticism of others and be suspicious of it; he must accept the praise of others and be even more suspicious of it. He cannot depend on others. He must detach himself from his own page so that he can apply both his caring and his craft to his own work.

5   Detachment is not easy. Science fiction writer Ray Bradbury supposedly puts each manuscript away for a year and then rereads it as a stranger. Not many writers can afford the time to do this. We must read when our judgment may be at its worst, when we are close to the euphoric moment of creation. The writer "should be critical of everything that seems to him most delightful in his style," advises novelist Nancy Hale. "He should excise what he most admires, because he wouldn't thus admire it if he weren't . . . in a sense protecting it from criticism."

6   The writer must learn to protect himself from his own ego, when it takes the form of uncritical pride or uncritical self-destruction. As poet John Ciardi points out, " . . . the last act of the writing must be to become one's own reader. It is, I suppose, a schizophrenic process, to begin passionately and to end critically, to begin hot and to end cold; and, more important, to be passion-hot and critic-cold at the same time."

7   Just as dangerous as the protective writer is the despairing one, who thinks everything he does is terrible, dreadful, awful. If he is to publish, he must save what is effective on his page while he cuts away what doesn't work. The writer must hear and respect his own voice.

8   Remember how each craftsman you have seen—the carpenter eyeing the level of a shelf, the mechanic listening to the motor—takes the instinctive step back. This is what the writer has to do when he reads his own work. "The writer must survey his work critically, coolly, and as though he were a stranger to it," says children's book writer Eleanor Estes. "He must be willing to prune, expertly and hard-heartedly.

At the end of each revision, a manuscript may look like a battered old hive, worked over, torn apart, pinned together, added to, deleted from, words changed and words changed back. Yet the book must maintain its original freshness and spontaneity."

9   It is far easier for most beginning writers to understand the need for rereading and rewriting than it is to understand how to go about it. The publishing writer doesn't necessarily break down the various stages of rewriting and editing, he just goes ahead and does it. One of our most prolific fiction writers, Anthony Burgess, says, "I might revise a page twenty times." Short story and children's writer Roald Dahl states, "By the time I'm nearing the end of a story, the first part will have been reread and altered and corrected at least 150 times. . . . Good writing is essentially rewriting. I am positive of this."

10   There is nothing virtuous in the rewriting process. It is simply an essential condition of life for most writers. There are writers who do very little rewriting, mostly because they have the capacity and experience to create and review a large number of invisible drafts in their minds before they get to the page. And many writers perform all of the tasks of revision simultaneously, page by page, rather than draft by draft. But it is still possible to break down the process of rereading one's own work into the sequence most published writers follow and which the beginning writer should follow as he studies his own page.

11   Many writers at first just scan their manuscript, reading as quickly as possible for problems of subject and form. In this way, they stand back from the more technical details of language so they can spot any weaknesses in content or in organization. When the writer reads his manuscript, he is usually looking for seven elements.

12   The first is *subject*. Do you have anything to say? If you are lucky, you will find that indeed you do have something to say, perhaps a little more than you expected, If the subject is not clear, or if it is not yet limited or defined enough for you to handle, don't go on. What you have to say is always more important than how you say it.

13   The next point to check is *audience*. It is true that you

should write primarily for yourself, in the sense that you should be true to yourself. But the aim of writing is communication, not just self-expression. You should, in reading your piece, ask yourself if there is an audience for what you have written, if anyone will need or enjoy what you have to say.

14 *Form* should then be considered after audience. Form, or genre, is the vehicle which will carry what you have to say to your audience, and it should grow out of your subject. If you have a character, your subject may grow into a short story, a magazine profile, a novel, a biography, or a play. It depends on what you have to say and to whom you wish to say it. When you reread your own manuscript, you must ask yourself if the form is suitable, if it works, and if it will carry your meaning to your reader.

15 Once you have the appropriate form, look at the *structure,* the order of what you have to say. Every good piece of writing is built on a solid framework of logic or argument or narrative or motivation; it is a line which runs through the entire piece of writing and holds it together. If you read your own manuscript and cannot spot this essential thread, stop writing until you have found something to hold your writing together.

16 The manuscript which has order must also have *development.* Each part of it must be built in a way that will prepare the reader for the next part. Description, documentation, action, dialogue, metaphor—these and many other devices flesh out the skeleton so that the reader will be able to understand what is written. How much development? That's like asking how much lipstick or how much garlic. It depends on the girl or on the casserole. This is the question that the writer will be answering as he reads his piece of writing through from beginning to end, and answering it will lead him to the sixth element.

17 The writer must be sure of his *dimensions.* This means that there should be something more than structure and development, that there should be a pleasing proportion between all of the parts. You cannot decide on a dimension without seeing all of the parts of writing together. You have to examine each section of the writing in its relationship to all of the other sections.

18 Finally, the writer has to listen for *tone*. Any piece of writing is held together by that invisible force, the writer's voice. Tone is his style, tone is all that is on the page and off the page, tone is grace, wit, anger—the spirit which drives a piece of writing forward. Look back to those manuscripts you most admire, and you will discover that there is a coherent tone, an authoritative voice holding the whole thing together.

19 When the writer feels that he has a draft which has subject, audience, form, structure, development, dimension, and tone, then he is ready to begin the careful process of line-by-line editing. Each line, each word has to be right. As Paul Gallico has said, " . . . every successful writer is primarily a good editor."

20 Now the writer reads his own copy with infinite care. He often reads aloud, calling on his ear's experience with language. Does this sound right—or this? He reads and listens and revises, back and forth from eye to page to ear to page. I find I must do this careful editing at short runs, fifteen or twenty minutes, or I become too kind with myself.

21 Slowly the writer moves from word to word, looking through the word to see the subject. Good writing is, in a sense, invisible. It should enable the reader to see the subject, not the writer. Every word should be true—true to what the writer has to say. And each word must be precise in its relation to the words which have gone before and the words which will follow.

22 This sounds tedious, but it isn't. Making something right is immensely satisfying, and the writer who once was lost in a swamp of potentialities now has the chance to work with the most technical skills of language. And even in the process of the most careful editing, there is the joy of language. Words have double meanings, even triple and quadruple meanings. Each word has its own tone, its opportunity for connotation and denotation and nuance. And when you connect words, there is always the chance of the sudden insight, the unexpected clarification.

23 The maker's eye moves back and forth from word to phrase to sentence to paragraph to sentence to phrase to word. He looks at his sentences for variety and balance in form and structure, and at the interior of the paragraph for

coherence, unity and emphasis. He plays with figurative language, decides to repeat or not, to create a parallelism for emphasis. He works over his copy until he achieves a manuscript which appears effortless to the reader.

24 I learned something about this process when I first wore bifocals. I thought that when I was editing I was working line by line. But I discovered that I had to order reading (or, in my case, editing) glasses, even though the bottom sections of my bifocals have a greater expanse of glass than ordinary glasses. While I am editing, my eyes are unconsciously flicking back and forth across the whole page, or back to another page, or forward to another page. The limited bifocal view through the lower half of my glasses is not enough. Each line must be seen in its relationship to every other line.

25 When does this process end? Most writers agree with the great Russian novelist Tolstoy, who said, "I scarcely ever reread my published writings, but if by chance I come across a page, it always strikes me: all this must be rewritten; this is how I should have written it."

26 The maker's eye is never satisfied, for he knows that each word in his copy is tentative. Writing, to the writer, is alive, something that is full of potential and alternative, something which can grow beyond its own dream. The writer reads to discover what he has said—and then to say it better.

27 A piece of writing is never finished. It is delivered to a deadline, torn out of the typewriter on demand, sent off with a sense of frustration and incompleteness. Just as the writer knows he must stop avoiding writing and write, he also knows he must send his copy off to be published, although it is not quite right yet—if only he had another couple of days, just another run at it, perhaps . . . .

Questions for Discussion

1. Murray's original audience for this essay on advice about writing was beginning writers—people wanting to publish what they write. Find evidence that this was his intended audience. Then name several instances of how his advice can apply also to student writers.

2. Summarize what Murray says about each of the seven elements writers must look for when revising their work.
3. What does the "maker's eye" do in revision?
4. When does revision end?

Appendixes

Appendix A

Connectors and Their Uses

Coordinating Conjunctions

Used to join two independent clauses. Preceded by a comma.

Contrast	*Addition*
but	and
yet	
	Alternatives
Result	or
so	nor
for	

EXAMPLE

Twenty-five people arrived for the lecture, *but* the speaker was not one of them.

Do NOT use a comma when the second subject is omitted:

Twenty-five people arrived for the lecture *but* had to return home without hearing the speaker.

Subordinating Conjunctions

Used to join an independent and a subordinate clause. Ordinarily, use a comma if the conjunction comes before the first clause; usually no comma if before the second clause.

Time	*Contrast*	*Purpose*
after	although	so as
as	even though	so that

as long as	though	in order that
as soon as	whereas	
before		*Condition*
since	*Cause*	if
until	as	unless
when	because	
whenever	since	*Degree*
while		as far as
		so far as

EXAMPLE

Although twenty-five people arrived for the lecture, they had to return home again *because* the speaker didn't arrive.

Transitional Adverbs

NOT conjunctions. If they are used to link a second clause with a first, they *must* be preceded by a *semicolon*.

Example	*Contrast*	*Addition*
for example	however	also
for instance	instead	finally
(*not* such as)	nevertheless	furthermore
	on the other hand	in addition
Result	otherwise	indeed
accordingly		in fact
consequently		likewise
therefore		meanwhile
thus		moreover
		then

EXAMPLE

Twenty-five people arrived for the lecture; *however,* they had to return home because the speaker didn't arrive.

Prepositions

NOT conjunctions. Prepositions are followed by objects: *at home, during lunch hour, at any time, for the moment.*

at	down	on
about	during	over
above	except	since
across	for	through
before	from	to
behind	in	under
below	into	until
between	like	with
by	of	without

EXAMPLE

Although twenty-five people arrived *for the lecture,* they were unable to hear it because the speaker's plane couldn't land *during the snowstorm.*

Appendix B

Glossary of Key Terms

Note: Cross-references to words defined in this glossary (or related words) are given in boldface. Examples of the term being defined are underlined.

analogy   a type of **comparison** that refers to a familiar thing for the purpose of explaining something else:

> Light waves act like waves of water when they encounter an obstacle.

appositive   a noun (or noun phrase) that precedes or follows another noun and renames that noun:

> Sheba, a Welsh Corgi, barks at anyone who walks down the alley.

cause and effect   a means of developing an idea by showing how one thing brings about another. It may be one cause and several effects, one effect with several causes, or a chain reaction of causes and effects.

classification   a means of developing a subject through arranging it in classes or groups; for example, contact lenses may be classified as hard, soft, and extended-wear.

clause   a grammatical element made up of a group of words containing a subject and a verb plus **modifiers** and **complements**. An independent clause can stand grammatically as a sentence; a **subordinate** clause cannot.

coherence   the quality of being logically integrated. An essay that has coherence "hangs together": all of its parts are clearly interrelated to make up a logical whole. A writer uses a number of devices to achieve coherence, the most common being a clearly stated **thesis,** logical organization, **transitions** (words, phrases, and sentences), and **repetition** of key words.

comparison   a means of developing an idea by showing similarities and differences between two subjects. It may address one subject first and then the other, or both subjects together point-by-point.

complement   a word or group of words that follows a verb and completes the idea begun by the subject and verb. The complements are underlined in these sentences:

> One of the first things a skier learns is <u>how to fall</u>.
> David has become the best <u>skier</u> on the slopes.
> He has learned his <u>lesson</u> well.

conclusion   the ending of an **essay,** usually a single brief **paragraph.** It can restate the **thesis, summarize** the major points, refer to material brought up in the **introduction,** and/or in some other way drive home the point of the essay.

coordination   the grammatical procedure of tying together two or more similar sentence elements with one of these conjunctions: *and, but, or, nor, for, so, yet.* Any sentence elements (nouns, verbs, phrases, **clauses,** for example) can be joined, as long as those joined are of the same kind (nouns, verbs, etc.).

editing   a procedure performed on a rough draft for the purpose of revising words and sentences and correcting errors.

emphasis   stress on a word, sentence, idea, etc., commonly achieved by (1) order of arrangement (final position usually being strongest), (2) contrast (a brief sentence or **paragraph** surrounded by others of greater length), or (3) **repetition.**

essay a short piece of non-fictional writing that presents and supports a single idea. It is usually characterized by an **introduction** that includes a **thesis statement,** a **conclusion** that reiterates the point, and several **paragraphs** in between that develop the idea. Essays may be **expository,** persuasive, argumentative, narrative, or descriptive.

exposition a kind of **essay** that explains a point by means of such organizational patterns as **classification, comparison, cause and effect,** process analysis, example, definition, and **analogy.**

free writing a pre-writing technique used to bring out the writer's ideas on a subject. It is usually done fast, without interruptions, and without concern for form.

imitation trying to do something the way someone else does. Writers may observe how others write—how they use words and sentences, how they arrange their ideas, how they achieve **coherence,** etc.—and then try to write in a similar way.

introduction the beginning of an **essay,** usually several sentences long. It usually presents the subject, states the **thesis,** and clarifies the writer's attitude toward the subject. It may also address the reader, describe the setting, give background information, or in other ways lead the reader into the subject.

modifier a word, phrase, or **clause** that describes another word. An adjective modifies (or describes) a noun or pronoun; an adverb modifies (or describes the action of) a verb and may also modify an adjective or another adverb.

narrative or narration, the story of how something happened. It may make up an entire **essay** or be a portion of an essay that develops one aspect of a subject. Sometimes an essay begins with a short narrative in order to catch the reader's interest.

non-restrictive usually refers to modifying **clauses** (like those beginning with *who* or *which*) and **appositives**. A non-restrictive clause or appositive is not essential to the meaning of a sentence and is therefore treated as an interruption, set off with commas, dashes, or parentheses. See also **restrictive**.

> **non-restrictive clause:** Brian, <u>who is a theater major,</u> rehearses the new play every night until 1:00 A.M.
>
> **non-restrictive appositive:** Brian, <u>a theater major</u>, rehearses the new play every night until 1:00 A.M.

paragraph a unit of writing, usually made up of several related sentences as part of a larger piece. A paragraph has unity of thought, completeness in discussing a given aspect of a subject, and **coherence**. One of its sentences often is its **topic sentence**.

participial phrase a group of words consisting of a **participle** and its **modifiers** and/or **complements**. The phrase functions as a modifier of a noun. In both examples below, the participial phrase modifies *organizers*.

> <u>Concerned about nuclear arms proliferation</u>, organizers of peace movements throughout the country try to increase citizen awareness.
>
> Organizers of peace movements throughout the country, <u>seeing the continued proliferation of nuclear arms</u>, try to increase citizen awareness.

participle a verb form that, in regular verbs, ends in *-ed* or *-ing*. (For irregular verbs, participles are shown in dictionaries with the verb they derive from. Under *begin,* for example, the past participle is *begun.*) To be a verb, a participle must be accompanied by an auxiliary verb. That is, a past participle (*-ed*) must be accompanied by a form of *have* (<u>has talked</u>, <u>had typed</u>), and a present participle (*-ing*) must have a form of *be* (is singing, are going, was drying, were discussing, etc.). Without one of these auxiliary verbs, a participle functions as an adjective **modifier** or as a noun (a gerund). With the addition of related words, participles can make up **participial phrases** and gerund phrases. The sentences below illustrate participles as (1) verb, (2) gerund, and (3) modifier.

(1) Bart has guessed wrong nine times out of ten in his office football pool. (verb)
(2) Guessing is productive only when backed up by knowledge. (gerund—a noun functioning as subject of the sentence)
(3) Bart has decided to give up the guessing game. (modifier—adjective describing *game*)

proofreading a final, meticulous reading of a piece of writing, done for the purpose of discovering errors. Proofreading should not be confused with **editing** or **revising,** which are done at an earlier stage in the writing process.

repetition repeated words and phrases, often done to achieve **emphasis** and **coherence.** Since repeated sentence elements draw attention to themselves, unimportant items should not be repeated unnecessarily.

restrictive usually refers to modifying **clauses** (like those beginning with *who* or *that*) and **appositives.** A restrictive clause or appositive is essential to the meaning of a sentence and is therefore not set off as an interruption. That is, it is not enclosed in commas (or dashes or parentheses). See also **non-restrictive.**

restrictive clause: The water-cooled breeze that blows off of Lake Michigan is a chilling tribulation in the spring but a welcome relief in the summer.

restrictive appositive: My brother Karl was one of the last people to have polio before vaccines were produced.

Glossary of Key Terms

revise literally, to "see again"—to reread and rework a piece of writing in order to improve it. Revision may consist of addition, deletion, or substitution and may be done at the levels of words, sentences, **paragraphs,** and the entire work. Revision is done while the writer is composing and after a first draft has been completed. Successive drafts will receive further revision.

subordination a grammatical procedure that makes one sentence element dependent on another. Less important ideas may be subordinated, whereas main ideas are stated in independent **clauses.** A subordinate clause does not stand alone as a sentence; it must be connected to an independent clause.

> When the union members made their wage concessions, they expected to be able to keep their jobs.

summary a short restatement of the important ideas in a piece of writing. It is sometimes used at the **conclusion** of one's own writing to restate major points. It is also used to convey in a brief form the ideas of another person.

thesis statement a sentence that conveys the main idea of an **essay,** usually occurring near the end of the **introduction.** A well-phrased thesis will present not only the subject of the essay but also the point, as this sentence illustrates:

> Values learned at the video arcade are not the kind that will benefit society.

The first part of the sentence (up to *are*) states the subject, and the second part the point.

tone the style of an **essay** that results from a writer's attitude toward the subject. By choice of words, phrasing, and details, and in other ways, a writer conveys humor, seriousness, anger, cynicism, and so on.

topic sentence a sentence that conveys the main idea of a **paragraph,** occurring often at the beginning of a paragraph but in other positions as well.

transition a link between what follows and what went before, showing how the two are related. It can be a word (like *but, therefore, because*), a phrase (like *on the other hand*), a **clause,** a complete sentence, or even sometimes a brief **paragraph.** A piece of writing achieves **coherence** in part through effective use of transitions.

Index

Abstract writing, 252–256
Analogy, 90–98
Angelou, Maya, "Mr. McElroy," 57–63
Appositives, 185–186
"Arctic Storm, The" (Russell), 113–120
Asimov, Isaac, "Beginning," 215–224
Attitude of author, 18, 78, 101. *See also* Tone
Audience, 51, 55, 102, 133–134, 155, 190, 201, 259–260. *See also* Readers
Authority of writer, 56, 93, 97, 116, 143, 190, 235

"Beginning" (Asimov), 215–224
"Beginning of a Word, The" (Hamilton), 22–29
"Blubber on Ice" (Murphy), 83–89
"Bounty of the Sea, The" (Cousteau), 188–196

Cause and effect, 99–105, 139–146, 188–196, 202, 228, 231, 232, 239–243
Chitwood, Frances, and David Skwire, "Specific Details," 252–256
Classification and division, 129–138, 229, 231, 239–243
Coherence, 9, 26, 125, 128, 192–193

Colons, 52–53
Comma splices, 26–27, 36. *See also* Coordination
Commas, 11, 60–62, 71–72, 94–95
Comparison and contrast, 90–98, 121–128, 147–157, 202, 215–224, 228, 232, 239–243
Compound sentences, 26–27, 35–36, 43–45
Conjunctions
  adverbial, 125–127
  coordinating, 10, 19, 26, 71
Controlling idea, 117. *See also* Thesis statement *and* Point of an essay
Coordination, 11, 19, 71–72, 79–80, 103, 185–186, 203, 229–230
Corder, Jim W., "Developing a Paragraph from a Topic Sentence," 244–251
Correctness, 49–52
Cousteau, Jacques, "The Bounty of the Sea," 188–196

D'Angelo, Frank, "Probing for Ideas," 239–243
Definition, 22–29, 197–206
Description, 57–63, 75–82, 158–167, 239–243
"Developing a Paragraph from a Topic Sentence" (Corder), 244–251

Index

Development, 260, *See also* Modes of writing
Dialogue, 20, 211
Dimensions, 260
Dyslexia, 139–143

"Echoes of Grief" (Lessing), 75–82
Eiseley, Loren, "The Hidden Teacher," 207–214
Emphasis, 80
Essay preview, 2. *See also each chapter*
Examples, 25, 134, 229, 232, 239–243, 248
Exploring ideas. *See* Invention
Exposition, 5–13, 142, 225–232

Figurative language, 162–164, 182
Fisher, Dorothy Canfield, "Theme Writing," 235–238
Form, 108, 110–111, 153, 211, 237, 260
Fragments, 60, 153–155
Free writing, 46, 62, 81–82, 166–167, 213, 235–236

Generalizations, 245, 252–256
"Good and Bad" (Roberts), 48–56
Goodman, Ellen, "The New Ambidexters," 147–157
"Great Process, The" (Schwabe), 39–47

Habitual action, 86, 89
Hamilton, Edith, "Play in Ancient Greece," 225–232
Hamilton, J. Wallace, "The Beginning of a Word," 22–29
Heuristics. *See* Invention
"Hidden Teacher, The" (Eiseley), 207–214

Holt, John, "Three Disciplines for Children," 129–138

Imitation, 1–2, 3–4, 229. *See also each chapter*
Independent clauses, 11, 26–27, 35, 44, 52–53
Introductions, 43, 70, 85, 151, 237
Invention, 239–243. *See also* Free writing
 lists, 37, 137, 152
 questions, 20, 88, 127–128, 145, 204
 topics of, 239–243

Jeans, Sir James, "Why the Sky Looks Blue," 90–98

Key words, repetition of, for coherence, 9, 26, 125, 128, 193, 219

Lessing, Doris, "Echoes of Grief," 75–82
"Letter of Complaint," 106–112
"Lift Your Feet" (Ward), 99–105

McCarthy, Michael D., "Ticaspleeze and Trees," 158–167
 "Ticaspleeze and Trees (Revision)," 168–187
McPhee, John, "What Color Is an Orange?" 121–128
"Maker's Eye, The: Revising Your Own Manuscripts" (Murray), 257–263
Meaning of an essay, 8, 20–21, 213. *See also* Point of an essay
Metaphor, 92, 163, 164
Models, 1–2, 4, 12–13. *See also each chapter*

Index

Modes of writing, 240. *See also* Cause and effect; Classification and division; Comparison and contrast; Description; Exposition, Narration; Persuasion; Process analysis
"Mr. McElroy" (Angelou), 57–63
Murphy, Robert Cushman, "Blubber on Ice," 83–89
Murray, Donald M., "The Maker's Eye: Revising Your Own Manuscripts," 257–263

Narration, 14–21, 75–82, 113–120, 158–167, 207–214, 239–243
"New Ambidexters, The" (Goodman), 147–157
Newspaper column, writing assignment, 155–157
Nominative absolutes, 117–118

Observation, 64–70, 116, 119
Organization, 20, 25, 34, 37, 43, 46, 78, 82, 93, 98, 136–137, 152, 191, 213. *See also* Outlines *and* Modes of writing
Outlines, 7, 25, 34, 36, 51, 55, 78, 88, 94, 98, 101, 124, 132, 146, 192, 202, 211, 213, 218, 229, 231

Paragraphs, 133, 153, 156, 185, 244–251
Parallel structure, 79–80, 185–186, 193–194
Participles, 86–87, 102–103, 117–118, 165–166
Persona of writer. *See* Authority of writer
Persuasion, 48–56, 188–196

"Play in Ancient Greece" (Hamilton), 225–232
Point of an essay, 8–9, 59, 62–63, 70, 73, 132–133, 150–151, 211, 231. *See also* Meaning of an essay *and* Thesis statement
Pollution, 189–193
"Preface to Reversals" (Simpson), 139–146
Prepositions, 79–80
Prewriting, 40, 42, 45, 46. *See also* Invention *and* Free writing
"Probing for Ideas" (D'Angelo), 239–243
Process analysis, 30–38, 39–47, 83–89, 202, 239–243
Process of writing, 39–47, 168–187, 235–238, 239–243, 244–251, 252–256, 257–263
Proofreading, 13, 206
Purpose for writing, 18, 25, 51, 70, 73, 85, 93, 117, 150. *See also* Point of an essay

Questions for discussion, 3
Questions for exploring ideas. *See* Invention
Quotations, 17, 18–19, 20, 70, 143, 146, 205, 211

Readers, 29, 37–38, 63, 248. *See also* Audience
"Reading by Leaps and Bounds" (Smith), 197–206
Reference, citing of, 205
Relative clauses, 60–62, 94–96, 202–203
Repetition, 9, 26, 72, 79, 125, 193, 212, 219, 220–221
Revision, 41–42, 168–187, 236–237, 257–263. *See also* end of each writing assignment

Roberts, Paul, "Good and Bad," 48–56
Rosin, L. Daniel, "Summary of 'Take This Fish,' " 64–74
Russell, Bertrand, "What I Have Lived For," 5–13
Russell, Franklin, "The Arctic Storm," 113–120

Saccades, 198–202
Schwabe, Tom, "The Great Process," 39–47
Scudder, Samuel H., "Take This Fish and Look at It," 66–70
Semicolons, 26, 35, 44, 52–53
Sentence patterning, 3–4. *See also each chapter*
Serendipity, 22–24
Setting, 88, 210, 214
"Shearing Sheep in Patagonia" (Simpson), 14–21
Simile, 92, 164
Simpson, Eileen, "Preface to *Reversals*," 139–146
Simpson, George Gaylord, "Shearing Sheep in Patagonia," 14–21
Skwire, David, and Frances Chitwood, "Specific Details," 252–256
Smith, Donald E. P., ed., "Spelling Is Nonsense," 30–38
Smith, Frank, "Reading by Leaps and Bounds," 197–206
Specific details, 17, 25, 59, 63, 77, 85, 108, 110, 116, 134, 164–165, 187, 191, 252–256
"Specific Details" (Skwire and Chitwood), 252–256
Specific words, 8, 13, 82, 116
Speech communities, 48–56

Spelling, 30–35, 184–185
"Spelling Is Nonsense" (Smith, ed.), 30–38
Structure, 260. *See also* Outlines
Style, 79, 124–125, 165
Subject of an essay, 51, 151–152, 213, 259
Subordination, 125–127, 134–136, 144, 194, 202–203, 220–221
"Summary of 'Take This Fish' " (Rosin), 64–74

"Take This Fish and Look at It" (Scudder), 66–70
"Theme Writing" (Fisher), 235–238
Thesis statement, 8–9, 12, 18, 21, 34, 43, 73, 94, 117, 124, 132–133, 142–143, 150, 151–152, 161–162, 191, 202, 211, 218, 228–229
"This," avoiding vagueness of, 108–109
"Three Disciplines for Children" (Holt), 129–138
"Ticaspleeze and Trees" (McCarthy), 158–167
"Ticaspleeze and Trees (Revision)" (McCarthy), 168–187
Tone, 18, 42, 85, 108, 261. *See also* Attitude of author
Topic sentences, 28–29, 133, 244–251
Transitions, 43–45, 70–71, 85–86, 151, 192–193, 223–224. *See also* Coherence

Verbs, 71–72, 82, 86, 89, 103, 117
Vocabulary preview, 2. *See also each chapter*

Index

Ward, Andrew, "Lift Your Feet," 99–105
"What" clauses, 144
"What Color Is an Orange?" (McPhee), 121–128
"What I Have Lived For" (Russell), 5–13

"Why the Sky Looks Blue" (Jeans), 90–98
Writer, role of. *See* Authority of writer
Writing assignments, 4. *See also each chapter*

Acknowledgments

Bertrand Russell, "What I Have Lived For." From *The Autobiography of Bertrand Russell, 1872–1914.* © George Allen and Unwin Ltd., 1967. Reprinted by permission of George Allen & Unwin (Publishers) Ltd.

George Gaylord Simpson, "Shearing Sheep in Patagonia." Reprinted with permission of Macmillan Publishing Company from *Attending Marvels: A Patagonian Journal* by George Gaylord Simpson. Copyright 1934 by Macmillan Publishing Co., Inc., renewed 1962 by George Gaylord Simpson.

J. Wallace Hamilton, "The Beginning of a Word." From *Serendipity* by J. Wallace Hamilton. Copyright © 1965 by Florence Newlan Hamilton. Reprinted by permission.

Donald E. P. Smith, "Spelling Is Nonsense." From *Learning to Learn* by Donald E. P. Smith, © 1961 by Harcourt Brace Jovanovich, Inc. Reprinted by permission of the publisher.

Tom Schwabe, "The Great Process." Copyright © 1985 by Tom Schwabe. Used by permission of the author.

Paul Roberts, "Good and Bad." From *Understanding English* by Paul Roberts. Copyright © 1958 by Paul Roberts. Reprinted by permission of Harper & Row, Publishers, Inc.

Maya Angelou, "Mr. McElroy." From *I Know Why the Caged Bird Sings* by Maya Angelou. Copyright © 1969 by Maya Angelou. Reprinted by permission of Random House, Inc.

L. Daniel Rosin, "Summary of 'Take This Fish.' " Copyright © 1985 by J. Daniel Rosin. Used by permission of the author.

Doris Lessing, "Echoes of Grief." From *Particularly Cats* by Doris Lessing. Copyright © 1967 by Doris Lessing Productions Ltd. Reprinted by permission of Simon & Schuster, Inc., and Michael Joseph Ltd.

Robert Cushman Murphy, "Blubber on Ice." Reprinted with permission of Macmillan Publishing Company and Robert Hale Ltd. from *Logbook for Grace* by Robert Cushman Murphy. Copyright 1947 by Robert Cushman Murphy, renewed 1975 by Grace E. Barston Murphy.

Sir James Jeans, "Why the Sky Looks Blue." From *The Stars in Their Courses* by Sir James Jeans, copyright 1931. Reprinted by permission of the publisher, Cambridge University Press.

Acknowledgments

Andrew Ward, "Lift Your Feet." Excerpted from *Fits and Starts: The Premature Memoirs of Andrew Ward* by Andrew Ward. Copyright © 1970 by Andrew Ward. Reprinted by permission.

Franklin Russell, "The Arctic Storm." From *Watchers at the Pond* by Franklin Russell. Copyright © 1961 by Franklin Russell. Reprinted by permission of Alfred A. Knopf, Inc., and Curtis Brown Associates, Ltd.

John McPhee, "What Color Is an Orange?" Reprinted by permission of Farrar, Straus and Giroux. Excerpt adapted from *Oranges* by John McPhee. Copyright © 1966, 1967 by John McPhee. This material first appeared in *The New Yorker*.

John Holt, "Three Disciplines for Children." From *Freedom and Beyond*, pp. 102–104, copyright © 1972 by John Holt. Reprinted by permission of the publishers, E. P. Dutton, Inc., and Penguin Books Ltd.

Eileen Simpson, "Preface to *Reversals*." From *Reversals* by Eileen Simpson. Copyright © 1979 by Eileen Simpson. Reprinted by permission of Houghton Mifflin Company and Victor Golanez Ltd.

Ellen Goodman, "The New Ambidexters." From *Close to Home* by Ellen Goodman. Copyright © 1979 by the Washington Post Company. Reprinted by permission of Simon & Schuster, Inc., and the Washington Post Company.

Michael D. McCarthy, "Ticaspleeze and Trees." Copyright © 1985 by Michael D. McCarthy. Used by permission of the author.

Jacques Cousteau, "The Bounty of the Sea." © 1980 The Cousteau Society, Inc., a nonprofit membership organization located at 930 West 21st Street, Norfolk, VA 23517. Used by permission.

Frank Smith, "Reading by Leaps and Bounds." Adapted from *Understanding Reading*, 3rd ed., by Frank Smith. Copyright © 1982 by CBS College Publishing. Reprinted by permission of Holt, Rinehart and Winston, CBS College Publishing.

Loren Eiseley, "The Hidden Teacher." Copyright © 1978 by the Estate of Loren C. Eiseley. Reprinted by permission of Times Books/The New York Times Book Co., Inc., from *The Star Thrower*.

Acknowledgments

Isaac Asimov, "Beginning." Reprinted from *In the Beginning* by Isaac Asimov, copyright © 1981 by Isaac Asimov. Used with permission of Crown Publishers, Inc.

Theodor H. Gaster, "How Toothache Came Into the World." From *The Oldest Stories in the World* translated and retold by Theodor H. Gaster. Copyright 1952, renewed © 1980 by Theodor H. Gaster. Reprinted by permission of Viking Penguin Inc.

Edith Hamilton, "Play in Ancient Greece." From *The Greek Way* by Edith Hamilton. Copyright 1930, 1943 by W. W. Norton & Company, Inc., and renewed 1958, 1971 by D. Fielding Reid. Reprinted by permission of W. W. Norton & Company, Inc.

Dorothy Canfield Fisher, "Theme Writing." From Thomas R. Cook, ed., *Essays in Modern Thought* (1935). Reprinted by permission of the Estate of Dorothy Canfield Fisher.

Frank J. D'Angelo, "Probing for Ideas." From Frank J. D'Angelo, *Process and Thought in Composition*, 2nd ed. Copyright © 1980 by Little, Brown and Company (Inc.). Reprinted by Permission.

Jim W. Corder, "Developing a Paragraph from a Topic Sentence." From *Contemporary Writing: Process and Practice* by Jim Corder. Copyright © 1979 by Scott, Foresman and Co. Reprinted by permission.

Excerpt from "Showplace on the Prairie." Copyright 1977 Time Inc. All rights reserved. Reprinted by permission from *Time*.

Excerpt from John Muir, "Shadow Lake." From *The Mountains of California* by John Muir. Copyright 1982. Used with permission. Available from Ten Speed Press, Box 7123, Berkeley, CA 94707. $7.95 + $.75 for postage & handling.

Excerpt from "Giant Gas Gusher in Louisiana." Copyright 1977 Time Inc. All rights reserved. Reprinted by permission from *Time*.

Gail Sheehy, "Pulling Up Roots." From *Passages*, copyright © 1974, 1976 by Gail Sheehy. Reproduced by permission of the publisher, E. P. Dutton, Inc., and International Creative Management.

David Skwire and Frances Chitwood, "Specific Details." Reprinted with permission of Macmillan Publishing Company

Acknowledgments

and the authors from *Student's Book of College English,* 3rd Edn., by David Skwire and Frances Chitwood. Copyright © 1978, 1981 by Glencoe Publishing Co., Inc. Copyright © 1975 by Glencoe Press, a Division of Benziger, Bruce & Glencoe, Inc.

Donald M. Murray, "The Maker's Eye: Revising Your Own Manuscripts." From *The Writer,* October 1973. Copyright © 1973 by The Writer, Inc. Reprinted by permission of the publisher.

TO THE STUDENT

Please help us make Gorrell's *Bridges: Readings for Writers* an even better book. To improve our textbooks, we revise them every few years, taking into account the experiences of both instructors and students with the previous edition. At some time, your instructor will most likely be asked to comment extensively on Gorrell's *Bridges: Readings for Writers*. Now we would like to hear from you.

Complete this questionnaire and return it to:

College English Developmental Group
Little, Brown and Company
34 Beacon Street
Boston, MA 02106

School _____

City, State, Zip Code _____

Course title _____

Instructor's full name _____

Other books required _____

Please rate the selections:

	Liked best				Liked least	Didn't read
Bertrand Russell, "What I Have Lived For"	5	4	3	2	1	____
George Gaylord Simpson, "Shearing Sheep in Patagonia"	5	4	3	2	1	____
J. Wallace Hamilton, "The Beginning of a Word"	5	4	3	2	1	____
Donald E. P. Smith, "Spelling Is Nonsense"	5	4	3	2	1	____
Tom Schwabe, "The Great Process"	5	4	3	2	1	____
Paul Roberts, "Good and Bad"	5	4	3	2	1	____
Maya Angelou, "Mr. McElroy"	5	4	3	2	1	____
L. Daniel Rosin, "Summary of 'Take This Fish'"	5	4	3	2	1	____
Doris Lessing, "Echoes of Grief"	5	4	3	2	1	____
Robert Cushman Murphy, "Blubber on Ice"	5	4	3	2	1	____
Sir James Jeans, "Why the Sky Looks Blue"	5	4	3	2	1	____
Andrew Ward, "Lift Your Feet"	5	4	3	2	1	____
"Letter of Complaint"	5	4	3	2	1	____
Franklin Russell, "The Arctic Storm"	5	4	3	2	1	____
John McPhee, "What Color Is an Orange?"	5	4	3	2	1	____
John Holt, "Three Disciplines for Children"	5	4	3	2	1	____
Eileen Simpson, "Preface to *Reversals*"	5	4	3	2	1	____
Ellen Goodman, "The New Ambidexters"	5	4	3	2	1	____
Michael D. McCarthy, "Ticaspleeze and Trees"	5	4	3	2	1	____

	Liked best			Liked least		Didn't read
Michael D. McCarthy, "Ticaspleeze and Trees (Revision)"	5	4	3	2	1	_____
Jacques Cousteau, "The Bounty of the Sea"	5	4	3	2	1	_____
Frank Smith, "Reading by Leaps and Bounds"	5	4	3	2	1	_____
Loren Eiseley, "The Hidden Teacher"	5	4	3	2	1	_____
Isaac Asimov, "Beginning"	5	4	3	2	1	_____
Edith Hamilton, "Play in Ancient Greece"	5	4	3	2	1	_____
Dorothy Canfield Fisher, "Theme Writing"	5	4	3	2	1	_____
Frank J. D'Angelo, "Probing for Ideas"	5	4	3	2	1	_____
Jim W. Corder, "Developing a Paragraph from a Topic Sentence"	5	4	3	2	1	_____
David Skwire and Frances Chitwood, "Specific Details"	5	4	3	2	1	_____
Donald M. Murray, "The Maker's Eye: Revising Your Own Manuscripts"	5	4	3	2	1	_____

What did you think of the assignments following the readings?

_____

_____

Did the biographical material, vocabulary previews, and pre-reading questions help in your reading?

_____

Did you find the sentence patterning exercises useful? _____

Please add any comments or suggestions on how we might improve this book.

_____

_____

_____

Your name _____ Date _____

Mailing address _____

May we quote you in our promotion efforts for this book?

Yes _____ No _____

Thank you.